Every *Little* Thing

a memoir of faith and resilience

By

Melanie J. Makovsky

First paperback edition.
Paperback ISBN: 979-8-89185-048-4
Hardcover ISBN: 979-8-89185-049-1
Ebook ISBN: 979-8-89185-050-7
Library of Congress Number: 2024931114

hope*books
hopebooks.com

Endorsements

Melanie Makovsky writes her life story beautifully, interweaving the thoughts and heartbreak that come from being part of a family with an inherited genetic form of early-onset Alzheimer's disease. Everyone who cares about someone affected by this disease—friends, family members, and clinicians—should have *Every Little Thing* on their table.

—Lindsay Hohsfield, PhD, Neuroscientist, Co-Founder of Youngtimers

Melanie Makovsky splits the world open by telling the truth about her life in this intimate, raw memoir. She captures her own voice at age six or thirteen or forty with clarity and precision, exploring life's joys and struggles. Readers will resonate with her honest, brave reflections on asking big questions about God, caring for a seemingly inconsolable newborn, being a military wife, battling postpartum depression, raising neurodivergent kids, losing her dad to Alzheimer's, and more. Ultimately, they'll find hope, grace, forgiveness, and faith woven into her story.

—Keri Wyatt Kent, author of *Listen* and *Breathe*

Table of Contents

"American Woman," the Lenny Kravitz version

I'm driving. The driver's side window is down—rolled down because I'm driving an early 1980s Plymouth Sundance, the best car I could afford at the time, and only then with my dad's help. It cost me about $2,500. I'm wearing a tank top, old cotton shorts that I made myself (poorly) in my junior high home ec class, and a pair of sunglasses. I'm glad the other drivers can't see the ugly shorts. The music is loud, a CD playing from my CD Walkman, connected to the radio through the car's cassette deck. The wind is blowing through my pixie cut. In my imagination, though, I am driving a shiny '67 Mustang, wearing stylish clothes, and my hair is long and blowing just the right way as the other drivers and passengers stare at my beauty, my desirableness, with a mix of adrenaline and envy. I've spent all morning staining wooden posts for my father so I can make a few dollars for some late-summer fun, and I'm on my way to my friend Liz's house to continue painting. She and her new husband, Brian—her baby's father, whom she married only a month after we all graduated—are painting a spare bedroom in her parents' home where she, the baby girl, and Brian will be living for the foreseeable future. Hence, the ugly old shorts. It is early August, 1999.

When I arrive, I enter through the back door and announce myself so I don't scare anyone since they're in the back room downstairs. The rest of the afternoon is unremarkable, but it did get better when a few other

1

guys arrived. Liz is still a relatively new friend. Although we spent a lot of time together throughout senior year, her crowd was new to me then, which was exciting. I have other female friends, too, but when I hung around with Liz and Brian, it was always a mixed group of guys and girls, and that was more fun. Liz and I both enjoy the banter and teasing with the guys. We get to flirt with them—and they with us—without any expectation that it will go beyond flirting. In Liz's case, it's obvious that she is not seriously interested in them—she's married now. In my case, I suppose it's a little trickier, but I've made an effort to ensure that no emotional relationship attachments develop. In August, when I leave for college a couple of hours away, I don't want to have any emotional, relational ties to some guy back at home. I've spent the last several years eagerly anticipating the time when I can get out from under my parents' roof and my parents' eyes. I need my own space, a chance to make decisions without feeling like I may have to defend and justify them, and an opportunity to clear my mental slate and build my adult life without having to accommodate old baggage from the past.

Eventually the bedroom wall painting devolves into a group of four almost-adults chasing each other around with rollers full of wet seafoam green paint. At a certain point in the pleasant pandemonium, I suggest we all go outside and paint my ugly car since it certainly can't look any more junkyard than it already does. We run out to paint my car—but we don't do it. I chicken out at the last minute. I don't want to be the person who is scared of what her parents would think. I don't want their opinions to matter anymore, but they do. So I chicken out and only paint the tailpipe seafoam green—and even then, I worry that the exhaust fumes and the paint fumes will make the poor old thing explode.

When we come back in through the back door, an older guy named Eric is in the kitchen and my anxiety skyrockets. I'd met Eric at Liz's wedding rehearsal dinner, but I knew of him quite a while before that. A few years before Liz and I met and became friends, Liz's older sister, Jen, passed away in a car accident. Eric was in the car with her, in the passenger seat, and was severely hurt but recovered. Jen and Eric were engaged at the time of the accident. Liz had told me all this months ago because Eric was going to sing at her wedding. She also told me that since the time of the car accident, Eric had become engaged to another person, Angie, and they'd had a little girl together. They'd been living in South Carolina for at least a year, but a few months ago, Angie had returned to Pennsylvania with the little girl, Abigail, while Eric had stayed in South Carolina. They'd broken up, and Angie and Abigail had moved back to Pennsylvania because they were from this area, too. The whole story made my head spin a bit. Big drama.

But there was more head-spinning for me when I officially met Eric at the rehearsal dinner for the wedding. To be fair, I was in my best form that particular night. I'd taken a few afternoons earlier in July to get a genuine, dark tan—lying on a towel in my backyard wearing a bikini and SPF 8 and listening to Sarah McLaughlin—and I had gotten my pixie cut trimmed and a new, more modest dress for the occasion. During the rehearsal, I got googly-eyed by the two cute little girls—Liz and Brian's daughter, Libby, and Eric and Angie's daughter, Abigail—but other than waving at the babies, I didn't interact with anyone but my friends. So, later at the rehearsal dinner in the church basement, when Eric walked over and sat next to me, staring at me intensely, it was very awkward.

I was talking with another bridesmaid who had just graduated with Liz, Brian, and me, and I was being generally silly and loud. Then, out of the corner of my eye, I saw him come up to the table, pull out the chair next to mine, turn it, and sit down directly facing me—not the table. He leaned against the table and stared at me. I'm not a person who naturally blushes, but his stare was so intense that my left ear felt like it was on fire.

When I finished telling my goofy story, I was so freaked out by his staring that I couldn't look at him directly. I'd gone from feeling confident to feeling embarrassed or exposed—in a bad way. And for some reason, I felt like I had to explain myself, as if he was adjudicating me somehow. But he didn't move, so I had to say something.

I said, "Sorry. Weird story. I'm kind of weird."

He smiled and said, "Don't ever change." Then he got up and walked away.

So, after painting my car's tailpipe seafoam green, I feel weird about going back into Liz's house because Eric is there, and I may have to talk to him again. He is definitely weird. He dresses like it is still 1992. He is an adult, a father. He isn't a part of my world. I know what is in my world, but his world is like another galaxy. Yet he is opening a big Columbia House box full of new CDs and is holding the new Garth Brooks *Double Live*. I want that CD, but I am not going to talk to him. And just as I make that decision, I'm talking to him.

I don't remember what we talked about; I know it was something about the CDs. "What CDs did you get? I like country, too. I really want to get that Garth Brooks one. I've liked Garth Brooks since I was little. Yeah, I like classical, too. It's nice that the CDs are cheap." Something like that. The whole thing is incredibly uncomfortable. There is one moment where we both kind of geek out about how much we like Garth Brooks. He has that same huge smile on his face and is looking directly into my eyes. I feel myself smiling, too, but at the same time, there is the sudden embarrassment again, like a scared little girl. It is the worst kind of embarrassment. And yet, I have wanted to talk to him. I get comfortable there for a minute, and I smile and talk excitedly about music. Music is my passion, so that makes sense. He likes music, too; he teaches music. He is a teacher, and I just graduated. Ick. I have to get out of here—so I do.

I am back at Liz's house a few weeks later. I had laid low for a while at home, keeping busy or not so much. I imagined all I needed to pack for my first trip to college—my first trip to move out and never come back—but I don't really have anything to pack. I have all the presents I received at my graduation party—mostly school supplies, money, decorations for my dorm room, and several shower caddies.

I don't talk to Liz about that when I visit her and her mother for lunch before I leave for school. I shy away from talking about my future college life and my excitement for leaving town, something that grew increasingly more difficult as my first day of school orientation drew closer. But Liz and her mom wanted to take me out for lunch because I was leaving in three days.

Lunch is awkward. Liz and I were best friends, but we weren't good at connecting emotionally with each other. We were good at having fun in groups—usually groups that were mostly guys other than us. And we both knew that this was goodbye. But we ate lunch with mixed emotions at a TGIFridays near their house, and they gave me a bookmark with an Irish prayer written on it. I still have it to this day.

As awkward as it was, I was comfortable enough to ask if I could go back to their house from the restaurant. I'd developed a pounding headache, one that began developing that morning before I'd even left and had only grown as we had chatted and eaten. As the meal ended, I'd reached the point where I could no longer hide my pain. My parents' house was farther away, and driving there seemed impossible. So I asked if I could drive the short distance to their house and lie down until I could make the drive home. When we got there, my head was pounding so hard that I barely made it through the door and past the washing machine before I kicked off my shoes and fell mercifully asleep.

I don't remember much about that nap except that it was needed. When I woke up, I was disoriented. It took me several minutes to remember where I was and why. No one was around, but I could hear the TV in Liz and Brian's room, so I groggily wandered in that direction. The TV was blaring, and Liz was on the computer playing a game. All I remember and was aware of was the cacophony of noise coming from both machines. But I needed to say thank you before I left and get awake and alert so I could drive. I needed to get back home and go to bed.

I'd been shooting the breeze with Liz for a while as we leaned on the back of the couch behind her computer before my foggy, throbbing brain realized there was something on the couch; it took even longer for me to realize it was a person.

It was Eric. He was fast asleep, even with all the binging and pinging from the TV and the computer. His mouth was hanging open, and his shaggy blond hair was covering his face. I don't remember what I said when I noticed him, but Liz and I laughed, and I was proud of my witty observations about him. And he heard us. He woke up, squinting his eyes shut despite his glasses. He was wearing black pants and a white button-down shirt, so I thought he must have had a music gig. He was a music teacher—or at least that's what he was in South Carolina until he moved back here to see his kid. Anyway, he squinted, pushed his hair out of his eyes, and turned his head back and forth like he was trying to cross a busy street. And then he opened the outer corner of his left eye to see me, seeing him. Then he started squinting and blinking even more.

"Oh. Oh. Oh, it's you."

He was visibly blushing, pushing his hair out of his face, trying to sit up and recover from the surprise. Only I wasn't sure why it was a big deal. Why had he approached me and stared at me the way he did at the wedding rehearsal? Why had he wanted to talk to me about a bunch of CDs? Why was he blushing?

He recovered quickly and sat up, still visibly tired, and started a whole new conversation with me, leaving Liz standing there watching us talk.

"Sorry. I worked late last night and just kinda fell asleep right here when I got back."

I had assumed he was living there, but Liz nor anyone else had ever said anything that made that clear. I knew he'd moved back to Pennsylvania from South Carolina to be near his daughter, but I'd assumed he had a job lined up and was teaching at a school somewhere. Why was he working late at night? I couldn't ask that. It wasn't my business, and more importantly, I didn't want to get drawn into a conversation again—not when my head was pounding. Not when I was starting a new life in a few days.

"Sorry we woke you. Liz and her mom took me out to lunch for my birthday, but I got a headache, so I came back here and slept on the other couch."

"Oh. Your birthday."

"Yeah." And then, I said, "I gotta go. Bye."

Weirdo.

"Somewhere a Place for Us," Barbara Streisand

Sleep is an enigma. This is a new word for me, and I like it. It means something weird that I can't understand. I have a pretty good vocabulary for a seven-year-old. Mom makes me go to bed at nine every night, but I'm not tired at nine. Sometimes I'm not even tired until 11:00, and it's boring just to lie here in the dark. Some nights I try to convince Mom that I don't need to go to bed yet, but she always insists that I do. I fight with her about it when I'm in the right mood. One time, I even screamed and held on to the sofa as she yelled and threatened me, but eventually, I always end up here. When I'm feeling daring, I turn the light on and play in my room, making up songs or dances, or reading, or writing in my diary. This works especially well if I can wait until after Mom and Dad go to bed. Their bedroom is far enough away that they will never know I'm awake unless I get too loud. I like to sing to myself, too.

A lot of nights I just lie here, though, because it's easier. I make up stories and dream about being a famous singer and dancer like Paula Abdul. I'm thankful that Mom at least lets me listen to the radio while I'm in bed. The radio looks like it's made of wood, but it isn't, and it has a little light on top so I can see the clock in the dark. That's how I know when I make it to 11:00. When the little cards with the numbers on them turn to a new time, they make a nice little clicking noise, and I like that, too.

The song that's playing now is one of Grammy's favorites. Grammy loves Barbra Streisand, and she loves this song so much that she had its title engraved into Grandpa's cemetery stone. I guess she likes this song now because she and Grandpa aren't in the same place anymore—she's in her house up the road, but Grandpa's in heaven.

Grandpa went to heaven last November, but I've been missing him for longer than that. Grandpa died of Old Timer's Disease. Old Timer's Disease is what happens when old people start forgetting things, even things kids know, like what someone's name is or that you're supposed to wear matching shoes. Once, when I was four, I asked Grandpa to read me a book. I liked this book so much that I had it memorized, but it was much nicer when someone read it to me. So I climbed up in his lap where he sat, and he read it to me—but he wasn't getting the words right. He was just looking at the pictures and making up a story to go with them. He had forgotten how to read.

I don't think I ever sat in Grandpa's lap again after that. I still loved him, but he was a little scary. Eventually, he moved to a big house that had lots of people with Old Timer's Disease. I visited once, and he was in a fancy cushioned wheelchair. I guess he forgot how to walk, too. He didn't talk to me then, and he didn't really look at me, either. This place was scary. It was a house, but big, and there were lots of people in cushioned wheelchairs. Some of them yelled things or cried loudly, and there didn't seem to be anyone around who could help them. All the rooms were almost dark, and the whole house stank. Grandpa didn't seem to know who I was. I didn't go to see him anymore after that. Then, one night, someone called from that house with all the Old Timer's people, and they said Grandpa died. Grammy cried a lot. I was wrestling with Scott in Dad's recliner chair when the phone rang. Scott hit me in the face and knocked out my loose tooth. But losing a tooth didn't seem very important after that phone call.

The lady singing this song is saying that somewhere there will be a place for them, so I understand why Grammy likes it and why it makes her think of Grandpa. They aren't in the same place anymore. I don't know much about heaven. I know it's where people go when they die, that it's up in the sky somewhere, and that Grandpa is there, along with my Uncle Dennis. I never met my Uncle Dennis because he was only

12 when he died. He was riding his bike and was hit by a man driving a truck.

Listening to this song makes me miss Grandpa. I want to see him again, but not in the dark, smelly house where he used to live. I want to see him in heaven. Maybe he can read again now.

I wonder if he can see me from up there. I don't know how high up it is, and even if it's close enough, I don't know if he can see me through the ceiling. But maybe that doesn't matter if he's a ghost or an angel or something. I reach my arm straight up toward the ceiling and hold out my hand. I want Grandpa to reach down from heaven and hold my hand—and he does.

Or maybe I just imagined it. Maybe I'm making this up so I have a cool ghost story to tell my friends at school or so I can sound like one of the poor orphan girls in the books I read. But I'm sure I felt a touch when I held up my hand. Maybe it was Grandpa, or maybe it was God. I can't be sure. But it did make me happy, and I did feel like whoever it was loves me. Whoever it was, he loves me so much that it makes me want to cry.

"Say My Name,"
Destiny's Child

My first week of college is over, and it's going great. I mean, I know it was only freshman orientation week. I haven't actually taken any classes yet, and I can't believe how much the books cost. But I'm here. I'm an adult, and my parents are almost two hours away. My roommates, Kyla and Erin, are great. They seem to know more people than I do, though. They got here the same day I did, so I'm not sure how.

One of the first things I figured out was there are things I need to orient to that aren't exactly a part of the orientation curriculum. Kyla and Erin like the same music, but it's not what I like. I like rock and classical; they like pop, R&B, and Broadway. We only have one CD player, so that could be a problem. It's easier to just pretend I like Destiny's Child and the *Chicago* soundtrack—for now. I don't know how long that's going to last.

The other thing I hadn't anticipated was the boys. Getting a boyfriend was on my to-do list for the week, but it hasn't happened yet. One of the older students who had already arrived in the dorm told me that I had to be patient but persistent. Maybe insistent. "There's only a handful of straight guys, so they go fast," she said. Only a handful of straight guys? How is that possible? I know it's a music school, but in high school, there was only one guy who was gay. I didn't think this was a very common thing. Apparently, I was wrong.

No matter, I would remain patient and persistent, and I already had my eye on someone who also seemed to have his eye on me. Definitely one of the straight ones.

With the orientation schedule complete for the day, I open up my laptop and let Kyla and Erin know that I'll be logging on to America Online, so the phone line will be busy for a while. They don't care; they're still hanging out with new friends.

"You've got mail!"

I've got mail. I don't get emails too often, and most of the ones I do get are silly forwarded messages, warnings about crazy or scary crimes or ghosts, and chain letters. All of these are from friends; only people I know personally have my AOL sign-in name. So I'm surprised to see an email from a sign-in name I don't recognize. Who the hell is cham20me?

It isn't a chain letter or junk mail, but it does manage to creep me out. It's Eric, Liz's late sister's old boyfriend who's living at her house. The one who has a kid. Why in the world would he email me?

I let Kyla and Erin read the email the next day. Eric is offering to do me favors for no apparent reason. He says that since freshmen can't keep their cars on campus, he would gladly drive up and give me a ride if I wanted to come home for a weekend and see my parents. He says that if I'd like a home-cooked meal, he would gladly drive up and cook me a meal in the dorm's shared kitchen. Why the hell is he making these offers? What does he want from me? Does he actually like me? Like, *like* me? Kyla and Erin seem sure of it, laughing about how weird and gross it is. Eric is nice, though, and I don't like them laughing. Their laughing at Eric is making me mad.

I write an email back to Eric.

Weirdo.

✥

November 12, 1993

Dear Diary,

Today at lunch, someone walked up behind me and said, "You have big boobs" really loud.

"Never Is a Promise," Fiona Apple

Christmas is a joke this year, only not the funny kind. It is a farce. We are sitting here in our pajamas, opening presents as if it's a normal Christmas, when it is anything but. I don't remember ever wishing that it wasn't Christmas, but today it is, and I do.

I mean, this is honestly ridiculous. I'm 14 and Scott is 12, but it isn't our ages that make this so awful. It's the fact that we are, all three of us, sitting here performing this ritual, pretending we are happy and celebrating the most wonderful day of the year. We are pretending we are happy to help each other feel happy, but we don't feel happy. None of us are happy, and none of us will be happy, no matter how hard we try—and we all know it. We're doing this for each other, but also because we don't know how else to do this.

It is Christmas morning, and my dad is in jail. I don't really want to talk about why. You can do the research yourself if you really want to know; it's not hard information to find. The whole town knows because the darn newspaper made a big deal out of it, which is the only reason my parents told us what was happening. They didn't want us to find out from everyone else.

Last summer, when I learned that my dad had been accused of committing a crime, I had what was probably the worst night of my life up to that point. There were just so many elements of it that hurt, but most of all, it hurt because I felt like I had done something wrong, too. The whole thing was ugly, but I had no knowledge of it until months into the judicial process; that night, it was revealed that I, without any knowledge of my own, was a part of this. I hadn't participated or even known about it, but I'd been attached to it by my parents, and by the newspaper, so now I would suffer for it. My parents, at that time, believed that the result would be a probation sort of situation, so they reassured me that he wouldn't go to jail and that the worst was behind us. But I knew better.

Sure, it was summer break, but all those people at school were still around. A couple of months of vacation didn't make them go away, and their parents read the paper, and their parents knew whose daughter I was. The closer it got to the first day, the worse it would get. And then I'd be back in the halls with those boys who harassed me.

In the second half of seventh grade, a group of boys began pursuing me. At first, it was just little comments here and there, mostly about my breasts, but then the comments started becoming more hurtful, more sexual, and more graphic. "Does your dad sell watermelons on his farm? 'Cause you sure have some." Then, in eighth grade, it turned evil. I was assigned to a different school bus that year, and the boys who'd made uncomfortable comments in passing the year before now had my captive attention—and each other's—for a full 45 minutes twice a day. In no time, they were offering to pay me for sexual favors, placing bets with each other to see who would be the first to touch me, and making obscene gestures. Eventually, they did begin touching me, and though, of course, I did what I could to prevent it, with so many kids stuffed on the bus, it was easy to press yourself up against someone and make it look like an accident. When nothing stopped them from that, they grew bolder, and one boy even leaned across several people to fondle me.

Through it all, I knew I was being bullied, and I knew it was wrong. But, in my mind, it wasn't entirely their fault. They were young teenage boys, and they had hormones taking them for a ride just like I did, and this is what happened to boys. They became so filled with sexual desire that they couldn't control themselves. Years ago, when I was ten and got my first period, my mother and I, of course, had "the talk." Other than the new anatomical knowledge, though, I only remembered what she said about boys and their urges. She told me that if I kissed a boy, he could get an erection, and then he would want sex. I had zero desire to kiss these boys, but somehow, they still wanted sex. That was unexpected. What was worse was the way they enjoyed talking about it with each other—about my body, discussing its merits like they were buying a car. I hated it, and depending on the day, I responded with either thinly disguised fear or rage covering up my fear. Neither was effective. But the part that scared me the most was that inside, I was hiding a secret, and that secret was that I liked it.

It was confusing to me to like something so wrong and so hurtful, but it wasn't that I liked the way they talked about me and touched me. It was because they'd chosen me as their object. There were lots of other girls on that bus, and many more in the school, and all of us were pressed together in a building too small to hold us, rubbing bodies at a time when rubbing bodies can cause problems. But they picked me. I didn't like that I'd been picked for this, but it meant that I was important; it meant that I had won. It meant I was sexy and valuable, in a way. Sex was not something I was interested in, but it was definitely on my mind.

The problem, now that I'm a ninth grader whose dad is in jail, is that they have a whole new angle to torment me and a whole other way of looking at me. Now, when they harass me, they ask about my dad, about how it feels to be his daughter, and not in a kind way. I'm no longer just a sexual object; I am a girl who has problems that make her weaker and more vulnerable, and they know that their arrows will pierce me deeper. And now that Dad has been in jail for a month, there is no one I can, or should, involve in it. No one cares. Even if I went to the vice-principal and told him what was going on now, it would be easy for him to assume that I was only looking for attention. Maybe I was.

That's what I'm thinking about this Christmas morning, sitting here in my very unfestive pajamas next to a three-foot-tall Christmas tree made of plastic and wire. This is not Christmas—it's a farce. Christmas is going to Ronald's Christmas Tree Farm on Thanksgiving and hiking around, pointing out all the good-looking trees until Dad decides one is good enough for him, too. Christmas is being in charge of checking the C9 bulbs and replacing the dead ones while feeding them carefully up to Dad on a step ladder, hanging them with precision, and usually complaining about it. Christmas is that big tree in the corner, cookies and milk for breakfast, and a fire in the fireplace where Dad burns up all the torn wrapping paper.

There is none of that this year because there is no Dad this year. No one wanted to put up a tree, but no one wanted to pretend Christmas wasn't happening, either. So, we set up these little trees in the living room— one for Scott and one for me. No one wanted to buy presents, and no one wanted to receive presents. I'm still a kid; I still love presents, and my mom still hides them from us, wraps them, and leaves them under the tree on Christmas morning for us to open. But this year, I'm so angry about having to try to be happy on my favorite day of the year when I know I can't be. I feel cheated out of something I should have, the expectation of a happy day with a happy family, and so I cheated myself out of surprise presents as well. Weeks ago, I snuck into my mom's bedroom closet and found all the unwrapped gifts, and I'm happy to report that at least I'm getting some good stuff out of this. I looked more than once to see if she bought any more, and Scott joined me. We're putting on a good show so we can have presents, and because that's what my mom wants. She's hurting, too, of course—in different ways, but she's trying to keep everything the same as much as possible. Which doesn't work. But it's what she wants; she wants us to have Christmas presents and open them, so we do, but I'm not even trying to hide my frustration. I hate anything fake.

The phone is ringing now, and I'm assuming it's going to be Dad. I'm annoyed by this because I haven't even opened my cherry-red Airwalkers yet, and I want to get this over with. *You have a collect call from . . . at the correctional facility, do you accept the charges?* I don't like talking to my dad on the phone this way, and watching my mom do it is pretty bad, too. But it's Christmas, and he's probably feeling the worst of all of us, so I talk to him for a few minutes when it's my turn. Then, there's a surprise. Dad wants to read to us on speakerphone, and he wants to read something from the Bible. This is new.

I remember on the night the Gulf War began, Dad heard what was going on and wanted to watch CNN—which he did for a good hour, but then Scott and I, still being little kids, started whining because we wanted to watch Nickelodeon. Dad quickly got angry about our complaining and yelled, "Our country is at war, and they want to watch Nickelodeon!" I felt pretty stupid when he said that. Mom tried to persuade him a bit, but he was unusually angry and worked up, so CNN stayed on. At some point that night, after staring at the newsreels of night vision views of bombings, Dad suddenly said, "How can anyone believe in a loving God in a world like this?!" It was loud and unexpected. He didn't say anything else, and then Mom put us to bed.

So now, feeling much more like an adult than I did then, I'm perplexed as to why my dad, who had so openly declared to us that he didn't believe in a loving God, wants to read the Bible. I'm listening to him now, mostly because I truly can't figure this man out. The stories are nice, though, and I can tell that he and Mom want this to make me happy, so I pretend to be happy. I'm getting good at that.

"You Had Me from Hello,"
Kenny Chesney

It's Labor Day weekend, and I've already kind of gotten sick of this tiny ugly dorm room and feeling boxed in by it. A couple of guy friends here are driving home for the weekend in the same direction as my house, so I hitched a ride. I'm not sure what I will do back at home this weekend other than sleep in my own bed and not have to negotiate when the lights get turned off. That, and I have to meet up with Eric.

I've been trying to keep things light, friendly, and aloof with Eric. I realize I need to just tell him I'm not interested, but I keep chickening out. I need to hurt his feelings. I need to reject him but don't want to, so we dance around the subject. It's like ring-around-the-rosy with a big elephant in the middle. He knows why he's pursuing me, and I do, too—and he knows that I do—but I haven't completely acknowledged it yet. But finally, a couple of days ago, he asked if I was coming home for the long weekend, and I told him I was. Actually, at the time he asked, I hadn't fully decided yet, but I told him I was. He asked if I would meet him at a Friendly's restaurant—one that Liz, Brian, and the rest of our group frequented after school events so that we could talk. You can't use italics in AOL Instant Messenger, but if you could, it definitely would have said *talk*. Because we've *been* talking. We've been emailing almost every day for a couple of weeks, chatting about the things and people we have in common, dancing around the elephant. But now he wants to *talk*. And by the way he flirts, the goofy compliments he tosses out, I know what he wants to talk about. Because Kyla and Erin were right; he wants a relationship, but that means that first, we have to *talk*.

Until now, I've kept our conversations entirely online and entirely about superficial subjects. Our mutual friends, his daughter, our old high school, and the teachers we shared—despite him graduating eight years earlier than I did—stuff like that. College life and what I was learning about it. He gives me a lot of advice. In that way, it's kind of like having a dad who actually had a college experience. It's nice to have someone who can tell me what things are really like without sugarcoating the dorm-life scenario like the orientation leaders did. I can complain about my classes to him, and he doesn't chide me for complaining or try to act like I should be enjoying all of this. I'm definitely not enjoying life here, and that doesn't seem to surprise Eric at all.

So my friends drop me off at home, and I'm there, ready to hibernate in my bedroom, sweating like a pig since our house has no air conditioning. But at least I don't have to socialize all the time. In the dorm, I feel like I always have to be ready to be friendly to people I've just met. There's no downtime. Even if I'm doing homework, I have to be ready to prioritize whoever knocks on the door and wants to talk. If Erin or Kyla come in, if they're in the mood to talk or listen to music, I feel bad saying I'm studying, so I have to wait. I can't study if they're not because it's too loud. So I end up doing all my classwork with a flashlight or by the light of my laptop at night when they're either away or sleeping. Four hours of sleep has been pretty standard for me for a good two weeks now, and the anxiety of people constantly coming in and out is becoming debilitating. I'm going to sleep all weekend with the door locked.

Until it gets to Sunday afternoon, the day that I need to meet Eric at Friendly's to *talk*. I'm nervous as hell, which seems stupid. Rejection is scary, even when I'm the one doing it. I've flirted with and enjoyed the attention of a lot of boys, but I haven't rejected many because I tend to crave their attention. When boys pay attention to me, when they're attracted to me, I feel beautiful and desirable—no matter who it is, really. Even catcalls are compliments. They're kind of scary and threatening, but at least I've got their attention. Boys may call me a slut, but at least they call me.

But Eric's attention and knowing he's interested in me feels very different. It feels good, and I feel desired and pursued in a great way, but this is a lot different than catcalls and being admired for my boobs or my butt. He doesn't talk about my body at all. He says I'm beautiful. He says I'm interesting and sweet. I don't really know how to respond to that because it's too friendly. I only know how to flirt aggressively— not that I want to be flirting.

I'm supposed to meet Eric at 1:00, and it's 11:00 right now. I've avoided this situation long enough, and now I have to face it. I have to go. I could just not show up, but I'd only end up making a dumb excuse, and he'd want to reschedule. I've got to do this now, like ripping off a band-aid. Show up, make conversation, present my gentle rejection, and move on with life. No more awkward conversations with Eric. He'll get back on ICQ and find someone else.

What will I say? I need to give him a reason for rejecting him, and it has to be a nice one since I've been trailing him along on email and AIM for weeks. I've been wasting his time, really, because he's been wooing me instead of looking for someone else. But Eric isn't a prowler. He's not the creepy guy I thought he was when Liz told me about him. Well, not entirely. He's actually really sweet. I like him, just not like that.

Okay. What do I say? I need to blame it on school, on being away and not living in my bedroom in my parents' house in Allentown anymore. My plan here was to move away, be a college girl with a boyfriend, sing, and become a music teacher. Maybe move to New York City or somewhere else and live on my own. "I need to settle in at school and make my life there now, so I don't want to be in a relationship with someone at home." Something like that. That will work.

I pick out an old pair of jeans that make my ass look great but aren't too sexy. Most of my jeans are bootcut, but bootcut jeans make my ass look better than great, and teasing him like that would be mean. I put on a blue tank top. My bra straps are sticking out, which I hate. It looks good, but not too good. That's the goal here—let him down easy.

I'm not ready to tell my parents this is happening yet, so I tell them I'm going to shop for groceries to bring back with me to school on Monday. I'm 18 now; it's not their business anymore where I am at every minute. I feel like I still should tell them, but I'm definitely not telling them that I'm going to see a 26-year-old guy with a 2-year-old daughter to tell him I don't want to be his girlfriend. Just the sound of that feels gross to me, as great as Eric is.

Being a full-grown man, I expected Eric to meet me at the door of the restaurant or at a table, but when I walk in, he's behind the counter. He works here? I thought he was a music teacher, but apparently, he's a waiter. Actually, he's walking quickly in and out of the kitchen and talking to the other staff like they're friends. They're all wearing white shirts and black pants like Eric was when I saw him at Liz's house on my birthday, so maybe this is what he's doing now. Eric is wearing tight jeans that he's rolled up at the ankles and a baggy green shirt, and when he sees me, he explains that he does, in fact, work at this Friendly's, but he's not working now. The staff needed someone to make a cake, though, so he came in early to take care of that.

A waitress leads me to a booth in the far back corner, and she's smiling one of those silly girl smiles that says, "I know something you don't know." But I do know, because I know that she knows I'm the girl Eric's meeting here because he wants to go out with me.

A few minutes later, Eric comes over, sits across from me, and starts talking. He's talking but just warming up. He tells me about Jen, Liz's sister and his late fiancé, and how he still misses her every day, even close to five years later. He tells me that, yes, he was in the car accident with her, but she was driving. She died on impact, and he found out only days later when he woke up in the hospital. I think I see tears in his eyes. Then he tells me about Abigail, his daughter, who just turned two. He loves her, and he moved back here from South Carolina because he wants to be a part of her life. His split with her mother, Angie, happened the year before, and it was a mutual decision. And then he gets to the point. "I like you. You're beautiful. When I saw you at the wedding rehearsal, I knew there was just something special about you. And I feel comfortable around you. With Angie, with Abigail's mom, I always felt like I couldn't be myself, like I had to be the knight in shining armor. With you, I feel like I can be myself." He stops, smiling so widely that his eyes are partially closed. He's blushing, and he looks me directly in the eye.

This is my cue, so I say my line—the only line I came up with and rehearsed for this date. The only date, the only one we will have. So I speak my line, telling him kindly that I don't want to be his girlfriend because he's got too much baggage and I don't live in Allentown anymore. And so it's done, and I can move on.

But I didn't think about what might happen after I said my line, and now it's awkward. Eric is smooth, though; I know that, and he simply changes the subject. Somehow, within minutes, we're talking about our experiences in our high school chorus. We went to the same high school, albeit years apart, but we had a lot of similar experiences. He's a pretty accomplished singer, and he's frighteningly smart. His smile makes me smile. After all that awful awkwardness, we are laughing together, telling stories about pranks and the crazy fun that was high school for both of us.

Then I see it. I am holding his hand. When did that happen? Why did that happen? I should stop. This isn't what I came here to do, and now I am only confusing him again and messing this all up. But I don't let go. I keep holding his hand, and I hold it tighter, my grip becoming more confident than my emotions. I don't want to let go of his hand because I am fully, happily in this moment, laughing with this man and holding his hand. I am happy here with Eric, and I am holding his hand.

And I am holding his hand because I am supposed to. Because my hand belongs in his. His hand belongs in mine.

We sit there, drinking sodas and laughing for more than an hour. Then I cut it off, too confused about why this man, who was not supposed to be a part of my life, is, in fact, a part of it. I didn't make this decision, and I don't think Eric did, either, because he only voiced his affection. But somehow, this decision was made. And when I let go of his hand, mine feels empty.

I tell him I need to go, and he asks if he may walk me to my car. So we walk together to my parking spot behind the restaurant. He is still smiling widely, and I notice that his eyes twinkle when he's happy. I notice that I, too, am smiling.

We get to my ugly old Sundance, and he thanks me for coming and asks if he can give me a hug. A hug works for me; it's friendly, so we hug. Then he pulls back from the hug, his arms still on my shoulder blades, and for a brief moment, he stares into my eyes. He's still smiling, but this smile is different—deeper.

And then he is kissing me. His kiss is soft and feels like love. It feels like acceptance, comfort, and care. It feels like coming home, like this is exactly where I belong. He starts to pull away, but I'm not ready for it to end; I'm not ready to say goodbye. So I do the only thing I know to do—I slip my tongue gently, hesitantly into his mouth. He accepts it hungrily, and for a few minutes, we are alone on our own little planet where it doesn't matter that he is 26 and has a kid, that I am barely 18 and in college, that he has lived and loved and experienced things that I will never understand, and that I am just beginning to enter the world. Because this kiss is our moment. From this moment, it is no longer the world. Now it is our world.

"He's Always Been Faithful,"
Sarah Groves

It wasn't supposed to go this way. I wasn't supposed to be flat on my back, legs in the air, pushing for minutes at a time, not breathing, and then passing out from exhaustion and a head rush despite being on my back. There weren't supposed to be three different women holding my legs in the air. I wanted them on the ground.

I am giving birth to my first child at a birth center, a choice I felt would be the only safe option for both my almost-out daughter and me, and one that I'm thinking now may not work out anyway. I can feel the liquid gushing out of my body, and I don't know if what is coming out of me is pee, poop, amniotic fluid, blood, or something else entirely. I just know that I am working harder and feeling more pain than I ever have in my life, and what isn't coming out is a baby. In the midst of my delirium, my mind flashes to the opening scene of *Dances With Wolves*, a movie I watched on VHS about a hundred times when I was in junior high because I had little else to do on hot summer days alone in the farmhouse. The movie opens in a small tent on a Civil War battlefield, with several soldiers on cots—some with bleeding wounds, others with festering ones. Kevin Costner is the lead actor, and one of his feet looks like a pile of black mud from the ankle down. As he looks on, another man on a cot, whose wound takes up most of his leg, is approached by someone holding a hand saw, who then proceeds to cut off the man's leg where the wound begins: no anesthesia, no painkillers, no antiseptic wipes. One man is sawing, and the other is screaming. Kevin Costner puts his boot on and limps away.

But I'm not Kevin Costner here, and I can't stand up, put on my pants, and stop what's happening. I need to have a baby. I need to push out this baby, and I can't stop doing it because even if I tried, my body wouldn't let me stop. I have no idea how long I've been in this position—it could be minutes or days. Time isn't relevant now; pain is the only thing I sense. Contractions aren't relevant, either, because I stopped having those before I ended up on my back. I feel betrayed by these midwives and nurses who promised me a beautiful, natural childbirth where I could soak in a tub, walk, moan, and squat down to deliver my baby. On my back with my legs in the air is exactly what I was trying to avoid. They stand there, staring at my nether regions, periodically commanding me to push, and I do, like it's the biggest crap I've ever taken in my life. But when I get to the point where I need to inhale, I blackout and stay blacked out until I hear them telling me to do it again.

In the brief seconds I have at the end of another push, I look at my husband, seated on the bed at my side, his head moving back and forth between my crotch and my face as if he were watching a tennis tournament. One of the nurses holding up my left leg makes a comment that is supposed to be funny, and my husband laughs. I am dying, but everyone else in the room is chatting and joking. I want to tell him to tell them to shut up, to realize that there is a good chance they may be witnessing the last minutes, or hours, of my life. I move my mouth, but only grunts and groans come out, and I can't think of the words I need. But I can move my left arm, and I use it to smack my husband.

At some point, minutes or hours or years later, I feel a tearing pain at the point of action, and I think of the man in *Dances With Wolves* who got his leg cut off. This is the pain I feel, both inside and out, but I remember that that means it's almost over. I breathe and push as long and hard as I can, and then suddenly, finally, there is a small amount of relief. I've birthed her head. But then the nurse, the one who kept chatting and joking through my impending death, sticks something just as big inside, stretching me even wider. The midwives are speaking, and they sound frightened. I wonder if my baby died even though

I didn't. One of the midwives, finally acknowledging that I'm there, tells me that her umbilical cord is around her neck, and they need to untangle it. They are literally unwinding one of my internal organs while it's still inside me. But in the midst of that, out of pure willpower, I push once more, and she, still tangled in the cord that connects her to me, emerges.

They lift her onto my stomach, and while I'm still very much aware of the pain, it's happening on another planet now. The midwives and nurses are working on it. I look at my first child, my little daughter. Her head, unsurprisingly, is round, with dark eyes, chubby cheeks, and a head full of dark hair. Her body appears pretty plump as well. She is staring at me, and I realize my face is the first thing she is seeing in the world. "You're so beautiful," I tell her. One of the nurses laughs and tells me that she is pooping on me, but that is irrelevant. I don't even realize that she is not breathing until one of the midwives leans over and forcibly sticks a plastic tube into her mouth, moving it around quickly as she squirms. "We need to get her breathing," she says, and for a brief moment, I recognize that she is blue in the face and that maybe she won't survive. I am terrified once more. She has been lying on me for at least a minute, which means she has gone way too long without taking her first breath.

The moment passes quickly, though, and she not only breathes, but screams. She screams and screams and screams. I smile at her screams. Someone suggests that my husband take her and hold her, saying that they need to help me stop bleeding, and he lifts her off of my stomach, which now feels both empty and cold. I'd forgotten he was even in the room.

He begins singing to her behind my head where I can't see them—since I am still flat on my back, legs in the air, vaguely aware of numerous needle pokes and pulling on pieces of anatomy between my legs. I'm listening to him singing and her screaming, more concerned about her screaming than whatever is happening at the other end of me. One of the nurses laughs. "You've got a good one!" she says about the screaming, and I wonder what she's imagining my daughter will be. A midwife smiles at me over my right knee, saying, "Relax now; the hardest part is over." I remind her that I now have to take this baby home and raise her. Then she asks me what we are naming her.

Ida Carol.

Hours later, I awake from a surprisingly comfortable sleep. I am still in the same bed at the birth center, and I am still naked, but now I am propped up with an insane number of pillows and blankets. I am alone in the room, except for Ida, and I wonder where everyone has gone. The baby—my baby, Ida—is naked except that someone has diapered her, and her otherwise nude body is pressed against mine. We are warming each other, skin to skin. She is sleeping, but every once in a while, her left eye opens a bit and looks at me.

I remember, then, that she will know my voice because she has heard me from the womb for the last nine months. I want her to hear my voice while she can see my face, but the moment seems beyond words. So I sing. I sing a song I've heard and enjoyed many times on the radio that I wasn't even aware I knew the words to. Faithful. This is the child I prayed for, the one that will change our lives forever. She already has.

"In This Life,"
Colin Raye

My dad's been home for a couple of weeks now. He was quiet for the first week, and he's still pretty quiet, but something is different.

Prison definitely took a toll on his body. He still had hair on the top of his head when he went in, but now it's gone, and even the hair on the sides is much thinner and grayer. Also, his skin is whiter than I've ever seen it before. His skin was always pretty dark, almost olive. At first, I wasn't sure why he looked so pale, but now I realize he's had a perpetual farmer's tan since before I was born.

I don't think it's just his appearance that's changed. He seems happy, which is unexpected for a man who just spent 11 months in jail. It's a happiness that's only obvious to us, his family, though, because it's a sort of quiet happiness, like he has a wonderful secret he's hiding. His personality and his habits are the same. He sits in his chair, he reads the newspaper, he watches the evening news, and he walks slowly through the orchard. Yet there is a sense of peace in him now where there used to be hurt and resentment. I get that he's grateful to be home, but this is something deeper, something that has given him peace from the pain I saw in him before.

He doesn't talk about it, and I'm afraid to ask. It's a deeper conversation than I'm ready to have at this point because I'm still angry and hurting, and I don't think I want to have peace just yet. Not after everything I went through as a part of the collateral damage from his actions.

Life on a farm of any kind is cyclical. My father's work changes with the seasons and the weather they bring. We don't go on summer vacations because summer is too busy on a farm. Summer is when the pick-your-own business is open, and there are days when the crowds become overwhelming. Mothers with children, Asian couples who bring their whole extended family, little old ladies in sun hats who pick multiple boxes of peaches, moving quickly, like picking peaches is their job. They're going home to make pies, they always say.

Fall is often even busier here. Apples, pears, and pumpkins are all available, which brings bigger crowds looking for the quintessential fall hayride. My dad's job, along with his hired crew of farm workers, is to harvest as much of the fruit that remains on the trees after the customers go through to be sold (hopefully) to companies that make juices or other products that don't require a visually perfect apple. Despite that, there's always a huge pile of fly-covered apples on the ground near my house by October, laying there to rot so that at least they can contribute nutrients to the ground for the next year. The smell is incredible.

My dad's work is essentially the same work his father did, on the same land with many of the same trees. In fact, there are a few rows of mismatched trees in the peach field, with some trees whose peaches ripen early next to trees that may not have ripe fruit until September. My grandfather planted those while he was in the early stages of his Alzheimer's.

My grandfather, and now my dad, do the same work as the great-grandfather I never met. He is the one who purchased this land, the barns we park the tractors in, and the house I live in. Winter, spring, summer, fall. The years on the farm are pretty much the same now as they were then, with only a few more modern tools that took the place of the hand saws and other rusted tools that still hang inside the barn walls. So many things change, but many more stay the same.

I used to believe that my dad was resentful of his work. My grandfather began teaching him the skills to keep trees and plants producing fruit over multiple years and the best ways to plant new ones when they stopped. My dad learned his work through an apprenticeship of sorts, which often meant hard work without pay. My dad didn't take over until the mismatched peach trees went in. At that point, he purchased the farm from his father because there was nothing else to do with it. I think that my dad knew his whole life that he would be the farmer one day, and that that knowledge kept him from exploring the other things he enjoyed as a kid. I assumed, I suppose, that he resented that, that he wanted something different, but that his parents' expectations that he take over, the pain of his father's untreatable disease, and a sense of familial obligation left him with no other option but to continue working in the same fields where he'd spent his life. By now, I know well the hurt that comes from the expectations of others, and I felt it from my father, too.

Now that's gone. Instead, the emotion surrounding him, his aura, is one of peace and comfort. He's doing the same things but almost seems to enjoy it all now. He looks at things that have always been here and smiles as if they are suddenly brand new. I love this new person he's become. I don't know how 11 months locked in a cement building with criminals could give him peace, but it did. It healed things that were broken inside.

I have broken things inside, too. I've tried therapy and books on self-improvement, but they only seem to tell me to do more and be different. They don't tell me how to do that. I'm sick of feeling like I'm not enough now, just as I am, a flawed 15-year-old who wants something to believe in.

One of my dad's reliable habits is to read the newspaper while he drinks a cup of coffee first thing in the morning. Since he's home, though, he saves the paper for the evening and reads his Bible instead. So I do the same.

I dig through the piles and rows of books on my shelf: *Nancy Drew, American Girl, The Babysitters Club*. Behind them, I find the black Bible I received when my mom forced me through a confirmation class at the church up the road.

I take it out, lie on my bed, and begin in Genesis.

"Forever Your Girl,"
Paula Abdul

I'm ten now, and for some reason being ten is hard and boring. Looking around at all my toys, I wonder why I still have them. My big Barbie dream house is taking up a lot of space, but I don't play with it anymore. I played with it for a long time, but now it's dusty, and all the little stickers are peeling off. I have a lot of toys, but I'm always bored at home. I get out my Barbies or My Little Ponies, but it's like I've forgotten how to enjoy playing with them, so I don't. I spend most of my time listening to tapes and singing along, or reading. I'm writing a lot in my diary, too, and some songs and poems in a different notebook. When I look back at the first diary entries I did in first grade, I don't even recognize myself. All I wrote then was a log of what I'd done that day; some of the entries are pretty much identical. I didn't talk about my thoughts or feelings or anything bad. I wonder what it felt like to be six because I can't remember anymore. In my diary, everything sounds like it was so normal and bland. But now, at ten, the blandness and normalness make me mad. Some days I'm just down in the dumps, but other days I'm mad. I'm so extremely bored and unhappy that I want to scream, or run away, or break a window, or scratch my skin off.

I read a book from the school library about a girl whose mother hit her. My mom slaps my face when I call her bad names or tell her to shut up. A few years ago, I would never have said things like that to her, but now I'm just so frustrated that when I think mean words, they come out of my mouth right away—so I get smacked. But the girl in the book's mom was way worse. She hit her with spoons, pushed her down, locked her in her room for hours—stuff like that. And when she finally got help, she was comforted by her friends and teachers and other people who cared about her. The thing is, I think the person who wrote the book wanted me to feel bad for her, but I don't. I'm kind of jealous, actually. I hate when I get smacked, but I also know that I deserve it and that it isn't abuse. I'm pretty sure if I told another adult that my mom had smacked me when I yelled at her and called her a bitch, I would just be told that I shouldn't speak to my mom like that. The girl in the book got all this attention and sympathy, and that's the part I want. But I'm entirely too normal, and boring, and fat, and hairy, and ugly. I'm sure I'm the only girl in fifth grade with dark, hairy legs and a bra. Why does it have to be like this? I can't have fun anymore because nothing is fun, but I can't be pretty like the other girls in my class, either. I feel myself starting to cry.

I need to stop thinking about this. I need to go to sleep.

Finally, I am able to lie down, close my eyes, and feel my thoughts leaving me as I drift off.

And then I sit up quickly, so fast that I feel dizzy for a few seconds. There is no noise, but someone is here in my room. I can't hear them, but I can feel someone watching me. Then, when the dizziness and mental fog clear, I can see him.

My grandpa is here. He doesn't really look like my grandpa, but I still know it's him. He's kind of fuzzy around the edges, not quite in focus, like a blurry photo. He is sitting in my little rocking chair, the one he and Grammy got me a long time ago, but it doesn't make sense for him to be sitting in it because it's little, and even I'm too big for it now. A grown man wouldn't fit, but somehow, there he is—fitting.

I stare at him, trying to figure out why he is here in my room in the middle of the night. Then, as I wake up a little more, I realize that he can't be here. He's dead. He's been dead for years now. But there he is, smiling at me, and I'm not even scared. Even though I realize that he must be a ghost or a dream and that I should be scared, I'm not. He's just sitting there in the chair on the other side of the room, watching me sleep. He's my grandpa and he loves me, so he came from heaven to visit me; I decide that's what's happening. It's much easier to believe that than to believe something scary.

And then, just like magic, I'm fast asleep.

"I Cross My Heart,"
George Strait

Eric and I have been engaged for two weeks now. It all happened really quickly, and I wouldn't have it any other way. I'm still a bit flabbergasted by how unexpected this all was. After our kiss outside the restaurant, I got a ride back to school, and now Eric and I are talking every night on AOL, messaging for hours, sometimes into the early morning. I'm only getting about four hours of sleep a night, but I don't care. Then, about two weeks after we became an unexpected and unlikely couple, he told me he would have a whole weekend off work at the end of September. He was starting a new job at a nicer restaurant and planned his first day there for the beginning of the week, leaving the weekend free for us to be together. In the end, we decided that he would come to me in Princeton, and we'd take the small commuter train from town into New York City.

We spent September 25th walking around the city together, stopping at every street corner to kiss while we waited for the walk signal to cross. We saw *Les Miserables* in the morning and got tickets for *The Magic Flute* at the city opera for the evening. We ate cheeseburgers in a greasy-spoon diner. While we were eating, Eric suddenly got up and moved quickly toward the door. When I asked him what he was doing, he said, "Being spontaneous." He walked out and was back in five minutes with a long-stemmed red rose he'd purchased from a street vendor.

From there, we walked to Lincoln Center. It was early, but we figured we'd sit together and wait for the opera house doors to open. We sat on the edge of the fountain, and as I leaned on his shoulder, Eric described a dream he'd had. In the dream, it was our wedding day. In laughter over the absurdity of this silly dream that had come only weeks after we'd met, we joked about what the flowers would look like and the string quartet we'd hire to play.

When the moment became quiet again, I leaned into him, admiring the sound of the fountain, the city lights, and the amazing feeling of love I'd never experienced before. I wanted to freeze the moment and live in it.

Smiling, he nudged my shoulder and said simply, "Ya wanna?"

I stared at him for a few seconds. Did I want to what? I wasn't quite sure what he was asking me. But the last thing we'd talked about….

I giggled. "Okay."

He smiled so wide I thought his face might break.

And then I realized: we're going to get married.

The problem is, though, that no one wants to congratulate us. I was on top of the world when I came back late that night, and I think he was, too. He slept next to me in my little, hard dorm room bed. But in the morning, when Kyla and Erin came back to the room and asked us about our weekend together, I told them we're engaged now, and they gave me weird looks. And when I told the other girls in the dorm, I got the same look. No one said congratulations; if they did, they didn't mean it.

Later, after Eric leaves, Erin starts talking about Eric's age and his outdated clothes. She finds it hysterical that he's so old that he still uses the word "babe." As the days pass, Kyla starts telling me that I shouldn't talk to him every night on AOL. "You have to have a life. You can't rely on him. You have to keep it loose. If you talk to him for hours every night, you'll let him control you."

I look at her sheepishly. I want to talk to him every night. But Kyla thinks it's unhealthy, somehow. Is she right?

Another girl from down the hall talks to me in the bathroom. "Why would you want to agree to marry a person right now? He's an adult, yes, but you're 18. How can you possibly think this will work out?"

"We're planning to wait until I finish school to get married," I tell her. I don't mention that neither Eric nor I want to wait out four years of college for me, but I feel like we have to because my parents don't know about any of this yet, and I don't think they'll be happy.

"Well, how can you even know that this relationship will last that long? Will you still want to marry him in four years?"

I can't imagine ever not wanting to marry him. He is everything to me.

"I can't actually imagine marrying him yet," I say.

And she says, "Then why did you tell him you'd marry him?"

I'm so tired. My head is aching. I buy a Mountain Dew from the soda machine and go to class.

What am I doing?

✤

March 9, 1993

Dear Diary,

I've decided I'm going to keep writing in here (and all the diaries after this one) for the rest of my life. Even when I have kids, I'm always going to write in my diary. That way if something important happens, like with Anne Frank, I'll have it written down.

"Open the Eyes of my Heart," Michael W. Smith

So, I started attending the Christian fellowship group here at WCC, even though I'm still not entirely sure what I believe. I was 13 when I started trying to read that Bible I got from my confirmation class, but I haven't gotten very far. I don't actually get it. These stories of supposed history in the Old Testament somehow manage to be both dry and kind of hideous at the same time. What is there to love here? Why would God decide that he owns these people and that they have to follow pages and pages of specific rules—some of which seem completely random—or he'll kill them or make them suffer? I mean, he's requiring these people to do things like build an altar according to his exact instructions, right down to a specific number of "cubits," and to impose horrid punishments on people and even animals for not doing what he wants them to do.

I'm not opposed to following instructions, and I'm open to the idea that God knows stuff that people don't know, that he created people, and that, therefore, he's allowed to make the rules. But what I don't see in these long, boring books of stories and lists and measurements is love. There are places where he promises to take care of people, to let families grow bigger and bigger, and to provide for them—but, frankly, the level of obedience he is requiring here is kind of disgusting. There is zero forgiveness, no tolerance for mistakes, and no apologies are accepted.

But really, I'm not so much questioning the veracity of the stories in the Bible, or even why God did things the way he did in these stories, but why the heck this stuff means so much to my dad. What is it about all this stuff with cubits, gold, woven cloth, clans, and sacrificial blood sprinkled all over people that has made my dad seem so…I don't know. Peaceful? Thankful? Happy? It doesn't matter what it is; I just know that, whatever the right word is, I want to feel it, too, like my dad does. Although I'd rather not go to jail to find it.

So, basically, this is a research project. I take the information I have (which is very little), my observations of my father's behavior before and after he started believing the Bible, and the Bible itself, and figure out what happened and why it made this difference in him. Unfortunately, though, I'm so busy learning about Mussorgsky, the circle of fifths, how to develop a coloratura, and the right way to sing the vowel Ee that I don't have the brain space to think this through, nor the time to continue reading the Bible. I have less time and energy now than I did in high school; I haven't even made it out of Deuteronomy.

But I brought the silly Bible here and hid it in the back of a desk drawer in my dorm room. I've taken it out a few times. I go to the Christian fellowship, and I actually really love it. We sing these praise songs, and despite the fact that I spend hours singing every day with the same other people, I enjoy singing the praise songs. They're simple and happy and give me that "kum bi yah" feeling while we all sit around the overhead projector that gives me the words. The melodies are really simple, so typically, there are at least four different lines of harmony going with it, and sometimes the sopranos will throw in an impromptu descant of sorts. It's Westminster Choir College—they gotta make it fancy. But the songs don't make me think about God. Actually, they make me think about Eric: about how wonderful he is, how he loves me even though I'm not perfect and sometimes not even good, how he tells me my fat thighs are sexy, and how he's promised to love me forever. And when we sing the songs, I feel like this is my dirty little secret. Everyone else is singing about God, and I'm singing about my fiancé. I'm too embarrassed about this to even tell Eric. It seems shameful. Eric is wonderful, but he isn't God—although I'm not sure if God is wonderful. I only know that I like coming to the meetings and that God makes my dad happy.

Then, last weekend, I left the Bible sitting on my desk in the dorm on Friday before Eric arrived to pick me up. When we got back to the dorm on Sunday night around 2 a.m., we went right to sleep, as usual, but the next morning, when I came back from my 8 a.m. piano class, Eric was looking at it. I felt embarrassed. It seemed like a little girl thing to do, to bring my confirmation class Bible to college with me, and I still worry that Eric will decide I'm too immature for him.—but he simply asked me about it.

"I didn't know you read the Bible."

"I don't, really," I told him, "But I got it out after my dad came back because, like I said, he reads it all the time now, and he seems so happy, or different, or something. I'm trying to figure out why reading the Bible makes him different."

"What have you figured out?"

"Nothing. I don't get it. I can't even keep myself awake when I try to read it. It's been a long time since I started, and I haven't read it in a while." I hadn't told him that I was going to the Christian fellowship. I didn't know how he'd feel about that.

Over the next few days, we talked online about religion here and there. It wasn't a new topic for us, but before, we'd only talked about how we thought about God as kids—what our parents taught us or didn't teach us, what we had decided to believe for now, and mostly, whether or not it was truly God who brought us together. Personally, I do believe that the good, happy, loving God my dad seems to know is the one who brought us together, and I think Eric does, too. I just can't find that God in my Bible.

Since that conversation, Eric has said that he's reading the Bible now, too, and that he's going to help with this little research project of mine. He's always trying to help me and make things easier for me. He also said that Mr. Lewis—Jen and Liz's dad, who he's still living with— reads the Bible, too, and that he went with Mr. Lewis to a men's Bible study meeting that happens every week. Eric is so smart and knows so much more than me about everything. He's read stuff about Buddhism, Hinduism, Daoism, and all those 'isms that I only know about because of yoga and that one Asian history class I took. I figured that, since he's now working on the Bible research, too, I can rely on him to explain how the God in the Bible is related to those things. Eric doesn't believe in any of the 'isms, and he's just as confused as I am about God and the Bible right now. But we still talk about God like he's this sweet old grandpa who sits on a cloud and makes happy things happen. That's what we want him to be. We talk about how he designed us for each other, and how God knew we'd be together and designed everything perfectly to make us happy. That's the God I want to believe in, but the Bible God seems too angry and mean.

It's so frustrating that I have to analyze Chopin instead of figuring out the important stuff.

"Someday,"
Sugar Ray

Apart of me wants to clean up Angie's house, but I don't want her to think that I'm implying she's doing anything wrong. It's messy, and there's laundry and toys on the floor and dirty dishes in the sink. I'm not babysitting, though, and I have to keep reminding myself that. I'm just hanging out here while Eric's at work at the restaurant so Abigail can get to know me. And Angie, too, of course. I want her to be my friend, especially now that I've stopped trying to make friends at school. It's too hard now that I'm with Eric every weekend, and I feel different about everything now. Out of my classmates' league, I suppose.

I like talking to Angie, but she had a baby with my fiancé, and that kind of scares me since they're still friends. Unlike Eric's other previous girlfriends—all of them—Angie has a good reason to still be a part of his life. She had him first. It's kind of uncomfortable.

Abigail and I are sitting on the floor in a play and storage room at Angie and Jason's house. Abigail can talk, sometimes even in full sentences, but won't talk to me. I can't tell if she likes me, but she seems quite happy sticking Teletubbies stickers on my face. It's a good start.

✥

November 10, 1991

Dear Diary,

We are in the mountains. Last night, we went spotting. We saw 54 deer and a turkey in an hour and a half! Around 2 p.m. we're going to leave. I'd rather stay.

"Gymnopedies No.1,"
Erik Satie, performed on flute

It's so, so late. I am so, so tired. And she won't sleep. This baby girl, Ida, who I prayed for, who we wanted so much, is here—but it isn't what I thought it'd be, that's for sure. I am both terrified and terrorized by her presence because it is so much more than I can handle. Tomorrow will be six weeks since her birth. Tonight is Christmas Eve.

Knowing that tomorrow she will be six weeks old doesn't really compute in my tired, aching mind because my sweet, brown-eyed baby girl, whose giant cheeky smile stands in such sharp contrast to her piercing, blood-curdling screams, does not sleep for more than an hour at a time—and those hours that do come only come when I am holding her. The crib that Eric built for her, that we prayed over, is still made up as it was before she arrived because every attempt to lay her in it has erupted into auditory terrorism within minutes. I am suffering in a way I never knew possible.

I came down with a cold about two months ago, and the coughing fits steadily increased. I coughed through Braxton-Hicks contractions, and then I coughed through 12 hours of labor, and now I cough through the night, waking myself and waking this baby. Each time I cough, I feel a breath-taking gush of blood release itself from between my legs. When I stand up, too, the blood gushes, and I am immediately weakened, clutching the nearest chair or wall to keep from losing my balance, frantically clutching my tiny, dark-haired girl like a squirming sack of potatoes that's perpetually in my arms.

Our apartment is tiny; too tiny, we assume, for a couple who has now become a family. Certainly, our beautiful terrorist shouldn't need to sleep in a crib that only fits next to the kitchen refrigerator. She seems to feel the same way, judging by her aversion to it. We have a child now, and a child needs a bedroom, a nursery. So we are moving later this week into a rental home a few miles away. But right now, we are here, in this little basement studio apartment, and I wish I had the ability to sleep standing up, and I wish that the coughing would stop and the blood would stop and the crying would stop and everything would just stop.

We've run out of ideas, of course, just like we do every other night when we are desperate for sleep and she rips through the quiet with her long, howling cries, on and off every few minutes. Out of desperation, I purchased a brown fleece baby sling online last week, and had the shipping rushed. We have so many baby things, many of which I've determined at this point will never be touched, and this sling seems too thin, too soft, too flimsy to hold a wiggling newborn safely against a mother who may literally fall over with exhaustion at any moment. But so far, carrying her in it against our stomachs has been the only way to get her to sleep longer than a few minutes—at least some of the time.

Tonight, Eric is wearing the ugly brown sling, and this baby girl, who in five weeks and six days has led me to question every decision I've made in the last three years, is fighting exhaustion as much as we are. Even in the sling, we find that we can't sit down, or she will awaken and begin the terrible cycle all over again.

This is Christmas Eve, and we have our baby. We dreamed of this baby, talked about this baby, even named this baby years ago—even in my college dorm room, even in the first days after the ring was on my finger. For this child, we prayed. Now, we pray only for sleep.

The apartment is dark now except for the light glinting off the snow on the ground outside. It is silent except for the soft flute music playing on the CD player by the bed. We've stopped talking, even stopped thinking at this point, and in our desperate exhaustion, we are united in one mind with one goal: rest. My baby girl, snuggled in the sling against her father's chest, is wriggling but no longer crying as he tiredly sways slowly along with the music. It's the same music we used each night for months before her birth, working together to train my mind and body to relax as we practiced for the upcoming natural birth. As he sways, Eric—her father, the man I love when I have time to think about it—sees that I am the one crying now. I am crying from the exhaustion and the sense of failure and disbelief that has overcome me these last few weeks. Her crying, I believe, means that I'm not being the mother she needs, that I am not good enough to be her mother. I am afraid, even now in the dark, that I will never be good enough. And I don't want to be a mother that is just good enough; I want to be the best.

Eric, my husband, her father, sees my tears, or feels them, even as the exhaustion consumes him, too. In the dark room, in the reflection of light off the snow, I see him move slowly toward me, and he wraps me in his arms. He hugs me tightly, even with the tiny lump of an infant against his chest. He says nothing, and I know he doesn't need to because he feels just as I do.

In the tiny, dark apartment, on Christmas Eve, we dance. We dance a slow dirge of exhaustion, grief, love, and peace. We dance holding our baby, the child we prayed for and will continue to pray for, and in that foggy moment, as we sway her to sleep, there is a moment of clarity. This is our life. This is what we prayed for. It isn't perfect. We aren't perfect. She isn't perfect. What we have now is this one perfect moment. For tonight, it's enough.

"Shout To The Lord,"
Darlene Zschech

Last night, while I was singing the praise songs on the overhead projector at Westminster Christian Fellowship, I admitted—to myself, anyway—that I can't imagine God. I believe he's real and that he knows us, but I can't picture him or really know what he's like. If I can't get to know him the way I can get to know a real person, how can I—or anyone, for that matter—know what God's like? When I read the Bible, I get the information, the lessons Jesus teaches and how they apply even now, but in my mind, it's hard to imagine how Christians build their whole life around these words. There seem to be passages that get really specific about rituals and sacrifices and special ways and reasons to wash yourself, but these only applied a long time ago and don't even make sense in some cases. There are a lot of instructions about right and wrong in the New Testament, but there are even more about grace and forgiveness. The laws are viewed differently and applied differently because of Jesus' teaching, crucifixion, and resurrection. I get all that, but I really just want someone to tell me what to do if I want to be a Christian, and how to pray in a way that doesn't feel like I'm talking to myself.

There are things about me, feelings I've had, empty places inside me, and an inner world I have that no one, not even my parents, has ever been aware of, let alone appreciated. But when I open up that inner world that exists purely in my mind and describe my thoughts and inspirations to Eric, he doesn't just listen to them—he appreciates them. It's not quite the same as my dad's new calmer, quieter demeanor, but the intentional listening without judgment is the same: the possibility of thinking and exploring ideas without having to come to a conclusion or a change that needs to be made. There are long pauses in conversation that aren't awkward at all—pauses that feel reflective and safe. So when we sing about how God fully knows us and fully loves us, even the uglier parts, it's like getting a single bite of something sweet but being unable to have more. I am chasing the peaceful feeling that the Bible, Christian fellowship, prayer, and love in general give to me. But if that in itself were Christianity, it wouldn't satisfy me. I need solid truth; I need to know that it is truth, and I need to feel that truth is not just true in the Bible or true in the world. I need to know that it is truth for me, in me, and all around me. I need God to be in me, but in order for that to happen, I need to be in God.

I'm doing all the right things and starting to feel the right feelings even if I don't totally understand them the way the others do, so I guess I'm a Christian now, but I'm not really sure. This still doesn't feel like the same thing I see in my dad.

On Friday, Eric arrives again and parks his car in front of my dorm. It's illegal to park there, but the campus is too small to park anywhere else. I've been waiting for his arrival, though, so I'm quickly out the door and at his car. It's Friday, and it's cold, but I've been watching for him, just like I do every Friday when he comes to drive me home. My parents don't know I'm coming back this weekend, though, so that means I'll get to spend the entire weekend unhampered by their expectations. I'll stay with Eric in his rented bedroom in Liz's parents' house. We may not even leave the room.

He gets out of the car, walks to the passenger side, kisses me, and starts talking about God—which is not normal. We've had long discussions, usually in bed, about what we believe, know, and don't know about God. He knows I am still trying to read the Bible; he knows my dad is different than he was a few years ago and that it's because he read the Bible while he was in prison. He knows I'm trying to figure out why the Bible changed him. We also toss around the idea of God a lot, kind of flippantly. "God wanted us to be together," "God smiles when we kiss," silly things like that.

But today, I can immediately tell that something about this particular day, and something about Eric himself, is different. He's got that big smile on his face that I love so much—the one that even pinches his eyes a little, the one that I know to be a natural reaction when he feels joyful. And he is joyful, but not just to see me this time.

"I know what it is! I found what you're looking for in the Bible, that thing your dad has that changed him!" he says, and now his whole body seems to be smiling. He's energized; he looks like he did after we kissed the first time in that Friendly's parking lot, like he has electricity running through him. But it's cold, and we have a good two-hour drive ahead of us in Friday rush hour traffic, so I ask him to tell me in the car.

An hour later, he's trying to explain to me what he learned at a men's Bible study he went to with Jen's dad the previous morning, but I'm not clear on how what he's telling me is so invigorating to him yet puzzling to me. He's saying he loves Jesus and that Jesus died for our sins—but I've read all that before, and my dad has told me about it with much the same look on his face. What I don't understand is how to connect the information to that look and the excitement and love in it. It's like my quest to learn what happened to my dad in jail is beginning all over again, only this time it's Eric, and this frustrates me because I want what they have, but I don't quite understand what it is. I want to love God that way, and I want to be this excited and this happy about Jesus dying on the cross, but knowing all that isn't making me happy. It's making me think that maybe God is picking and choosing some people, and I'm not one of them, even though my dad is, and now Eric is.

"I want to feel the way you do," I tell Eric, "but I just don't. I can't just decide that something's true or that God loves me and Jesus died for me because you tell me to and it says so in the Bible. I can't manufacture a relationship with God out of information about him. I'm trying to, and I'm praying, but I still don't have this…thing."

"You need to talk to Al," he says. "And we're meeting him for lunch tomorrow."

Al's stature and quiet demeanor contrast sharply with the image I have built in my mind over the last 24 hours. I imagined a sage, deeply spiritual man whose very presence exuded his separation from the heathen surrounding him. Instead, the man I shake hands with and sit across from in a diner booth is much more of a Mr. Rogers than a Dalai Lama. There is, though, a feeling that this man, this conversation, is significant, that it's marked in my life before it even occurs. It feels more like an audition or a job interview, and I am incredibly anxious in front of this man.

All of this is compounded by Eric's presence next to me in the booth. I can see that Eric feels a sense of thankfulness and love for this person, whom he himself only met a few weeks ago. On top of that, this is the man who led my fiancé to a set of religious beliefs that I have not yet entirely swallowed myself, so the flow of this conversation could have a huge impact on my future. If I don't like what Al has to say, will it mean the end of my engagement, the loss of the most important person in my life right now? Does this change mean that Eric is pressuring me into joining an organization that will change the framework of the way I think and shape our future the way he wants it to go? If I choose this, if I choose Christianity and church and Jesus, I will need to figure out how to be both a Christian woman and a Christian wife at the same time, and I wonder if Eric has already formed an idea of what he wants me to say and do and be in those roles. If I don't choose this, or if I don't live up to his expectations, my engagement could end.

At Al's request, I tell him why I'm here: how I became interested in the Bible, what I've learned about it in the nice but uninspiring church experiences I've had at my parents' church and Westminster Christian Fellowship. I explain about my dad's time in prison and the foundational and personal change I see in him since his release two whole years ago now, and I admit that what I've seen in Eric over the last few days is remarkably similar. I tell Al that these two men, my father and my fiancé, are the two people I admire most and that I feel a sense of lost-ness, a curiosity about who I am and why I'm here, a need to ensure that my past is somehow redeemable despite the moments that I still grieve—and that, more than anything else, I want to be sure that my life counts for something because my grandfather began losing his memory at age 50 and was gone before he turned 60, and I think that I might not have as much lifetime as most other people do; I have to squeeze it all in now.

As often happens, I feel like I've talked and revealed too much when I lay this all out for this man who I know next to nothing about, but he doesn't seem surprised and doesn't tell me not to worry or feel bad about myself. He tells me that we all do bad things and we all have bad things happen to us, and that this anger/fear/guilt/hurt I feel is universal. "We all feel these things," he says, "it's the human condition. Even Adam and Eve once felt this way." I know this is supposed to reassure me, but actually, I feel a bit belittled by this idea. If everyone feels like this, I'm not as unique as I thought.

The conversation goes on like this for some time, and I realize I'm getting comfortable, even charged up the more I speak and ask. His answers make me want to ask more and defend more. I've turned it into a mild debate. Later, I would question if I'd been disrespectful or if Eric thought I had been, but being able to answer this man as he answers me and fire back questions at him helps me feel smart and strong in a situation that otherwise terrifies me.

In the end, after a couple of hours, Al tells me that no one, including Eric, is expecting me to sit there and commit my entire life to being a Christian right here in the restaurant. I look at Eric to be sure this is true, but I can't read his intentions here. Instead of continuing our mild argument, Al presents me with a pink softcover book and asks me to read it when I have time to focus my mind on it in a quiet space. I agree, and we say goodbye. And when we get out the door, Eric changes the subject immediately, so I know things are going to be uncomfortable for a while.

"Wide Open Spaces,"
Dixie Chicks

Everything sucks, and I don't know why. Maybe because it's just not good enough; I'm not living up to my own standards. My grades are mostly Bs, but I'm about one more B away from a C. My voice teacher is mean to me, chiding me when I make mistakes. She makes me cry during my weekly lessons and then chides me for that, too. I had to find—and pay—my own accompanist for the lessons. I like her, but I can't afford her, although she charges me much less than her time is worth. My voice teacher insists that the accompanist and I practice together at least once a week between lessons, so I have to pay for her time then, too. I've "forgotten" to pay her a few times, and she never says anything.

I have an on-campus job, but because work-study is a part of my financial aid plan, part of that money goes toward my tuition—leaving me with only a few bucks a month. The job is nice, though, and provides me with the only peace and quiet I can get here. I sit in a little basement library that houses only sheet music and scores; when someone, usually a graduate student, comes in to borrow some, I find the piece they want in the storage room, bring it to them, and they fill out a card that says they borrowed it. If they return something, I mark the card that they signed when they borrowed it and put the score back on the shelves. It's silent when I'm alone here, and my time on-shift is heavenly. Other times, for busier shifts, I work with a girl named Jen, who's a freshman like me. She's probably the only person here that I feel almost completely comfortable talking to, especially about Eric. When we work together, we spend most of our time taking silly quizzes on the internet. Either way, the job is worth my time just to let me hide in the basement office.

I went to see an on-campus mental health counselor, and it was helpful enough that I saw her once a week for a while. I talked to her about how the comments from the other girls in my dorm make me question my relationship with Eric, about how I don't really have any friends here, about why I go back home every weekend with Eric, and about how my parents don't know I do that. Some weekends, I stay with Eric in his room at Liz's parents' house, but my parents think I'm still at school.

The counselor is great, and it's nice to say these things out loud because otherwise it feels like it's all stuck inside. When all my frustration stays in my mind for weeks at a time, it feels like it starts to boil after a while, and I reach a point where I yell, scream, or start crying and can't stop. Telling the counselor helps, but it doesn't stop the stuff from bottling up in me between my appointments. I need to find another way to vent, or I'm going to do something stupid.

Weekends with Eric—and sometimes Abigail—are the highlight of my life right now. The only time I feel completely happy. That said, we argue sometimes. I feel like Abigail's mom has way too much control over him, and it seems like many of his decisions are made based on whether or not she will get mad at him. He's afraid that if he makes her mad, she won't let him visit Abigail anymore, so he loans her money that he doesn't really have. Sometimes we have to spend time with Abigail, her mom, and her mom's boyfriend, instead of having Abigail to ourselves. I understand why he feels the way he does, but it isn't fair to us that she controls so much of his life—our life. But neither of us knows what to do about it.

Weekends with Eric and Abigail are so important to me that I refuse to study or do work for my classes when I'm with them. They are my family, the two people I love most in this world, and I won't let my classes get in the way of the few hours I have with them each week. But my teachers don't care. They assume all of us are sitting around in the dorms all weekend or drinking at Princeton on Thursday nights. They don't understand that I'm not that person.

The result is that I do all my work for the following week while the dorm is relatively quiet on Thursday party nights at Princeton. It's a nightmare every time, and I hate it, but I can't complain about it to anyone else. No one here understands what it's like to be so completely in love with a person—an imperfect, made-just-for-me person—that you change your life, your goals, and all your plans so that you can devote every possible minute to him. I don't even care about my degree anymore, honestly. I wanted the name "Westminster Choir College" on a framed bachelor's degree one day, but not anymore. I don't belong here. I belong with Eric and with Abigail. I would quit school if I could, and we would get married right now. But my parents have already said that it's out of the question. They're dead-set on me not only getting my music degree but getting it here, at Westminster. Over Christmas break, they assured me with their words that they like Eric and Abigail, but they've made it clear that they aren't confident that our relationship will last. I brought up the idea of transferring to Moravian College, which was my backup choice when I applied for Westminster, citing the fact that I don't feel like I fit in here, supplies and accompanists and CDs and books are sucking up any money I make, and I hate living in a dorm. But it was out of the question. They didn't want to listen to my argument because they thought it was made up, that I was only wanting to make the change to be closer to Eric. I do want to be closer to Eric, but more than anything else, I don't want to be here. If it weren't for Eric's comfort and love and Abigail's cute little smile, I'd want to be dead.

✛

September 2, 1995

"The Opposite Side"
Sitting around, trying to write
About an experience I had
But my emotions are too strong.
You didn't know how to show it,
But you were always there for me.
But then you needed me to be there,
But I couldn't seem to be.
I didn't understand that you could make mistakes
And when you told me about it, it brought back some bad memories.
I tried to make sense of what you were going through,
But I couldn't manage to.

You see, the last time I was on the other side.

I'm not sure what's going to happen.
I'll take each day at a time.
Sometimes I think too much.
And there is punishment for that crime.
On that night life crumbled around me
And you left me to put it together like a jigsaw puzzle.
For a while you were unforgivable to me,
But then I came to see,
This time you needed me.

The world confuses you, too, just like anybody else.
I'm learning to notice how we're alike, you and me.

"Come Away with Me," Norah Jones

Of all the places I could take Ida, the library is not a good choice. Even after two weeks, I have no idea how to predict when she's going to cry, and when she cries, she screams. It's all she does. I have to hold her all the time because the only thing I know about this baby so far is that she is less likely to cry and scream when she is being held close to me. I bought an expensive pocket sling carrier from some lady's private website for that purpose, and I even had it rush-shipped, running the bill up to $75, which seems astronomical. So that's where she is now, tucked way down into the sling with just the very end of her face showing; the sling is strapped so tightly around my body that it's uncomfortable. She's asleep, but I'm rocking back and forth while I scan the shelves of books in the childcare section—which is right next to the children's section, naturally. If I keep rocking and keep quiet, and if every other person in this entire building keeps quiet, she might stay asleep long enough for me to find this book and get out of here.

Thankfully, I was able to check online before I made the 15-minute drive over here. Strapping my tiny, wailing, red-faced baby into a car seat and driving away with her still freaks me out every time. I spent my entire pregnancy preparing for her birth, but I didn't do much to prepare for a baby. I guess I thought some kind of instinct would kick in, but the only thing that feels instinctual is the anxiety. I know this nervous feeling from singing solos at events and auditions: it's stage fright. Only that's over once you get started, and I'm not on a stage; I'm in the county library checking out Dr. Sears' *The Fussy Baby Book*, because that's what I have, and that's why I am so terrified right now. I don't want Ida to wake up because if she screams here the way she does at home, everyone in the library will see that I have no idea what I'm doing and that I have zero ability to take care of my baby. I don't want anyone to know how clueless I am, and I don't want to ask for help. I don't have anyone to ask, anyway.

I make it out of the library, but she screams the whole way home in the car.

I can't do this, I think to myself. This isn't what I wanted. It's been two weeks, and I'm still as clueless as I was the day she was born. I want help, but I know that if I ask for it and receive it from anyone, I will have to go along with their way of doing things and their way of handling my baby. All the pregnancy and natural childbirth books warned me about this part. People who want to help might tell me what I should do for her, but what they think is right may not be right for her or me. I fantasize all the time about one of the older, experienced women from our church walking in the door with a hot meal and then happily taking Ida out of my arms and into her own while I eat and take a long nap. Yet, asking that theoretical church lady for help would open the door for her and would give her the prerogative to tell me what I'm doing wrong and to do things her way while I'm taking that nap. I don't feel like I'm doing anything right at all, but if someone else said it, it would push me over the edge. So whenever someone asks how we're doing, I'm vague about it. "We're tired, but we're doing well." No one is doing well. "Oh yes, I love carrying her this way all the time. I almost never put her down; she's so sweet when she's sleeping." When she's not sleeping, she screams so loudly I'm terrified of her.

Naturally, after sleeping in the sling for 45 minutes and then screaming in the car for ten, she needs to nurse as soon as we walk in the door. So we plop down on the couch, and I carefully arrange her heavy little body on my breastfeeding pillow and even more carefully latch her onto my nipple. It takes a few tries to get her to latch correctly, but once she does, I can relax. I don't have to work at this part, so I lean my head back on the couch and close my eyes. Fifteen minutes of sleep is better than none.

"Clocks," Coldplay

We're in our own rental house now; it's old and quirky—but in a cute way. The living room carpet is mint green, and there's no dishwasher. The master bedroom has the world's ugliest wallpaper border, and the only place we found where we could hook up our TV was in the unfinished basement. So now, when we rent DVDs from Netflix by mail, we watch them in the dark basement alongside all the weird jumping spiders and boxes of stuff that belong to strangers. There's a smaller bedroom, the nursery, next to the master bedroom, with cute mint green walls. We put Ida's crib in there, although she still hasn't slept in it for longer than three hours.

But Ida is taking it a little easier on us right now. She still scream-cries several times a day, but her bright, ear-to-ear smile and huge brown eyes make her very endearing. Eric ran a 5K nearby on Valentine's Day, and everyone was enamored with her sweet, round face and big smile. Over the last month, we've also discovered that there is a neighborhood cat—a long, skinny, orange-striped male who seems to think he lives in our house. One day, I propped the front door open, and he walked in and laid on the carpet. Ida seems to love him and gets wide-eyed when she sees him. She will happily sit on the carpet next to the cat, although I have to watch her carefully so she doesn't try to pull his fur or tail.

Mom and Dad are visiting, too, but they're staying in a nearby hotel. Mainly, they're here to see Ida's baby dedication at church this Sunday, but we somewhat slyly put in a request that they also help us start getting the overgrown plants in the yard into shape. I thought that one side and the entire back of the house was lined with dead shrubs, but when the weather warmed up, they sprouted heart-shaped leaves and balls of pink blossoms. According to Dad, they're hydrangeas, and if we prune the bushes back to a smaller size and don't let them get this big again, we could even add fertilizer to the roots and change the color of the flowers.

Dad showed Eric and me how to prune them so we'd get as many blooms as possible, and then he helped with the lawn and thinned out some of the plants in the front. We've never had a landscape to take care of before—or any land at all, really—but just like that, I'm ready to till soil, buy seedlings, and plant a tree. I didn't realize that Dad knew things like how to prune a hydrangea bush so it blooms more. He trimmed the big, plain green bushes at the farmhouse, but this week, he had so much to tell us about how to beautify the yard.

Ida is seven months now, and she's chilled out enough to let Grandma and Pop Pop hold her without crying. Dad is Pop Pop because Ida can kind of say that.

I feel at home. Settled. Comfortable for the first time in a house with my husband and daughter. I'm actually kind of happy. We have so little; the move only required three full minivan trips of stuff from the basement apartment. But this little house on this little road with this little baby and my incredible husband is perfect right now. It's all I want.

"The Star-Spangled Banner," played poorly on the piano

It's late, as always. What do I do all day that keeps me up working until the early morning hours? School. I do school all day. I get up a few hours after going to bed, drive in the dark, sitting in traffic, to get to Westminster, and then spend the entire day sitting in class after class, or having my voice lesson or choir practice. I'm in my third semester now, but my schedule is still packed: five days a week. Then, at the end of my last class, I drive to a childcare business, where I pick up the two children I am babysitting in the afternoons. They're great kids, and it's a great job, but by the afternoon, I am both worn out from the long day and anxious about all the work I need to get done at night, so I know they're not getting me at my best. I'm pretty sure their mom knows, too.

I'm in an apartment now, but I'm only really in it from 8 p.m. to 6:30 a.m. It's definitely better than the dorms since I have more space and privacy, but it's still not where I want to be. Or, rather, it *is* where I want to be all day long while I'm trying to get through my classes, lessons, and rehearsals on four hours of sleep a night. During classes, the apartment and my bed inside it are the pot of gold at the end of a rainbow, as far as I'm concerned. But I still don't want to be here, at this school, on my own, when everyone I love is somewhere else, and no one I love is here.

I've made that very clear to my mom and dad, but they won't hear it. For three semesters, I've been trying to convince them to let me transfer to Moravian, my second-choice school that I was also accepted to, so I can move back home and at least be able to return to my actual home at the end of the day. But whenever I bring it up, it's like they close their ears. Like they literally won't hear it. They still think I want to transfer because I want to be near Eric—and that's true, but the problem is they think it is the only reason, no matter how many times I tell them that the environment here, the professors and other students and schedules, is just too much for me. They keep reminding me that two years ago, when I was 16, this school was what I wanted.

I'm so angry about this that it even comes out in my piano practice, which is happening at 1 a.m. on my roommate's electric keyboard. I have to be able to play the national anthem in 4-part harmony by the end of next semester because I'm a music education major. It's assumed that this skill is necessary to teach music in a public school, so this is my project right now—even though my interest in teaching music, and in music itself, is questionable right now. I'm so tired and frustrated that I'm making simple mistakes, and banging so hard on the keys that the upstairs neighbors are stamping on the floor, trying to get me to stop. The rocket's red glare, the bombs bursting in air. That's how I feel right now. Angry, like a bomb.

On Friday afternoons, I get done a bit early. Classes end earlier on Fridays because the teachers don't want to be there any more than the students do, and my babysitting job is off for the day because the kids' mom took a day off herself. So here I am, back in the apartment—but it's finally during daylight hours, and I may even be able to squeeze in some sleep. The sun coming through the windows is giving me a rare rush of optimism.

Yet I know this isn't the norm. One good day is not going to fix everything, and I shouldn't pretend it will. I still don't like it here, and I still want to transfer to Moravian, but I'm stuck. Mom called a few days ago, and I told her again that I would be happier living at home and going to Moravian as a commuter student; she just kept saying that, yes, this is hard work, but she knows I can work hard, and my grades are pretty good so it can't be that bad. She tried to fill me up with unrealistic optimism, talking about "fulfilling my dreams," but I've reached the point where that kind of talk from her only makes me more angry. I've spoken to Eric about it, too, of course, and he loves the idea of me being nearby, but it's not like he's going to pay my tuition, and he's still living in that tiny bedroom in Liz's parents' house. He actually offered to pay my tuition if my parents got angry with me and refused to continue—but Eric is a waiter. He can't pay full-time college tuition for someone else from the piles of change he's accumulated in tip money. He shouldn't have to. I know this is my problem to figure out.

In the morning, something about the sunlight turns my thoughts toward Jesus, and it occurs to me for the first time that God may care about my problem. And God is probably the only one who could change my stubborn parents' minds. Plus, if I tell them I transferred schools because God told me to, they can't argue with me.

No, no, I can't think like that. That isn't how it works. I don't get to tell God what I want to do and expect him to make it happen. That's the same as when I was six and asked him to bring me a Lady Lovely Locks doll. He's not a genie in a bottle. He's God, and He is the one who knows my future: whether or not I will stay here and struggle through my degree until it's done, or transfer, or quit. I know what I want, but he knows what it will actually be. I won't get anywhere by assuming that what I want and what God will do are the same thing. But the glinting sun coming through the window on this November morning gives me hope and reminds me that if he died for me, he surely cares about even this.

So, in the afternoon, I put all my classwork on hold and decide to spend the next few hours meditating, praying, and asking him what I should do. I still don't really know how to pray, but I like to think that God honors my efforts anyway. So I sit cross-legged on the carpet in my room, my CD player filling the air with Chopin, and I do my best to clear my mind and just talk to him. I tell him why I'm unhappy. I tell him what my parents think and why I think they're wrong. I tell him that I'm angry, scared, and tired. I tell him that, deep down, I just want to go home.

There's no booming voice from the sky, and I knew not to expect one, but I was sort of hoping that spending a good, long time making the effort to pray would suddenly give me all the answers. It didn't, but it did give me peace and remind me of how tired I was. Praying always feels like one step away from rest for me. So that's what I do. I lay down in my bed just as the evening colors begin to appear in the sky, and I go to sleep. Just before I drift off, I think that maybe this sleep—indulgent as it seems, given my schedule—is exactly what I need for now and that once I've rested, God will answer me.

Four hours later, I awake in the dark, and I know what I need to do.

"The Sign," Ace of Base

We're sitting here in English class diagramming sentences, and everyone has to participate. It's the most boring activity ever, yet I am incredibly nervous. Everyone has to participate, and we are reading the sentences out loud, adding the appropriate punctuations, and identifying the parts of the sentence, one sentence at a time. Ms. Carn is calling on us systematically, snaking vertically through the rows of desks. I'm not nervous because this is a hard thing to do—because it isn't. We've been learning parts of a sentence since third grade, adding new parts each year for the last five years. But I know that if I do mess up, someone will laugh, especially if it's something simple.

And the line is ticking my way. I'm the second person in the second row from the door. And…here we go. My turn.

"Rebecca's grandmother likes to knit, sew, and crochet. The subject is Rebecca's grandmother. The verb is 'likes.' The full predicate is 'likes to knit, sew, and crochet.' 'To knit, sew, and crochet' is a prepositional phrase."

And…yep, there it is: the snickering everywhere around me. What did I mess up this time? As I look around, a number of students are laughing silently, a few are snickering, and one is repeating "crochet" over and over—and that's when I realize what I did. I didn't say "crochet." I said, "crotch it." And I'm mortified. It will take weeks for this to stop being a constant joke, with me as its butt. I can hear the voices already, saying "crotch it" under a mimed cough or sneeze. Boys yelling, "Hang on, I gotta fix my crotch it," in the halls as I walk by. There is nothing, no mistake at all, that I could make that would be overlooked. This is junior high; that's how things work here.

I do have one saving grace, though—I think. Because I'm "gifted," I am with the same group of students for every class, every day, so we're a bit isolated. Chances are pretty good that the "crotch it" incident won't be interesting enough to get around to the general ed. students. The other "gifted" section will probably hear about it, but at least it's not a whole school thing. And at least the guys on my bus, the ones who look at me and see a floating set of boobs, won't know this happened. That's not a fire I want to add fuel to.

Then, just two days later, I am rescued from the shame of the "crotch it" incident when my friend, Amy, who's also in my classes, makes a similar mistake. While taking turns reading the answers to a fill-in-the-blank worksheet in history class, Amy mispronounces "gentiles," and the entire class roars with laughter. "Crotch it" won't stick around much longer now.

In the ten minutes it takes for all of us to let the joke go and reluctantly return to reading the answers to a worksheet we've all completed and will forget about when we walk out the door, I notice something in Amy. Not only is she laughing so hard at her own mistake that she's enjoying herself, but she's repeating it like a joke as much as anyone else. Did she say it wrong on purpose? Why would she do that? Does she want to become the new "crotch it" girl? Maybe she does.

Junior high is weird.

"Hey Ya," Outkast

I'm trying to be patient, sitting in an exam room waiting for a doctor, but it's hard since I had to bring Ida with me. I really have no choice but to bring her everywhere I go. I tried giving her a bottle of milk a few times, but she barely let us put the bottle nipple in her mouth before she spit it out again. We tried everything—I hid in the basement while Daddy gave her the bottle so she wouldn't expect milk from me. We waited until we knew she had to be hungry and wrapped her in a shirt I'd been wearing so she could smell me, but nothing. I want to keep trying, but for now, it's a no-go, and the breast pump is a beast, anyway. It's painful when it squeezes my nipples, and putting my breasts into a battery-operated machine feels obscene. Apparently, my boobs don't like the pump, either, because it takes forever to get just two or three ounces of milk out.

Despite the fact that I've been sleep-deprived for almost five months ever since Ida was born, I'm actually feeling pretty good today— mentally. I finally broke down and started seeing a psychologist at the clinic inside the Naval Academy base, and seeing her has made a big difference for me. To my happy surprise, the doctor herself has twins who are only a month older than Ida, so her insight on how to think and feel at this point in my life is aided by having a full hour to talk to another woman going through the same ordeal. I'm so thankful for her and thankful that God led me to suck it up and admit that I needed help. Of course, the medication I'm taking helps, too.

Unfortunately, all the trauma during Ida's dramatic birth—the physical trauma, that is—did a number on my nether regions, which is what brought me here, to the same clinic, to see a medical doctor. Between exhaustion, hours of nursing, and having a baby who screams any time I put her down, I seem to have a bladder infection that just won't go away. I already did a round of antibiotics, but the pain returned a few days later. My stupid body won't give me a break.

The medical assistant who took my vital signs and led me into this exam room also handed me the standard urine cup, and I obediently did my business, leaving Ida screaming on the floor because I had nowhere else to put her. She doesn't tolerate the stroller well, either, so I didn't bring it. With all the bladder infections I've had over the last five years, giving a sample seems pointless. I know well enough that when it burns to pee, I need antibiotics. But I need more medication, and I have to go through the process, so I provide the sample and hand it back to the HM. I feel ridiculous handing a clear cup full of my pee to a man I've never met before, and I wonder if he finds my flabby, overweight, post-baby body as disgusting as I do.

The doctor finally comes in, and I'm thankful it's a woman, even if she is super fit, skinny, and more educated than me. Amazingly, they already have the results of my urine analysis—which is also a pleasant surprise because I am beyond ready to go home. But what she says next is unbelievable and very unwelcome.

I'm pregnant.

Dumbfounded, I stare at her and explain that there must be a mistake. Ida won't be even five months old until next week. I did have a period since she was born, but only one, and after that, it stopped again because she is nursing every 2-3 hours around the clock. The urine analysis I did three weeks ago was just fine.

Furthermore, I'd also taken three different pregnancy tests in the time since my period stopped again, and they were all negative. So she must be incorrect. They made a mistake during the analysis; they mistook my motherly breastfeeding hormones for HCG, or they looked at some other woman's pee instead of mine.

No, she says. I'm pregnant, she says. If I got my period back once since Ida's birth, that means I am—was—fertile. My period didn't stop again because of Ida's breastfeeding; it stopped because we'd conceived. Again.

We've had sex twice since Ida was born, and both times, it was still kind of painful.

When it finally sinks in that this is reality, I get up and walk out of the exam room and out of the clinic office without saying anything to anyone and without filling out the paperwork that I need to sign. Carrying Ida, I go straight to the elevator and ride up to the third floor, the mental health clinic's floor.

I bust through the door of the clinic, shaking and yelling from the sheer anxiety and terror running through me, and demand to see my therapist immediately. This is an emergency. But I have to wait a few minutes.

This isn't fair. Why would God do this? Why would he allow me to get pregnant again? I am a terrible mother. I can't get my baby to take a bottle, sleep more than four hours at a time, or sleep somewhere other than on top of her father's chest. I can't even set her down without hearing her piercing screams.

I don't want to have another baby, ever. This whole experience since Ida's birth has been more than difficult. It's been traumatizing. Any confidence I ever had in my ability to care for a baby, adapt to new situations, think clearly on a few hours of sleep, or even love my child is gone. I can't think about loving her when I'm so tired, sore, and helpless. I am more helpless than she is since she knows that she can scream and cry, and I'll give her whatever she wants just to make the sound stop. I can scream all I want—and I do, every day—but no one is going to comfort me.

And now there will be two of them. Two mouths demanding milk, two bodies demanding to be held, two squalling little humans demanding sleep and yet fighting it off. I can't do this. I don't want to do this.

I have to do this.

✣

January 1995

A lot has changed since last November 27th, but nothing that really matters. Dad is still in jail, and I hate visiting him. I don't want to see him, but I'm not sure why. I hate it so much that when Mom goes this week, I'm not even going. I don't like talking to him on the phone every night, either. I don't know why. I don't understand anything about myself anymore. Christmas came and went, and it sucked the whole time. Now I think I have the flu. I'm just trying to decide whether or not the world sucks. I think it does. I'm going to throw up now.

"Fly Away," Lenny Kravitz

If I'd known it would be this easy, I would have done this last year.

I am transferring to a different school without my parents' permission. After a few days of solid prayer, I called the admissions office at Moravian College—my second-choice school, where I'd been accepted during my senior year of high school. At that time, I'd thought of it as only an emergency backup plan. The audition had been too easy, the music teachers and professors too obscure and much less dramatic, and although its music program was known for its quality instruction and talented students, it was known locally, whereas Westminster Choir College was known nationally.

So, my emergency backup plan has become *the* plan, and it's happening. After a few calls with the admissions office, I learned I didn't need to reapply or re-audition because all my information, including my acceptance, was still filed and waiting for me. I filled out and mailed the paperwork and told my roommate I was moving out at the end of the fall semester, and it was done.

Telling my parents had been another story. It took them some time to understand that I wasn't asking permission, that I was acting on my own because I could do that now. Then it took longer for them to understand that I'd already done it, including withdrawing from Westminster, and that it wasn't going to be undone. I tend to be good at shocking them. I told them, point blank, that if they would not allow me to move back into my bedroom (which hadn't changed a speck since I'd left it), I would move in with Eric, and he and I would get our own apartment, if necessary. I told them that if they weren't willing to pay for it, I would take out more loans, if necessary, and repay them as I could. Those were the only two areas where they had any decision, and even that decision was a power play on my part. They could punish me by not allowing me to move back in, but then I would get what I really wanted—again—and what they really didn't want by moving in with Eric. They could refuse to pay my tuition, but whatever loans they'd taken out were in their name, so either way, that part was on them. Naturally, they agreed that I could move back in and go to Moravian as a commuter student. Living in their house was the only sliver of control they had left over me. Mom even said she'd send checks to my old roommate in New Jersey each month to cover my half of the rent for the rest of the year.

Even though I will have to live under their roof and won't have the freedom I had before, this is a big win. I took my stance, made an adult decision, and followed through with it on my own, including having a plan and a backup plan for my living arrangements. Having a fiancé with a full-time job helped, but the point is that this is the first time, I think, that I made it completely clear that I had made a major decision for myself and acted on it without their permission—because I didn't need it.

Freedom feels like hope and flying.

"U Can't Touch This,"
MC Hammer

Summers at my house aren't too much fun. The centuries-old farmhouse doesn't have air conditioning, and even the box kind that you attach to a window doesn't fit. There wasn't a standard measurement for manufactured windows in 1801. There's no wiring for ceiling fans, either. So while Mom and Dad are working all day at our farm business, Scott and I are on our own to sweat and watch TV. Sometimes we separate and go to friends' houses for most of the day. I'm especially partial to my friends whose houses *do* have air conditioning, and bonus points for good food. Sometimes Muz and Suz, my mom's parents, pick us up and take us to their house. They have air conditioning, and we can play with our two younger cousins who live nearby, but we're getting older, and it's getting harder to find things to do there as well.

We spend most days watching TV. I read sometimes, too, but TV is easier. We watch our VHS movies: *E.T.*, *Sister Act*, and *Home Alone*, even though it's not Christmas. I like to watch the game shows we always watch with Muz and Suz, but in the afternoon, the choices on cable TV become Nickelodeon, reruns of movies from the 70s and 80s, or talk shows. I generally pick movies since I haven't seen most of the ones from that far back. Today, I watched *Stand By Me*, and it made me cry. Those boys were the best kind of friends. They loved each other so much, but in the end, they went their separate ways. Friendships can be thick and beautiful and steadfast, but they're also so delicate that even a little wind can break them.

It's 8:30 p.m. now, and the sky is mostly dark, with just a few little bits of color on the horizon. I'm not looking at them, though, because I am suddenly very sick and can't open my eyes. When I try, I see my bedroom spinning around me and strobe lights everywhere like I'm at a nightclub. But I know my lights are off, and my room isn't moving, so in addition to being very sick, I'm scared. I am lying here in the almost dark, flat on my back, with my eyes closed because it is the only way I can minimize the pain, nausea, and fear of what's happening.

Late this afternoon, when it seemed like the worst of the day's heat was past, Scott and I decided to fish in the pond. We drug out all the usual stuff Dad uses when we fish with him, which was a pain in the butt, and by the time we were done, we were hot, sweaty, and tired of the idea. Scott tried to cast for a while, but he couldn't get the hook and bobber out very far. So, for whatever reason, we started log-rolling down the hill next to the far side of the pond, which had recently been mowed. It's our sledding hill in the winter, but in the summer we sometimes roll down it, too.

On my third roll, though, I bumped my head against the ground a little harder than I usually do when I'm rolling and suddenly felt awful. I lay there on my back, staring at the blue sky, trying to figure out what was wrong. The sky was swirling, the blue and the clouds curling up in spirals and bumps like that painting *The Starry Night*, except it was still day. I could move my arms and legs, but if I tried to sit up, my head throbbed so much it seemed like it would explode, and if I tried to stand up, I couldn't quite get both my feet to stick to the ground. I've had headaches before—lots, actually—but this was different. My headaches hurt, but they don't start all of a sudden, or make my legs wobbly, or cause me to see the sky like a mentally disturbed painter.

I told Scott to get Mom, that I couldn't get up on my own, that I'd bumped my head and it hurt. He did, thank goodness, but when Mom came out to where I was lying, she was mad at me. When she saw that I hadn't broken my ankle again and wasn't bleeding, she said I was being silly. If I got a headache, that was fine, she said, but acting like I need an ambulance and saying I can't move was ridiculous.

I knew how this would go because Mom often tells me I make a big deal out of things that aren't: I cry too much, yell too much, let things bother me too much, think about things too much, and am generally melodramatic. I've been hearing that quite a bit lately. So to her, it seemed like this time, instead of overdoing my emotions, I was overdoing my headache. But she did help me up, walk me to my room, and get a bucket for me in case I needed to throw up. But I knew she had plenty to do after a full day of farmwork, so I figured it'd be quite a while before she checked on me.

I may have slept a while, but I'm not sure. I'm assuming I did because it's dark now, and I can hear the crickets and frogs doing their thing outside my window. I remember throwing up at some point, but it's not there now, so maybe Mom cleaned out the bucket and put it back.

I'm still trying to figure out what time it might be, without trying to roll over and look at the clock, when Mom comes in. She's less angry now, but I can hear in her voice that she's still frustrated with me. I get that she's hot and tired from being out on her feet working, lifting, and making customers happy all day; I really do. But I didn't do this on purpose, and I'm not being over dramatic—this time, anyway.

Mom tells me it's just a bad headache and I need to sleep so it will be gone in the morning. "But what if I have to go to the bathroom?" I ask. "I'm too dizzy. I'll fall down the stairs."

I feel her eye roll and accompanying sigh more than I see them. Nevertheless, I convince her that I'm scared and need her to stay in my room. She'll probably leave if I fall asleep again, but if I pee in my bed or fall down the stairs, maybe she'll believe I really do feel as bad as I'm telling her.

Now, it's been two days since I bumped my head rolling down the hill. I've been able to get up and move around a little, but after a few minutes, everything starts spinning again, and I can't tell up from down, floor from ceiling, and I crawl or drag myself back to bed or the couch. I've never had a headache last this long—but my head doesn't even really hurt. I'm just very, very dizzy, and I'm still throwing up when I try to eat. If I stand up even long enough to make myself some food, my eyes and my brain conspire against me, and the room is suddenly a spiral again, and the floor feels like standing on the ocean at high tide. And then everything starts to go black, and I sit down, stick my head between my knees, and just breathe until I have enough nerve to move back to my bed.

I'd love to see a doctor or call a darn ambulance, for goodness' sake, but I won't. Mom and Dad are both still saying it will pass—and it will, of course—but in the meantime, I feel like I'm being flushed down the toilet. They think I'm just being dramatic again, that I'm intentionally making too big a deal about a headache. It's hard to convince someone that you're really feeling what you say you're feeling because you can't actually prove it. As long as they're convinced that I'm a hypochondriac, I guess I am. I can't change it. So I crawl up the stairs, I crawl down the stairs, I keep my lights off, I read or watch TV when my eyes stop turning everything in circles for a while, I sleep, and I think. I'm very angry and want to scream at them, or call my friend's mom and tell her this is happening, but if I really am overdramatizing how I feel, hearing it from someone else would make things worse. It hurts a lot when someone who you love and who loves you decides that your emotions are lies designed to hurt them. This is happening because they are working hard, because business is good right now. Days when they're at the farm all day and come home weary and dirty mean lots of customers and good profit. Days like that also mean I'm on my own. Which is fine until I need them.

"Higher," Creed

I roll over in bed, but it takes me a minute or two to realize I'm alone in it. It's a twin-sized bed; if Eric were still in it, I wouldn't have been able to roll over. But within the same minute, I recognize the sound of his computer keyboard.

He's on this site that posts music-related jobs. I recognize it only because he looked at it around this time last year hoping to find a choir somewhere that needed a strong singer or a *Messiah* soloist for Christmas time, so I guess it's time for him to try again. 'Tis the season.

As he scrolls through each of the job posts, most of them too far away or unable to pay real money, there's one that stands out—mostly because it's short and doesn't divulge any information about the organization that's hiring or even a location. "Experienced tenor vocalist needed for full-time professional chorus. Must be willing to travel and commit to at least four years of service. Salaried position with additional allowance for housing and travel costs. Full background check required. Please contact this number for more details."

We both recognize the peculiarities of the ad simultaneously. What kind of business hires professional singers for full-time salary work? It seems like a joke or a scam, something illegal and dangerous. I laugh and tell Eric that perhaps they're hiring singing men for adult entertainment. He says, "I don't know, but okay, I'll bite," and sends a response to the email address listed.

"Clair de Lune," Claude Debussy

It's late, and I'm alone in my bedroom, sitting on the scratchy blue carpet with a book. I can't imagine the number of hours I've spent here since this became my room when I was two years old. Most of them, I realize, were exactly like this: sitting in the quiet, reading a book, imagining a life and a personality that I wanted but didn't have, or didn't have yet.

I'm playing the Debussy CD I bought at the Princeton Record Exchange during a walk through town with Eric. This piece is a comfort to me, and that's why I'm listening to it right now. This piece is a warm, dark night full of stars, the gentle touch of someone who loves me, a voice telling me I am beautiful, I am loved, and I will be cared for. A lullaby sung to me by someone perfect, who loves and cares for me, and who promises to never let me go. I need this person; I long for him, but I know people. No person could fit into this ideal. No person could ever love me like that.

But I am listening to this piece for a reason. I am imagining this person because I need him. I need to have someone who I won't ever have doubts about, who will love me perfectly, who will forgive me for being so faulty and broken, who will see my brokenness right along with my yearning to be wholesome and loving and full of love. I need someone who will pronounce all of that beautiful.

I imagine myself, three years old, sitting in my father's lap in his plush, reclining rocking chair while he watches the news on TV. I am tired, but I don't want to admit it. Mommy is busy doing something else, and Daddy's been outside working all day and is tired like me. So I lean my head on his shoulder and just sit, and I am happy just being there with him. This is what I want, but I want the impossible, perfect version. As much as I treasure this memory, it is far from perfect. My dad is tired himself and smells a little like gasoline. He is drinking beer, smoking a cigarette, and eating potato chips. It's a happy memory, but I know now that it isn't perfect because I stole a sip of the beer, inhaled the secondhand smoke, and developed a weakness for potato chips. Yet I know in my heart that I want to be held this way, wrapped in the security of a perfect father who will never fail me and never stop loving me.

As I sit alone in my bedroom on the scratchy blue carpet, listening to Debussy and imagining a perfect loving father, I read the book that Eric's new friend Al gave me a few weeks ago. The end of my fall semester has given me the time I need to read it, to excavate my heart and discover what it is that I'm looking for, and why the changes in my dad—and now Eric, too—are the outward expressions of my inward need for a love I haven't yet experienced.

Though I haven't encountered the perfect loving father that I sought and that my father and Eric spoke of in the Old Testament so far, the author of this book, in between her descriptions of what a Christian wife and a Christian marriage should look like, is describing this perfect, loving, eternal father that I've looked for in so many faces. I couldn't find him in those faces—the faces of my father, my mother, Eric, or the short but complicated line of boyfriends that came before him—but this *thing* that I see in my dad since he came home from prison, and the *thing* that I see in Eric are the same. I am right about that, but it isn't a *thing* at all. It is a person. It is Jesus.

"…purpose to make things right with Him. Spend time in prayer. Confess and deal with any sin. Invite Jesus to be your Savior, and by doing so, welcome Christ into your life and become a new creature in Him (2 Corinthians 5:17)…"

I want to be different. I want to know that my life has meaning, that my choices matter, and that I am truly, wholly good, but nothing I've tried has gotten me anywhere close. Nothing I've tried has ever made me whole. But this book that I've been trying to read, the Bible, is actually trying to tell me that it isn't a change I can make myself. It's a person I need to love. It's the Son of God. It's his lap I need to crawl into, and his heart I need to trust with my own.

"Your prayer might go something like this...," the author writes. I don't know how to pray, I realize. I remember my childhood prayers, "God, if you're real, make a Lady Lovely Locks doll appear in the living room for me when I wake up tomorrow." I am selfish to the core, even without Lady Lovely Locks. So I pray what the author suggests, word for word. I pray earnestly and thoughtfully, with just a tinge of desperation and doubt. I pray, sitting there on the scratchy blue carpet. And now I have the thing. The thing is Jesus.

When I open my eyes, everything looks the same. Debussy is still playing. The carpet is still scratchy. But I am different, and I can feel a warmth in my chest that tells me that this is real and that it changes everything.

"Heaven's Gate," 1997

How do I find heaven's gate?

How can I know where it is?

Have I lost it on my way?

"Fallin'," Alicia Keys

Cham2Ome: So you remember that weird job post that wanted tenors for a full-time salaried job?

Melly01: Yes...

Cham2Ome: It's the Navy Band. That's why it mentioned all the background checks and a housing allowance.

Melly01: I'm lost. What's the Navy Band?

Cham2Ome: A military band. Each of the military branches has one. They're in DC.

Melly01: I didn't know the military had bands still. I would have thought that went away like 200 years ago. And they have a full-time chorus? That's weird.

Cham2Ome: A full-time, active duty, salaried, enlisted chorus, yes. I'd have to go to boot camp and everything. But once I'm done with boot camp I'd be a first class petty officer.

Melly01: Why do you have to go to boot camp if you're going to be a singer?

Cham2Ome: I don't know, because it's the military. Everyone goes to boot camp. You just have to.

Melly01: So you're interested in this?

Cham20me: I'm driving there to audition next week.

Melly01: I thought you were going to audition for that grad school adjunct position at U Del?

Cham20me: I'll still do that. I have to have a backup plan.

Melly01: Wait, so this Navy chorus thing is your first choice now?

Cham20me: $50K a year and a housing allowance. And we won't have to move around. They're permanently stationed in DC. There are people in the band who've been there for 20+ years.

Melly01: So basically they've been in the Navy Band forever. They were there before I was born.

Cham20me: Yes.

Melly01: OK. I guess. You're excited. OK.

Cham20me: I'll get more info at the audition and we'll have time to think about it.

Melly01: But this is really your 1st choice now? U Del is your backup?

Cham20me: Yes

Melly01: …

✥

February 19, 1993

Dear Diary,

Last night, we slept over at Muz and Suz's house. Muz and Suz got lots of stuff to eat, and it's going to make me even fatter than I am now.

"Where I Come From,"
Alan Jackson

I hate this job, and I hate who I have to be to keep it. I'm working as a "counselor" at a local weight loss center, but the counselor title is a joke. I'm really a salesperson, and what I sell is memberships and dietary supplements, like juices, chocolate protein bars, and capsules that supposedly contain an herb that helps you burn fat faster. It seemed like a great idea at the beginning because I'm also a customer here. I've taken (and paid for) all those supplements and chocolate bars. (Not the juice, though. Ick.) This racket of a weight loss program helped me lose the 30 pounds I gained by stress-eating while I was at the music school for college, going from a pudgy size 12 jeans to a size 4. But now I'm a size 6, and they're starting to feel tight.

I know I won't be working here much longer. I wanted to make it work until I finish school, but it's only been a few months, and I'm already getting the hint that they need me to work more hours and make more sales. But ten hours a week is all I want to give here, and I refuse to go through the snake-oil salesman routine that the others do to sell products. I'm not making the quota to keep the job, so I know they'll confront me at some point and tell me to do more or leave, but I'll take the minimum wage until that time comes.

I see Eric's car pulling up now, thank God. I'm sucking up every moment I can with him right now because this summer, he's headed to Navy boot camp. In the last two months, he auditioned for both the graduate student assistant position at the college music department and for the Navy Band Sea Chanters, a small singing group that does concerts and promotional stuff for the Navy. He was offered both positions, and each represented a different view of our future together—after our wedding, that is. In the end, he chose the Navy. It's a full-time job and active duty military benefits for as long as he stays enlisted. But it also means he's going to boot camp this summer. All summer.

Seeing his car pull up with Abigail in her booster seat in the back brings out my first real smile all day. When I open the passenger door, I hear Alan Jackson turned up loud, and Eric and Abigail singing along. Abigail is only four and can't catch all the lyrics, so instead she sings the last word of every line. "Chicken! Sittin! Livin!" It's overwhelmingly adorable.

Eric gives me some time to complain about work, which segues directly into complaining about my weight gain. I mean, how long did I manage to look good before all 30 pounds piled back on? Two months? Two weeks? It's ridiculous. Clearly, the maintenance portion of this weight loss system needs to be fixed. Well, actually, I'm not following the maintenance program at all. I'm just eating what I want when I want it. It's me who needs to be fixed, and I know it, so my complaining about work turns into complaining about my body. This happens quite often. Eric does all the right things, of course. He holds my hand and says I am beautiful at any size, that I'm perfect the way I am, and that I'm still me no matter what number is printed on my jeans' tag. But this has all become a worn-out routine at this point, and it's a routine I was sick of before it even started. My mom whined about gaining and losing weight all the time, and there were times when her weight went up or down 30 pounds or more in a single year. My dad isn't nearly as flattering and kind about it as Eric is, but he does make it clear that he'd "rather she be fat and happy than skinny and miserable." I hate that I'm joining this body weight war that she's been fighting all my life, but I'm a woman, I have a curvy body, and I like fast food and dessert. The only women who are truly happy in their bodies are the ones who can eat whatever they want and not gain more than five or ten easily-shed pounds. Right?

✥

April 9, 1993

Mom called my school guidance counselor and told her about the boys on my bus bothering me and grabbing me. The counselor said I should talk to the vice principal. When I spoke to him, he said that since they touched me, and it's been going on for like seven months, he could actually call the cops because it was a crime—but that probably wasn't necessary. So a couple of guys got in-school suspension, and a few others got one day of detention. I'm not sure if that will make them stop.

I was sick for a while. I had a sinus infection, but when it started going away, I kept getting tired all the time. One day, I fainted at school and another time at church, too. The doctor said it was orthostatic hypotension and that it was normal to feel dizzy when you stand up at my age.

I smoked a cigarette in the barn a week before Easter, but I haven't kissed a boy yet.

"Whoop! There It Is," Tag Team

This school is so crowded it's virtually impossible to get to class on time. We've only got three grades in this building—seventh, eighth, and ninth—but we're still packed in like sardines. To get through the halls between classes, I either have to push and shove or just stand and wait, looking for an opening I can squeeze through. Today, coming out of 3rd period, this weird, greasy guy in my English class pushed past me in the hall, and at the last second, before he slid his way past me, he put up a palm that consequently slid over my boobs. Unlike the guys on my bus, though, he seemed to be trying to hide it. He said, "Excuse me," like it was unavoidable, and he just *had* to rub my boob in order to walk past me. And he's done it before. But maybe it really is just an accident? Like I said, these hallways are extremely crowded; you can't help bumping people around a bit. The guys on the bus certainly do it on purpose, but this guy is quiet and kind of shy. Jeez, am I so self-centered that I think that anyone who bumps me must be trying to feel me up? It's probably my fault. Maybe I should be trying harder not to bump into other people.

But the bus ride home is a whole other story with the way these boys talk to me, and for as long as this has been going on, I am starting to feel unsafe—and not just on the bus. They've done the bump-and-grope routine to me in the hallway, too, even shoving me up against a wall so I can't get away. They always make it look like an accident, like the other guy, so the teachers monitoring the halls must think it's just an innocent move that happened by chance because of how full the halls are. I know the teachers can see it. I'm pretty sure the math teacher I had last year saw it, but she didn't say anything. Plus, she never liked me; she thought my struggles with math were intentional or something. She seemed to think I wasn't taking the class seriously enough, even though I was taking it seriously enough to cry when I couldn't do the equations as quickly as everyone else. So she probably thought that if it was my choice to be bad at math, it was my choice to get felt up in the hallway, too.

Anyway, the bus is where things get scary with these guys. Last week, the red-headed guy—part of the group that likes to taunt me—sat across the aisle from me, and when I wasn't looking, he leaned all the way across the aisle and tweaked my left boob, making sure the others in the seats just behind him saw his prank and saw me push his hand away, too. I mean, he made a serious effort just to touch me. Maybe I should be proud that they think I'm that hot. I don't want them to grab me or call me names or offer to do graphic sex stuff to me, but a few of my friends have said that they can't get attention from any decent guy, so at least I got noticed. I guess.

While the other guys high-fived and congratulated him on the long-distance grope, I moved my backpack to the left side of my body, blocking myself off in case any of the others tried it. I lean my forehead against the window. It feels cool and soothing. I've had a headache since 5th period, and now I'm feeling a little hot and dizzy, too—even though it's only 45 degrees outside. I get headaches all the time now.

"Heart of Worship,"
Matt Redman

"I have to push."

"No you don't!"

I don't understand how Eric can scold me at a time like this. I'm about to push out a second child for him, and the first one can't even walk yet. In fact, she's crying loudly right now, which is really pissing me off. The crying and the baby who is trying to get out of me while we're still driving on the freeway.

"*Uuunnnnnnuuuhhh.*"

"Don't push!" Eric scolds again. He needs to understand that I can't *not* push. The best I can do right now, in the freezing cold car going 90 miles an hour, is hold back some of my strength to keep my body from pushing this baby out onto the floor mat while we're still out here on the highway.

"It's okay, sweetie. You're okay. Mommy's going to have a new baby," my mom coos to Ida in the back seat. If I could laugh right now, I would. She is trying to calm my poor, confused baby girl, but I can tell from her tone that she's scared and worried enough to scream herself. And, of course, I *am* screaming.

Finally, we pull up to the birth center and take the parking space in the back. Whenever a car is in that space, someone is having a baby inside, and now it's me. Again. As we get out, Eric runs ahead of me to the door, and I briefly envision the baby falling right out of me while I'm still waddling my way inside. But, of course, the baby stays where he is—which is no longer my stomach but my pelvis.

Two midwives meet us and rush us into one of the birthing rooms, a different one than the one I'd become a mother in 15 months ago, which feels like it may as well have been yesterday. David, the male midwife, tells me to bend over the side of the bed so he can check my cervix even before I've taken my shoes off. *There is no cervix; there isn't even a uterus,* I think. *Everything from my waist down is just baby.* And David realizes this quickly, without me having to say it. "The baby's coming now," he says.

As I follow his instructions and climb onto the bed faster than they can get the blankets down, I hear the back door I just came in open and shut again, and I realize that it's only been a couple of minutes since we got in the door. Mom is just now carrying Ida into the waiting room.

Then, *finally,* I'm de-pantsed, and I can push. There is a brief rush of terror that I recognize. The baby's head is crowning, stretching my vaginal opening several inches across and likely tearing it a bit as well. They call this "the ring of fire." For a split second, I think of *Dances With Wolves* again, and then I push on the pain, howling like an injured wolf, and for a few seconds, every muscle in my body is entirely dedicated to this one effort. And then, the ripping, exploding feeling comes as if a knife blade is coming out of me. And then the head is out, and there is relief, and I can breathe for a moment.

The other midwife, Jessica, is sitting by my feet, directly facing me. She tells me that she's going to use a small suctioning machine to clean some of the sticky fluids off the baby's face, and I nod. Eric, sitting on my left, nods as well. I can see him looking down, and I realize he can see the baby's head and face, but all I can see is my enormous, slightly deflated belly. Then, just as I see Jessica leaning over the side of the bed to gather up the suctioning machine, I feel the sensation of movement inside me, and then a push initiates itself. The baby is pushing *himself* out. I add a little push of my own to the effort and immediately feel the sudden emptiness in my body and hear a scream. Jessica hasn't even finished getting the machine up onto the bed yet.

For a few moments, I can only hear the wailing, and I'm not quite sure what's happening. Then I realize it's the baby wailing and that he is loud and healthy and breathing. I muster the strength to push myself back a bit on the bed so I can see this little screamer who swam out from between my legs. As I do this, Eric is staring at the baby, smiling the smile he reserves only for moments of true joy.

"You were right," he says. "It's a boy."

Within minutes, my mom walks into the room, carrying a sleepy, confused-looking Ida. I'm holding the baby boy against my chest now to warm him, and as I look up at my daughter, who was in the same place on my chest so recently that it seems like yesterday, I realize she is big. At 15 months old, and with all the accusations against me of starving her and refusing medical care, she still seemed so tiny and new to me. But no, she is a toddler, even though she's not toddling yet.

Mom smiles at me and laughs a bit. "I hadn't even gotten her out of her snowsuit yet." Ida is sucking on the inside of one of her hands—her signal that she wants to nurse, but she will have to wait. We have baby food packed for her so Mom can keep her fed and happy while we work on getting the baby nursing well. Eventually, later this afternoon, I will need to let them take turns, but her little brother will always need to go first.

Mom says, "You never told me what you were going to name him if he was a boy."

"Daniel," I tell her. "We're naming him after Dad."

As I rest and breathe deeply, taking in the amazing feeling of accomplishment and gratitude and love, I have a brief flashback memory. Eric and I, sitting at the Lincoln Center fountain, realizing that we had just become engaged, only five years ago. This is what we'd dreamed of, I know, but in the back of my mind I know that in a few days, the reality of raising two babies on my own all day, with the added pressure of being under careful watch by Child Protective Services, will make this all seem very overwhelming. But for now, I take that realization and set it aside to deal with another time. Now, for just one afternoon, I want to rest in Eric's arms while our babies rest in my arms, and thank God for all the things he's done for us in only five years.

Ida Carol.

Daniel Joseph.

"Violet," Hole

I'm pressing the blade of a pair of scissors into my wrist because I am a coward. How do other girls actually cut themselves? How do they willingly and intentionally slide a razor blade across their skin? I can't do this because I am too afraid of the pain. The best I can do is sit here in my bedroom, wailing and crying and yelling and pressing the dull blade of the scissors into my forearm. I've only thought about cutting myself a few times over the last seven or eight years of my life. When I first heard of it, it seemed insane, and I couldn't imagine how slicing my skin could make me feel better. It didn't really make sense to me. What makes sense to me is the scars the cutting leaves behind. Cutting scars are like visible evidence of invisible trauma. Most girls who cut, I'm told, wear clothing that covers their scars so others don't see them. But scars, I think, are a badge of honor. They scream, "Look, this is how life has treated me. These are the burdens I carry with me everywhere I go, yet you all still expect me to do the things everyone else can do." I want the scars, but I don't actually want to cut myself, and that's why I'm using the scissors to release my anger, fear, and hurt right now.

I have my books spread out across the bed, and I was truly trying to study, but I can't think straight because I don't know where Eric is. No one seems to know where he is. I've called his landline phone at Ellie's house, and I've called Ellie's parents to see if they know where he is or what he's doing. The last time I talked to him was last night, just before he left for his night shift job at the hotel he works at now.

And now he's nowhere. Worse, there's been continuous, heavy snow coming down since the middle of the morning, and now it's almost dark. I imagine him trapped in his car, hurt, unable to get free, stuck in a snowbank on a deserted road, and I cry and scream, imagining that the life we dreamed of together, the wedding we are slowly planning, will never be.

But, naturally, my imagination can do better than that. As shameful as I feel about it, I can't shake the idea, the pictures flowing through my mind. I am afraid that he is with another woman. I'm afraid that he is making love to someone thinner, more beautiful, more mature, and just plain better than me. Someone with some level of emotional security. He could even still be at the hotel, shacked up in an unclaimed room with a goddess—strong and confident and cellulite-free—who is slowly taking my place, one orgasm at a time.

Among the forgotten textbooks on my bed is my Bible. It was a gift from Eric for my 19th birthday, and he had the cover engraved with my name, including a hyphenated last name, *Haas-Makovsky.* But I don't know how to find hope in it. I know it's there, but I don't know the right page or book or verse for this. The concordance doesn't have a listing for "afraid my fiancé is screwing someone better than me and my life is over." I can barely think straight now, so I settle for a repetitive prayer, "God, please have him call me. Please tell me he's okay and he loves me and he isn't cheating. Please God. Please God."

As I perform my remix, prayer and screaming, I turn my stereo up louder, drowning out my fear so my parents don't hear me and try to intervene.

When he finally calls, it's almost 10 p.m. He says that after his night shift ended, he drove immediately to the University of Delaware, where he'd scheduled an audition for a potential entrance into a master's degree program with a graduate assistant position. As he explains, I feel the edge coming off my terror and the very welcome flow of emotional exhaustion taking over. But I'm not relieved.

Why didn't he just tell me? I knew that he'd been thinking of auditioning, that he was aware the position was available, that it paid enough to live on, and that he'd prepared music for the audition. But he never told me he'd scheduled it. I thought this was still an idea, but apparently it was a plan. A plan that didn't include me, that I didn't even need to know about. Slowly, as I listen to him talking to me in his calming voice about how he's sorry I was so worried, and in his excited voice about how well the audition went, the intensity of my emotions starts to boil again. But this time, it boils with anger.

I long for the deepest possible connection with Eric. I want to be his wife, his lover, his best friend, his confidante, his everything. And I want to be the only one holding every one of those positions. I want to be his everything until the day I die. And after I die, I want him to mourn me, long for me, feel depressed and lonely and empty without me, while also refusing to find joy in anyone or anything else. All or nothing. This is what I'm expecting. Demanding. Yet here I am, listening to him describe all the possibilities and the kind people he met and the information they gave him, planning his future. And the fact that I'm going to be there, too, that I'm coming along on this ride, is an afterthought. He hadn't forgotten to tell me he was going to do this; he just didn't tell me. It wasn't even a choice he made. *He didn't think it mattered.* He didn't think I mattered.

After we say our goodbyes, the aftermath of my terror ebbs and the exhaustion of an emotional hangover takes control. I toss all the books on the floor and turn out my lights. The anger is still there but has settled to an even simmer—for now. And the scissors didn't even leave a mark.

It's hard to fall asleep when I'm angry, no matter how tired I am. And I am angry because I'm hurt. This hurt my feelings. It hurt my heart. I am mourning a missed opportunity to pray for him, to cheer him on, to meet his potential future instructors and employers, to dream together of what life could be like a year from now in a new place. And I missed that opportunity because he chose not to offer it.

I haven't been my best for a while now. As glad as I am to be back at home, in my own bed, in my own room, and attending a school that doesn't make perfection a graduation requirement, it has taken some adjusting. I'm learning to relate to my parents as an adult child living in their house. I'm learning the ins and outs of a new school and a new environment. I'm exploring my newfound faith in Jesus. And I want Eric to help me with all of this as my security, my solid foundation. But now it feels like he's ripped the rug out from under me. This is hardly our first argument or the first burst of rage he's gotten from me, and it also isn't the first time he's lied to me about something. But it also won't be the last, and that's precisely the problem.

"Emotions," Mariah Carey

I am locked in my bedroom, making a mixtape. I recently discovered that my double-decker boom box can record songs from one tape to another *and* that it doesn't record any of the sounds from my room in the process. Which is good because I'm singing like no one is watching, and I can *almost* reach the high notes. The windows are open, and I know all of my dad's farmhand employees can hear me, but I don't care because I am an amazing singer, and I'm going to be famous one day.

When I'm alone in my room, I can think things like this, but being 12 now, I also know it's pretty unlikely that I'll be a famous rock star. It's like there are two voices inside my head; one is telling me that singing and dancing and being rich and famous is my destiny and that it's just a matter of waiting for the right person to hear my fabulous voice. But the other voice says that I have no idea where to find the right person, and that very few people who want to be rock stars ever achieve their dream, and that I'm not special, and not important, and I'm fat and ugly, so why would anyone want to listen to me or pay money to see me, anyway?

The singers on my tapes have photos of themselves on the covers, and they're all wearing skin-tight mini skirts over their amazing, perfectly proportioned bodies, and I already know that I don't, and will never, have that kind of body. Mini skirts will never be a part of my life because no one wants to see my big, wide hips or my jiggly thighs. No, what I need to wear is exactly what I'm wearing: black leggings, sneakers, and a giant black T-shirt that goes almost to my knees. I have to make sure that no one is really looking at me or that if someone does look at me, they will only see my face and ignore me from the neck down.

Not that there's anything good about me from the neck up, either. The haircut that I begged my mom for before the beginning of this school year looks more like an afro than the stylish, curly cut I saw on a TV show, and my eyebrows grow together in the middle, and I have pimples and a mustache. I'm disgusting. Sometimes, I cover up the mirror in my room; other times, I imagine someone else looking back from it.

I'm pretending; that's what it is. I'm dreaming of being a singer, a dancer, an actress, a beauty—but pretending is for little kids, which I am not. I wish I were still little sometimes, but most of the time, I just wish I were someone else. Not necessarily someone rich and famous and beautiful, though. I'd happily settle to have the life of one of the cool girls in my class. The cool girls are thin. They don't have pimples or hair on their faces; they have long, flowing hair that they can wear a million different ways, and they're good at sports and wear Umbro shorts and soccer team T-shirts. I'm on a softball team, but I didn't have to try out for it, and I'm so bad that I'm beginning to think I'm a liability to the girls who are good. They're all nice to me, but I can see them whispering when I miss a catch or can't get a hit. I play right field most games, and I know that's because I'm terrible, and the ball rarely comes that way. Even my parents know I suck. After the last game, my mom told me that one thing I was really good at was playing with my earring backs while I watched the game from right field.

When I pretend, it's an escape from my ugly, fat self, but it's not as fun as it once was. I can't really *feel* like the person I want to be anymore. I just keep thinking about my giant T-shirts that my mom suggested would hide my hips and thighs, the facial hair and armpit hair that is visible on last year's ballet portrait, the shame I felt when I couldn't run even half of the required mile in gym, and that time last June when I wore shorts to school and one girl commented on the hair on my legs and called me a gorilla. Sometimes that stuff is the only thing I can think about, and I think the encouraging posters at school ("You can do anything if you think positively!" "Reach for the stars!") are complete crap. There, I said it. It's all a big lie to make us work harder on learning things we don't really care about. I get good grades and go to "gifted class" once a week, but none of that matters. I suck at math, and I'm never going to get anywhere because I'm fat and ugly and hairy.

Sometimes I wonder if it's like sleeping when you're dead, and you get to live in your dreams. Maybe the good people get to live in their good dreams, and the bad people have to live in their nightmares. I wonder where Grandpa is right now—other than the white box—and if he can see me, or anything, from there. I wonder if he still *is* at all.

If the good people get to live in their good dreams when they're dead, that's awesome because I'm mostly good. I say bad words sometimes, and sometimes I spend a long time in the bathroom during math class so I don't have to do the work, but I'm nice, I do charity stuff, and I'm a Girl Scout. If good people get to live in their good dreams when they're dead, then I want to be dead because being fat and ugly is worse than any nightmare I've ever had.

I can't wait to be dead.

"I'm Already There," Lonestar

Much to my chagrin, Eric got his head shaved. He's headed to boot camp in a few days, and he said having a hairdresser do it here made a lot more sense than waiting until the Navy did it for him. He'll be gone for eight weeks, which will seem like eight years.

We spent the weekend wandering around Washington, D.C., where we'll be living someday soon. He said we'll probably have to live somewhere in Maryland, though, because even though the salary and benefits he'll have once he's in the Sea Chanters seem like riches to me, it also costs more to live here than it does in Pennsylvania. I wouldn't know, but he always knows things like that. I only know how to look things up on the internet.

I'm disappointed and a little apprehensive when he pulls the car up to the address the recruiter gave him, where I was going to leave him so he could fly to Great Lakes for boot camp. This is a Days Inn, and it's dingy and crowded—not a place for launching a long-term military career. Too many sketchy vibes. I sit there in the lobby with him, a few other recruits, and some uniformed guys, too. The only available seats are outside in the heat on benches that are really just big slabs of cement. This is like a third-world country, and I briefly consider the idea that maybe they're not going to take him to boot camp at all, that this is a trick used to collect poor young men to work for pennies or serve as lab rats for secret government experiments. I think I saw something like that on *Unsolved Mysteries* once.

I'm distracting myself, I realize, because I am sad and afraid. Sad about missing Eric for eight weeks and afraid that he might come back a different person. He doesn't really need—and for the most part, won't experience—the rougher, "Do it because I say so" part of the military in the Sea Chanters, but at boot camp, he'll get all of that attitude, the full restriction of his independence in order to support and defend freedom for everyone else. That's what the military is: a group of people willing to give up a portion of their own freedom to defend the rights of us all. Yet, sitting here on a cement block next to Eric, breathing in all the anxiety and hopefulness we're both hanging on to, we actually have nothing to say to each other.

Sitting here any longer, I suspect, would only succeed at multiplying my worries—and maybe his, too. It is time to go. I wrap my arms around him and kiss him deeply, awkwardly aware of the presence of the other recruits and passersby but unwilling to allow them to dilute the intensity of my sadness and fear of the unknown future. I walk back to the car, breathing deeply and feeling thankful for the long solo drive home.

Cosi Fan Tutte, Mozart

It's kind of weird that when you major in music in college, you don't have to do a senior project, an undergraduate thesis, or an internship to finish your degree. Instead, you have to do a recital. In a way, it seems too easy because my work for each class is done with a final exam, and some classes don't even require that. A recital is a final exam on my ability to perform, I suppose, but as long as I fulfill a few requirements, I could sound terrible and still pass. I don't get an A for being a fabulous singer or a C for being just an okay one. It's just, "You have fulfilled the requirement. Check," and I'm done.

After I made the change last year from a music education degree to just a plain old music degree, I realized, with a great deal of excitement, that because Westminster required so many credits in music-specific courses and because I'd used my summers to catch up on the humanities courses I would have taken in my first two years at a different school, I only needed a few more credits to graduate—and most of these were nothing more than "graduate credits," meaning that I could take whatever I wanted as long as I passed enough classes for Moravian to be willing to award me my degree. So, now I'm taking classes like "Ethics of Government" and "Survey of American Literature." I didn't pick the easy classes; I picked the ones that help me remember that I have interests other than music.

But, still, the recital is a requirement, so here I am, standing in the hallway, waiting to hear the applause go up for my recital partner,

Evelyn, who I am alternating with in performances. The first few pieces went fine, so I'm starting to get that ever-elusive performance buzz. I am doing well. I am good at this. My voice, and I, are beautiful. I can do something that not too many others can. I am loved.

Eric is here with me, too, because, on the suggestion of my voice teacher, who was also Eric's voice teacher for a little while last year, we are singing a duet from a Mozart opera, including some minor acting. It's all in Italian, which I can sing but not translate, but naturally, Eric knows exactly what's going on in this particular scene/song duet. He told me the whole story in context, but all I really needed to know was that I am playing a mildly self-righteous woman who has already turned down a romantic advance from Eric's character, and in the duet, I am turning him down again, while he turns up the charm and wins me in the end. I insult him in Italian through about three quarters of the song, then kiss him when it ends. *Cosi Fan Tutte* can be loosely translated as "Women Are Like That." And we are. But men are, too.

Eric and I have been having a lot of arguments; or, rather, I have been arguing and Eric has been listening smugly. Our wedding is now five months away, and deposits have been paid to caterers and rental companies who will bring chairs and tables and tablecloths and napkins—all of it. We made almost all of the decisions on these things together. But now he's…distant. But not just distant; he's difficult to talk to. No. He is aloof. More than that, too, though. He says all the right things, but he also says the wrong ones: sly remarks that hurt me, but covert and personal enough that I can't tell if he is hurting me intentionally with his words or if I'm just being…picky. Expecting him to whisper sweet nothings all the time like he did when we met almost three years ago. I knew even then that it was completely unrealistic to expect him to woo me that way for the rest of my life. But I expected it anyway.

And now we are less than a minute from walking out onto a little stage in front of a little audience to perform a song that is all about wooing. *I'm glad it's in Italian,* I think; *I won't have to know which parts of his lines are lies.* The performance ends when Eric wraps his arms around me, and we kiss. I am as nervous about this one kiss as I am about all the rest of the recital. Because this is a performance kiss, and I suspect that that is all it is for him.

The applause goes up, and I take my last few deep breaths as Evelyn, with her mature, experienced voice, takes her bow. My friend, Emily, who is waiting with us, is there to make sure I am ready for each entrance, but she is also my moral support. She has supported me—and, in turn, Eric—in my growth as a young child of God. She is truly my big sister in Christ.

As the applause goes up on the other side of the stage door, she looks at Eric and me, smiling, and says, "How is it that you two make that ending kiss look so romantic?"

"I'm a really good actor," Eric says.

Then the door opens.

"Complicated," Avril Lavigne

Looking for a church to call home is pretty much the same process as looking for a home to call home, but without the real estate agent.

Now that we're married and I've finally been able to hang my clothes in the closet here, finding a good church is our next step. But the only way we could think of to do the search was the internet. So a few days ago, we sat in our "office" room (which is really just a room with a desk, a computer, a chair, and a pile of boxes and milk crates to trip over) and typed "church near Glen Burnie, Maryland" in the search bar. We looked at a few different options, discussing whether or not we wanted to attach ourselves to a denomination (we don't), and how far we were willing to drive on a Sunday morning (maybe 30 minutes, but longer if we're sure it's worth it), and what type of worship music we want to hear (hymns vs. praise songs). The last is the one that becomes a research issue.

We both attended denominational churches as kids—Eric, Lutheran, me, UCC—but neither of us actually learned about what faith is in those churches. We both spent years going to churches because that's what you were supposed to do; it was part of being a good person. I even told my family I wanted to go at one point when I was ten because a kid at school said that you had to in order to be good, and up until then, we hadn't. But what Eric and I find as we look through church websites is that if you want traditional hymns, you have to go to a denominational church. Both of the churches we grew up in taught about Jesus, but neither of them taught about faith; so, since we want to grow our faith and we want Abigail to learn about faith in Jesus, nondenominational it is. And that means worship songs and a worship band. So we looked at nondenominational churches and landed on one closer to the Chesapeake Bay that was worth the visit. So here we are, two weeks after our wedding, going to church.

We've already figured out that nondenominational churches like to greet you when you walk in. That way, if you're new, they know it, and you end up getting an escort and a "getting to know you" conversation. But we'd like to lay low and stay off their radar for now. This church meets in a high school auditorium, so we figure that since we are particularly talented at late arrivals to pretty much everything, we can sneak in and sit in the back without drawing too much attention. The music is simple: a few worship songs I know, lead by a couple in their twenties, like us—her on vocals, and him on vocals and a keyboard. The sermon ends with an altar call, and a good number of people come forward to pray and ask Jesus to be their savior. Eric and I look at each other, smile, and agree that we're satisfied and will come back next week. We even like it enough to talk to the pastor and introduce ourselves, now that the service is over.

Pastor Peter is a good-looking guy in his 50s with a tan, blonde hair that's just starting to thin, and blue eyes. He tells us that they've been meeting in the auditorium for a couple of years now but that the church just purchased and broke ground on a piece of property that will become their church building. Again, my heart warms, and I feel like this is the place. A new-ish church family with a sure future ahead of them. This is the place.

And then Pastor Peter invites us to a picnic that afternoon at someone's home, so now we have to decide how committed we are to coming back. A service is one thing, but going to a picnic with casseroles and Dixie cups and cheap ice cream in plastic buckets is another. We have to decide if we're ready for real conversations with real people who will ask how we met, where we're from, and what we do. Mingling is scary. So we give him a noncommittal answer, but by the time we're in the car pulling out of the parking lot, we've decided to go, and to break in one of our new Pyrex casserole dishes, too.

Three hours later, we pull up to a huge old house in a quiet neighborhood full of huge old houses. We're only a little late, but we still have to shuffle around the countless casserole dishes spread out on the picnic tables. This person's backyard looks like a small park. It has a gazebo with multiple tables, a decorative pond, and a volleyball net. We're still in church clothes, and I feel overdressed. We grab paper plates, fill them, and awkwardly eat, standing against a bush and balancing our plates in one hand. We people watch and make polite conversation with the pastor again. Here and there, people introduce themselves, and I let Eric make conversation for the most part because I am very nervous. I loosen up gradually, though. Someone is selling church T-shirts that look like baseball jerseys, and we try to buy two just to show that we're serious about becoming a part of things, but they refuse to take our money and hand us the shirts like it's a privilege for them to do so. Then, as Eric and I are filling our paper plates, Pastor Peter calls everyone together to pray over the food and announces that there will be an immersion baptism in the decorative pond in an hour. I don't know if it's the celebrity status they seem to be giving us, the beautiful weather, or the remaining post-honeymoon glow Eric and I are still sporting, but something strange and wonderful flips a switch in my heart.

I look at Eric and tell him I want to get baptized. And he says he does, too.

So there we are, an hour later, standing in a deceptively deep decorative pond in a stranger's backyard, being baptized by strangers while more strangers cheer for us. I wore a white blouse, and there was a concern for my modesty if it got wet, so I was handed a men's blue polo shirt with the church name embroidered on the pocket. I volunteer to go first, mostly because if I wait any longer, my nerves will get to me and I will back out. But they bring Eric and I in together, step by step, into the water. It is almost shoulder-deep for me. I am trying to appear quietly confident, but I am scared to death. I know what baptism means from my reading of the Bible, from books that taught me about the Bible, and from other, older Christians who have guided Eric and me as we visited churches in Pennsylvania on the Sunday mornings prior to our wedding. But it occurs to me—although it's too late since I'm already boob-deep in the baptismal waters—that I don't really know what my choice to be baptized here will mean to the mass of strangers standing in the grass a few feet away. I am making a commitment to follow and live for Christ, but am I making a commitment to them as well? Jesus' expectations are clear, I think, but it's other people's expectations that worry me. People, I know, are incredibly needy and incredibly inconsistent.

Nevertheless, I feel a sense of peace and belonging as I am tipped backward into the water. I am not a stranger to Christ, and if I remain united to him by the Holy Spirit, I will be loved—by him, by my husband, and by these people.

These are the emotional, rapturous thoughts that flow through me, encompassing my heart, mind, and body as I step back, still in the pond, and watch Eric receive his baptism, thank the pastors, and kiss me before we even step out of the pond. We are forgiven, we are married, we are made new, and we are immersed.

I am my Beloved's, and my Beloved is mine.

"Rosanna," Toto

I am really terrible at small talk, probably because it requires talking about stuff that doesn't matter. If it doesn't matter, why talk about it? It's a way to get to know people, I suppose, but if you never get past that point, you don't really know them. And it's especially difficult with Eric's family. I just don't know them that well, and I'm too scared of them to take any risks, even conversationally. Sometimes I try to talk about something, but I always seem to get shut down with total silence, followed by a change back to people and memories I don't know about. Susan—Eric's sister, whom I've only met twice before today—has driven down to Pennsylvania from her home in Boston to visit their parents. Since we are usually up here to see Abigail every weekend, anyway, this was a good time for us to see her, too. I just sit and listen. Every time I visit with Eric's family, I feel like a fifth wheel, sitting in a chair and waiting until someone addresses me.

Susan is telling us about a friend who entered, trained, and ran the Boston Marathon last month—and not only finished it but loved it. Although Susan has never run it, she can describe it: the course, the crowds, the history, all of it. She's decided to train for it and run it herself next year and directs her description of her training plan to Eric specifically, who surprises me when he says, "Okay, I'll do it, too."

The only kind of running Eric does is running late. In fact, he's a champion at that. He *is* athletic; he played on his high school tennis team and coached the tennis team at the high school where he taught

107

in South Carolina. But now, as he's adjusting to the Navy, the Sea Chanters, and living in DC, his only real athletic concern is passing his physical "PT" testing and catching the train at rush hour. So, as Susan continues to explain that anyone who wants to run the Boston Marathon has to first run a different marathon and finish that marathon fast enough to meet a certain qualifying time, I am beginning to see some lonely weekends in my future. So it's actually two marathons, but Eric remains undaunted and ready to tackle the whole thing.

Eric's job with the Sea Chanters is definitely a comfortable one for all the rigamarole it took for him to get started. After he quit teaching and moved back to Pennsylvania from South Carolina, he'd been working shift jobs that paid by the hour, but in the Navy band, their responsibilities are directed toward attending rehearsals, being there for every performance in uniform and performing well, and one collateral duty that contributes to the administrative and publicity needs of the group. In description and on paper, it looks like a big job, but in reality—and factoring in the salary and benefits the Navy provides—it's an incredible deal. All that said, he is responsible for maintaining a certain physical fitness standard, and we're already living two states apart right now.

I make a rather sheepish attempt to be a part of the continuing conversation about running but almost immediately wish I hadn't. I said, "I used to jog all the time in junior high and high school. I was slow, and I walked a lot, though. It got me outside and helped me lose weight," But they just looked at me, and my mother-in-law said, "Yes, it's a great way to lose weight," then they shifted the conversation back to working out and old memories again. So I shifted back to my assigned role: the fifth wheel, the spare tire.

"Little Earthquakes," Tori Amos

A few weeks ago, just before Eric left for boot camp, Angie had said that I could come over and spend time with Abigail while he was gone, so I'm going to do that today. But I'm anticipating a lot of awkwardness, and I'm not very excited about it. Knowing what I do about Angie—specifically that she moves in with men who have jobs and lives off their income, and then when the money runs out, and she's asked to get a job herself, she gets pregnant instead—I'm anticipating an incredibly awkward day.

There are things about me that I love, know, and associate with myself because they were true at one time but aren't anymore. When I was 11 or 12, people knew I liked helping with little kids, and eventually, it seemed like everyone knew it. I got a reputation as a reliable babysitter, and at one point I had three regular client families that each had at least two kids. I even had an after-school nannying job last fall semester when I was still at Westminster. But when I'm honest with myself, the truth is that I don't like taking care of kids at all. I like their cuteness, their enthusiasm, and their hopefulness, but when I'm responsible for them, I also have to contend with their willfulness, their infinite energy, and their stubbornness. That's the bigger part of the job, which wears me down and makes me anxious and angry in a way that hurts and exhausts me, in a way that I don't know how to believe or even accept. On bad days, a little kid can bring out the worst parts of my inner monster.

I don't know how to be around Abigail without Eric around—or Angie, for that matter. Eric is the go-between in these relationships; I follow his lead in how I think about and interact with them. It's the same with his parents and sister. There are no real relationships between me and Eric's people; I'm like his office assistant who relays messages back and forth. If I had, or even wanted, an independent, personal relationship with Angie or Abigail or Ronnie or Terry or Susan, the entire dynamic of every other relationship—Eric and his family, Eric and Angie, Eric and Abigail—would be affected. I don't want to be responsible for shifting these tectonic plates; I've already dealt with too many earthquakes within my own family.

Everything goes pretty well for the first few hours hanging out with Abigail and Angie. Angie is actually fun to talk to, and once we get talking and I temporarily forget her history with Eric and all the money problems that came from it, we have a good time together. Then, around 3:00, Jason comes home from work to take Angie and baby Maximillian to the pediatrician, so I'll be here with Abigail alone for a while, with no actual plan for how to spend the time. Abigail doesn't want to be left alone with me either, which is typical for a four-year-old. She is surprisingly good at veiling her true feelings with the ones the people around her want to see. She gets that from Eric.

When the door shuts behind Angie, Jason, and Maximilian, Abigail runs into her bedroom and pulls out some toys without saying anything, so I give her a few minutes to get used to the idea that her mom left, but I'm here. I need to get used to it, too. After a little while, I quietly walk into her room and sit on the carpet. She turns her head and quickly looks at me, but then shifts her body so that her back blocks me from seeing her face. No problem. This is the easy part. I want her to love me, but I can't force it—nor do I want to try.

I wake up almost an hour later with my cheek on the carpet and two Beanie Boos sitting side-by-side on my back. Abigail isn't in the room. Oh no.

My panic lasts only long enough for me to get to the kitchen and find her pouring water into a plastic cup from an office-style dispenser. There is a small water puddle on the floor, presumably from the last few drips that come through after the cup is full, and maybe eight or so plastic kid cups on the floor under an open cabinet containing similar cups. I put away the cups and wipe up the dripping water. Abigail's shorts are damp, and although she could have sat in the puddle below the water tank, she does still have the occasional pee accident—particularly if she's feeling a little scared. So I take her to the toilet and have her sit while I bring clean shorts and underwear.

"Are you hungry?"

"Yes!" she tells me, so I look for stuff to make grilled cheese, but I can't find the right kind of pan, so I opt for SpaghettiOs instead. There's a pack of mini tomatoes in the fridge, and she loves those, so I hand her those as well and help her get up onto a stool at the kitchen island. Then I grab a handful of cookies for myself, but no plate—I don't want Angie and Jason to know I ate their food.

Just before dark, around 8:00, Angie, Jason, and baby Max come in with pizza. Abigail tells them, "I played and ate SpaghettiOs, and Mao took a nap and ate cookies." Angie just laughs when I apologize. Some stepmom I'm going to make. So I spend the next couple of hours cleaning up and holding the baby in the hopes of redeeming myself, but by 9:00, I'm tired and depressed. Nighttime is for quiet and deep thinking, but I'm sure that doesn't happen in a small house with a baby and a four-year-old. And I feel so scared and guilty. I did a crappy job watching my future stepdaughter, ate their food, and didn't clean up right. Worse, I don't think I made much effort to get Abigail to love me and see me as another parent, and the efforts I have made—today and over the last almost two years—aren't working. Abigail seems to see me more as an auxiliary person that comes with her dad. I want to love her, and I want her to love me, but I need time to create that, time for Abigail and me together.

I ask Angie if I can nap a bit here before I drive home, but she is getting irritated with me now. Nevertheless, she gets me a blanket and a spare pillow and tells Abigail that I'm going to have a sleepover with her in her bedroom.

We lay in Abigail's room, her in her bed and me on the floor for maybe 30 or 40 minutes, and I am crying quietly, overwhelmed. Eric has become my only friend, my only sounding board, willing to hear all the wonderful and terrible things I think about my parents, school, teachers, life, Angie, the world, and even himself—but he's been gone for over six weeks, and my frustration has built to maximum pressure. Now I am here with Abigail, my only connection to him until he returns, but I'm unwelcome with her. My hope had been to grow close and agile and more tolerant of Angie and Jason while he was away, but it seems I have made things worse.

Suddenly, Abigail jumps out of bed, runs out of the room, and slams the door. I can hear her crying, Angie consoling her while also telling her that just because I'm upset doesn't mean she can pee in her bed. Great. I sit on the carpet, trying to decide what my next move should be.

"Mommy, tell Mao to go home," I hear Abigail say, and a minute later the bedroom door flies open, revealing Angie, with Abigail in dry pajamas balanced on her hip and a set of sheets in her other hand. She tosses the sheets at me.

"Change her sheets. You're scaring her and keeping her up, and that's keeping me up."

"I'm sorry," I whine, getting big and beginning to remove the wet bed sheets in the dark. "It's just that I want her to like me and I miss Eric and I have no one to talk—"

"She doesn't want you here!" Angie says sharply. "Go home." And so I do.

Crying as I drive, I worry if I have damaged my relationship with Abigail, and thereby with Angie, and thereby with Eric, irreparably. I don't know how to do any of this. I don't know how to be without Eric because I'm still learning how to be with him, and his past, his family, and the people in it are daunting. Yet God is calling me to him and to all of them. I'm fully confident of this. So why am I fumbling all of it, and why is every step in these relationships so difficult? I am drained of frustration, drained of hope, drained of tears. Surely, loving the people God wants me to love shouldn't look like this, like failing.

"Eternal Father Strong to Save," William Whiting

Last spring semester, I went to my first student teaching experience at a local high school, but the high school chorus director I was sent to work with required me to do more leadership than my course required of me and more than I knew how to do. It was awful, and I wish I'd gone to my advisor sooner to explain what was going on, but in the end, I failed the course due to the weight of the high school teacher's poor evaluation of me. At that point, my options were to either do an extra semester beyond my fourth year of college in order to repeat the course next spring so I can get the teaching certificate a year after that, or to change my major to a B.A. in Music, skip the teaching certificate, and graduate in three years instead of four by taking a few summer courses to fill in a few required general ed. credits. Since I don't want to be a teacher anyway, it wasn't a hard choice.

So right now, I'm taking a two-week, six hours per day course in Latin-American fiction, and I love it. Back in 11th grade, Mom had asked me if I was sure I wanted to major in music, because maybe English would be better since I love to write. I turned down the idea immediately, though, mainly because I didn't want her to see me second-guess myself. I should have listened. Literature is more me than music is now.

Today, my Nokia phone rings in the middle of class and I feel like a jerk, but on some level I don't even care—or at least I don't want to care. I think I'm in the clear since I told the teacher ahead of time that I might get a call I needed to take, so I run out into the hallway and duck into this little faculty lounge room that's always empty.

This is Eric's last week of boot camp. I've only talked to him twice since he got there, for five minutes each time. Absence really does make the heart grow fonder, and beat faster. But this phone call can't go much longer than the others—I'm in class, and he has to limit the time so others can make their calls, too. But, God, is it good to hear his voice.

His graduation from boot camp will be the weekend of the Fourth of July, and we can arrive at Great Lakes and spend an hour or so together—in public only—on Friday evening, followed by the pass and review on Saturday morning. And he did it. He was the oldest recruit in his group by quite a few years and older than all but one of his leaders.

He gives me some instructions on buying plane tickets online for myself and Mom, something I've never done on my own, and that's it. His turn on the phone is done. So I give myself five minutes to sit and feel euphoric, then I head back to class. All this hard stuff—college, boot camp, not being married yet, the tension of being at home with my parents now—is almost done.

Silence.

Something isn't right. I was half asleep until a few minutes ago, but something is wrong at The Weather Channel.

The Weather Channel isn't something I'd normally find myself so focused on, but I'm sitting in a science lab classroom at 9:15 a.m., and I've been here for 45 minutes already, not even moving. An 8:00 a.m. weekly science lab for Meteorology class is one of the prices I've had to pay for my transfer to Moravian. I know it could be worse, but it's usually hard to look awake when you're half asleep.

Now, The Weather Channel has my attention. It's playing on a wall-mounted TV in the corner of the lab room, but it's muted because the teacher is lecturing. It looks like the typical Weather Channel content—someone is standing in front of a big, computerized, green screen map that shows satellite projections of some storm coming to the West Coast from the Pacific Ocean. The computerized picture reloads every few seconds, and I see the colorful pixelated blob of storm front move from left to right in jerky, 8-bit animation fashion. But what I'm really looking at is one of those special report banner updates running across the bottom of the screen, cutting the weather report person off at the waist. The banner is bright red with white print scrolling quickly from left to right in all capital letters.

"ALL COMMERCIAL AND PRIVATE FLIGHTS IN THE CONTINENTAL U.S. ARE CURRENTLY DELAYED OR

CANCELED. PLEASE SEE YOUR LOCAL NEWS FOR MORE INFORMATION AND CONTINUED COVERAGE."

What the hell?

Another student, who has also been staring at the screen instead of the instructor, raises his hand.

"Sir, there's a strange message banner on The Weather Channel."

The teacher stops, cranes his neck toward the ceiling-high TV mount, and watches long enough to read the message. "I don't think it's anything to worry about. There is probably an outage in the computer system that provides the radar signals to the airport towers."

The other student, satisfied with his answer, nods and refocuses on the chalkboard. But I can't. I just keep watching those words in the red box, scrolling over and over, over and over... *Something is wrong.*

I raise my hand and tell the instructor that I am going to the restroom. He nods, and when he turns his back to me again, I quickly slip my Nokia phone into my jeans pocket. The girl sitting to my right sees me but gives me a little smile. She won't say anything.

As soon as the lab door slams shut behind me, I am walking fast, trying to find a corner in the basement of this ancient building that is void of other people and also lets me get a signal to make a call. I dial my home phone number. Eric, who is on leave for a few days and is staying at my house with Abigail today, answers on the second ring. I don't bother with a hello.

"What's going on?"

He swallows. "What do you mean exactly?"

"I'm in the lab. The Weather Channel is on, but it's muted. There's some banner that says no planes are flying. What's going on?"

Eric pauses, then swallows again.

"Some terrorists hijacked a plane. They flew it directly into the north tower of the World Trade Center. It's on fire. Then, like 15 minutes later, another one hit the south tower. They're evacuating everyone and closing the bridges into the city. There was a third one, too. It hit the Pentagon."

I sit down on an old chair in the hallway with a cracked plastic seat. I pray. Then I go back to class. For the next hour, I am the only one in the room who knows.

At home that night, I cry a little, but mostly I'm just stunned. My dad, in his chair, stares silently at CNN for hours. My mom, finally home after closing the farm early, is still in her work clothes, making phone calls. I'm not sure where my brother, a senior in high school this year, is all night. Probably with his girlfriend. As long as he is safe. Eric is driving. He got a call from his new command that, because he's on active duty now, he needs to be within a certain number of miles from his duty station. He is driving into Washington, D.C., which scares me. He dropped Abigail off at her mom's before he left.

I wander around my house, room to room, in a daze. I have nothing to say. Schoolwork seems pointless; I don't know what the next hours will bring. I don't know what God is doing or where he is right now.

I collect candles, all that I can find in the house, and take my father's lighter from his desk. I distribute them and light them in every room, turning out the overhead lights as I do. Darkness everywhere.

"Crucify," Tori Amos

Doing my writing at my grandmother's house had been entirely my idea, and I'd had to convince my parents that it was necessary. I need quiet so I can do my schoolwork and write my paper because the sandblasting noise prevents me from concentrating and I can only get to my second-floor bedroom by climbing a ladder, and I've already fallen from it once. I still don't understand why this construction project had to happen now or how they could have thought that it wouldn't affect me that much. What started as a plan to sandblast a large wall in our late eighteenth-century farmhouse to reveal its original stone structure, and to enlarge our bathroom so its width would accommodate mine and my mother's ever-expanding hips, has turned into remodeling and restructuring most of the upstairs—including moving the staircase itself. My brother had moved out of his upstairs bedroom before the work even started since his bedroom was part of the project, but since my room would remain untouched, I could stay. That much has been true; my room isn't changing, but when they discovered an entire stone fireplace behind the staircase, the staircase naturally needed to be removed to expose this historical wonder. The staircase would be rebuilt somewhere else once they fully uncovered and restored the magical new/old fireplace, which would take some time. So I am living upstairs, but with no stairs—hence the ladder and my fall off of it.

The problem is that I'm also working on the biggest school project I've ever encountered. I am writing a research paper on *The Catcher in the Rye* for my honors English class. I don't know if other teachers I've had would agree that this is the biggest and most important project I've done or am doing, but I've decided it is because I'm madly, passionately in love with this book. It's me and J.D. Salinger, off to prove that rejecting people and living reclusively while mourning the loss of an idealistic culture that only ever existed in my mind is actually an act of heroism and selfless love. I want to marry, or worship, Holden Caulfield. In the paper, I compare him to Jesus. This paper is my life's work and will encompass all the wisdom of my 16 years.

My parents' relational boundaries with my Grammy have always been strained, and have always been something to complain about, too, but I won this battle in the end because it was about an important school project and because I got angry. I have learned that my anger and obstinance can be a weapon of both offense and defense and that, combined with my confidence that I am, in fact, wiser and smarter than my parents, the threat of my superior aggression is enough to get what I want.

Grammy's house is strange and quiet. When I get home from school and take a break from homework and Salinger, I wander around the house, peeking in cabinets and drawers and closets. It's 1998, and Grammy still has three Cabbage Patch Kids sealed in their boxes on a high shelf in one closet. In another closet are my grandfather's clothes. They have been hanging there, collecting dust, since his death in 1987—almost as long as the Cabbage Patch Kids. There's still a slightly dirty, working-man smell to them. My dad's clothes smell the same way.

There's also a heavy-looking marble box on a shelf. I've been looking at it for a few days now because I knew I'd seen it before but couldn't quite place where. Today, I remembered. This box contains Grandpa's ashes. Grandpa's been in that box since 1987. I'm sitting in a room with a dead body. The flakes of a dead body.

Part of me likes a good story, and I consider making up a ghost story to tell my friends: I wake up in the middle of the night to see my grandfather climbing out of the box. As I watch, he sits down in the desk chair across the room and watches me. The story isn't entirely made up. Several times since his death, I have woken to see my grandfather sitting in a chair in my bedroom. Sometimes he doesn't really look like my grandfather, but somehow, I instinctively know it's him. He doesn't talk; he just sits there and smiles at me. I'm not scared when I see him, but the following morning, when logic becomes accessible, I am terrified.

But this isn't happening now, so any story I tell wouldn't be true. Right now, I'm just sitting here trying to write, distracted by my awareness of that box. Grandpa is in that box; someday, when my grandmother dies, she, too, will be cremated, and her ashes will be mixed with his. Together forever, dust to dust, impossible to tell where one ends and the other begins. My grandmother and grandfather are a lovely tragedy. After they are mixed together, we, their family, will toss their ashes, a handful at a time, into the pond on the farm that my grandfather purchased from his father when my great-grandfather became ill, and that my father purchased from my grandfather when my grandfather became ill. Love, apples, Alzheimers, and ashes. A lovely tragedy.

"I Will Listen," Twila Paris

It hasn't been long, but I have stopped counting the days since I walked out of Eric's apartment, still wondering if I had been dumped or just threatened. It's hard to walk out of an apartment that already has a good portion of your own stuff in it, especially when it means driving alone with your thoughts for five hours, to return to your parents' house and tell them that the wedding for which they've been planning and shelling out money for a good year now might not be happening. It's almost as hard as spending the night alone in the bed that you and your supposed husband-to-be picked out together while he sleeps on the couch.

But there are good things about long drives alone, particularly when you're feeling afraid, angry, and hurt by the person you've built your life around for the last two and half years. The person who put a ring on your finger. The person who just dumped you while your wedding dress hung in the closet.

One of the good things is screaming. You can't scream when you're in a car with other people; they probably wouldn't appreciate that. And you can't move rapidly back and forth between blasting fast, crazy, fun music with the windows down and rolling up the windows and turning the radio off entirely. You also can't yell swear words about your potential future spouse while simultaneously ugly crying and pleading with God to make him love you again.

Of course, I did make the drive, and I did tell my parents what was happening when I got home. To their credit, they have been very careful around me—lots of hugs, but not so many that I'm uncomfortable, plenty of staying out of my way and letting me be alone, some gentle reassurance that they love me and that I shouldn't worry about the lost money that was already spent for the wedding, and a lot of patience and letting me cry in my room. I respect them a lot right now because they're respecting me.

Yesterday I went to the gym after my classes and lifted some weights, and a guy came over and talked to me. He asked about my degree program, what I liked about it, and what I planned to do after graduation. He was cute, and he was talking me up, I realized. I also realized that I'm still young, still attractive, and potentially single, and that this was a good reason to go to the gym more often. When I got home, I slipped my engagement ring off my finger and put it in my jewelry box—but before I did, I held it and prayed that I would wear it again soon. I haven't given up. I still love the man I am betrothed to, even if he is being a jerk, even if he has lied to me, even if he doesn't love me anymore, even while I am burning with anger at him. And I still want to marry him because I know that I'll feel all those things at different times after (if) we get married, too. I'm not naive about marriage, not after what my parents have been through. I still want Eric to call me from wherever he is and tell me he still wants to get married. I think I do.

But I also know that I am desperate to know that I'm still me, with or without him. I don't like that flirting with boys at the gym is a part of knowing that, but it is. And so is sending sad-but-kinda-flirty messages to an old flame on Instant Messenger, especially when this particular flame says that Eric would be missing out and that he himself is still interested. For a few hours a day, I want to be free of that engagement ring. I want to come back stronger and more confident because I was spurned just months before my wedding. Yes, I want to make Eric miss me, and I want to watch him hurt when I tell him he can't have me back.

But all the other hours in the day—and many hours into the night, too—I am crying, pounding my mattress and stomping my feet, running my ass off and lifting too heavy at the gym because I *want* to hurt and I *want* to feel pain because God has given me a raw deal: a two-and-a-half-year, love-filled, all-in, bait and switch. I'm not mad at God; I'm mad at Eric because he's the one doing this. But I *am* mad at God because he didn't stop it from happening.

Yet, just as I love Eric even while wishing him the fire of a thousand suns, I love God, and I know him well enough to know that, whatever happens, he isn't going anywhere and he isn't hurting me. He is growing me. He is forcing me to work harder, push my roots deeper into the ground that nourishes them, and collect the rain that I need to grow. God is telling me that there will never be a sure thing other than his love for me. He's telling me that he has loved me for eternity, called me his child before I was conceived, and cared for me before I ever took notice of him. And he is assuring me that he isn't going anywhere. He isn't changing his mind, and just because I don't know what will happen, that doesn't mean he isn't orchestrating a beautiful life for me. My job right now, he tells me, is to wait. I can feel my feelings and cry my tears, but I can't act. I must wait and listen for him.

Bad stuff doesn't stop happening when you're married and in love, and just because you get married doesn't mean that your spouse won't hurt you, *really hurt you,* ever again. I know that well. I think of my mom during my dad's dark period, with his name splashed all over the newspaper in accusation and hers printed next to it. When he went to jail and left her to run an already overwhelming business alone, to raise two pre-teens alone, to face the community alone. I thought she was crazy to still love him then because, to me, he was unlovable. But I realize now that that's what marriage is: loving a person when they give you no reason to, even when they give you every reason not to. And now my mom and dad are happier than ever, and they know you, Lord, and I, in turn, do too.

"And this is where I stand until He moves me on. And I will listen to His voice."

This is my job right now: to filter out everything but God's assurance of his love and care. To fully trust that even if Eric never calls or speaks to me again, if my parents struggle again, if I have to figure out how to be an adult on my own, even if I have to suffer and die, he is doing it all for me. His best for me. He loves me when all the rest of the world leaves me behind.

In the first six months of college, only two years ago, I moved away from home, met Eric, fell in love, and then met Jesus and fell in love again. Jesus is the one who's still here.

"And So It Goes," Billy Joel

Life is so good right now. Eric and I are definitely moving out of the honeymoon phase everybody talks about, and we've had a few arguments, but it's okay. Every morning, he gets up by 5:00 and kisses me goodbye before he catches the train into D.C., and most nights, we lay in bed reading the *Left Behind* book series. But I get bored during the day while he's at work. On good days, I go out and run—sometimes long runs so that maybe one day I can run a marathon, too—and other days, I do speed workouts in circles around our building. Some days, I go to the gym at Fort Meade and lift weights. Running is more important right now because I still need to lose 30 pounds to get back into my skinny jeans, but I'm told that muscle makes the fat burn faster.

The only other things I have to do are look for work and keep the apartment clean. It's a decent apartment, I guess, but we're already talking about finding a place with more kitchen room and space for our stuff in general. A lot of our wedding presents are stacked up in corners around the apartment, and some haven't even been unwrapped because we have nowhere else to put them.

Today, I'm cleaning up the bedroom dresser drawers. Eric has a lot of clothes that he doesn't wear too often, and when he pulls something out of one drawer, a bunch of other things usually get rumpled up in the drawer, and then he just leaves the drawers open. It drives me crazy, and we've been arguing about these kinds of things for over two years, but nothing has changed. So here I am, several days a week, doing my best to determine what's dirty and what's clean, folding and finding ways to stack the clothes to keep the drawers closed.

There are two smaller cube-shaped drawers that he puts socks, underwear, and random stuff in, so in an effort to clear up some space, I am sorting through those. Chances are, there is a bunch of trash and pocket change that he just tossed in, so if I sort it and clean it out, maybe the drawers will stay shut. At the bottom of the drawer, under all the mismatched socks and scraps of paper, are two velvety ring boxes. I don't recognize either of them. I'm already wearing both my engagement ring and my wedding band, so did he get me another ring? For my birthday, maybe? But when I try to stop the next thought before it comes, I fail. Did he buy a ring for someone else?

I've come too far at this point. I'm already full of fear, breathing faster, preparing myself to uncover a deep, long-lasting betrayal, a secret that I'm last to discover, that other people are all whispering about. When I open the first box, I find a ring I already know: Jen's ring, the one Eric had in his car that he gave me when he first proposed. Of course. I'm only surprised that I didn't think of it earlier. I can safely assume that the other ring box would be empty, then, because my engagement and wedding rings are always on my left hand.

But I open the other box anyway, against my better judgment, and I immediately regret it. Inside is another ring, fancier than the first, but also an emerald with small diamonds—and when I take it out and try it on, it is much too small. This ring was not intended for me.

I scream, cry, and throw things—pillows and silverware and shoes and clothing. It's tempting to smash the wedding china, but I don't, because perhaps I could return it and keep the money. How many times in the last four years have I worried that Eric was cheating on me? Several, honestly. That time with the scissors when he was gone all day during a snowstorm, not answering my calls, not caring that I was worried about him. The last time was when we separated before the wedding, which was only four months ago. All this time, he certainly knows that I have constantly worried that there was someone else. I had to worry. I thought that being on my guard every day and maintaining careful surveillance would keep me safe from this, yet I'm here again, betrayed by a man who showed me love and said he loved me. Another moment like before, lying on the cement outside the farmhouse, pounding my fists and crying because the man I loved most had betrayed my trust. It doesn't matter that Eric is my husband, not my dad; the hollow feeling within me is the same.

The next five hours are a blur of tears, yelling, and half-hearted revenge plans. Spinning scenarios in my head. Who is she? Was she living here with him before we got married? Did he break it off, or is he with her right now? And the last possibility seemed more and more likely as time went by. By 5:30 p.m., I had all but written him off because he was usually back by then.

At 6:45, he walks in wearing denim shorts and a polo shirt, carrying golf clubs. Of course, after almost three years together, plus all my efforts to call him, he knows what he's walking into, and I know him well enough to expect an excuse disguised as a story—which is exactly what I get. But it's not a pleasant one to hear. The smaller ring, the one I had only seen today, had been Jen's engagement ring, not the one he gave me the night we went to New York City, as he had told me at that time. The emerald ring that I had worn did indeed belong to someone else—not Jen, not even Angie. That ring had been one he purchased while living alone in South Carolina, and he had used it to propose to a different girl who was also just 18 at the time. She turned him down, and he tossed the ring into the console compartment in his car, where it remained for only two months, when he pulled it back out on September 25, 1999, and proposed to me with it.

Having already exhausted all the angry energy, there is no fight left in me, and all I can do is cry and tell him how incredibly hurtful this feels. The shame of knowing that with only one month of marriage complete, I have uncovered his lie and been so wounded that I have lost all the trust I had in him. If this had been his first lie to me, perhaps it wouldn't tear me up so much—but it isn't his first or even his second. What about the lies I haven't discovered or lies of omission, things I have no knowledge of and may never learn about at all?

Eric suggests we call Pastor Peter, the lead pastor who baptized us on the same day we first attended his church just two weeks ago. I agree, and 30 minutes later, we are sitting in folding chairs in a conference room outside his office. And Eric, having turned on his Prince Charming persona, has me smiling, laughing, and kissing him, despite my resolution to avoid it. It feels good to smile at my husband again, but I wish I hadn't made it quite so easy for him.

"You wanna know what I was thinking about earlier today?" he asks.

"You mean what you were thinking while I was at home angry at you and throwing a temper tantrum? Sure."

"I'm thinking let's have a baby."

I smile.

The meeting with the pastor was superfluous after that.

"It's Five O'Clock Somewhere,"
Alan Jackson

I'm finding it hard to understand all the hype around the Boston Marathon. Mid-April in Boston is often pretty cold, so I'm lucky that this year when Eric's running it, it's at least close to 55°F. Not that 55°F is warm, but it could be worse, I guess.

There also isn't much to see at the finish line. When Eric and Susan ran a marathon in San Diego last year, I was able to get to a couple different spots along the course, and at one point I got close enough to give Eric a kiss. After that, I got lost trying to find the finish line, realized it was 20 miles from where I was, and hitched a ride with a stranger to get to it. Another crazy life experience to tell our kids about one day, I guess. But here, there are piles of spectators on either side of the course, and I'm finding myself a good ten feet back from the course without any way to see much more than the backs of other spectators' coats. A few people comment on my now-conspicuous pregnancy, but no one lets me get any closer to the race course.

Another amazing feat of skill and prowess for my wonderful superhero husband, I think sarcastically. I've been reminding him that I used to go for two or three-mile runs while I was in high school, so I have, in fact, been a runner longer than he has. It's a pitiful comparison, but Eric does everything like an expert almost from the beginning and has so much experience in so many things that I often feel like he's teaching me how to be an adult. But now that my pregnancy is visible, I have something I can do that he can't, I suppose. I just hope that at some point, a day will come when someone who meets us will think that he's lucky to have me and not the other way around. I'm getting tired of hearing about how great he is. I'm not great at anything.

⁘

February 1996

I love my friends more than anything. They are my world. They have saved me from myself; without them, I would have killed myself. And I'm glad I'm still in junior high. Adults have nothing and no one to trust and nothing to believe in.

"Up on the Housetop," Gene Autry

I've read that young babies sleep a lot, nurse a lot, and in between sleeping and nursing, they cry. Literally every book I read, and every nurse, midwife, doula, and experienced mother told me this. But I still wasn't prepared. I know in my head—in my thinking brain, anyway—that Ida's shrieking is her normal, natural reaction to just about everything and that this is a part of her adjustment to life. I also know that Eric and I, and today Mom, too, are dealing with her crying in the right way. But a visceral, primal reaction in my body is telling me the exact opposite—to make the sound stop, to fix this problem, to run, to hide, to force this sound to just STOP. What kind of mother am I if I'm scared and even angry because my newborn is crying? And how will I be a mom to her if I find her cries terrifying and repulsive? She's six weeks old, for goodness' sake. And I'm already failing.

Someone I saw while I was out with her last week, a stranger in Walmart, asked how old Ida was, speaking loudly because Ida was wailing. I told her five weeks. This lady shook her head and said, "You've got her spoiled already." What the heck does that even mean? She's a baby, not a leftover meal forgotten in the back of the refrigerator. But I'd heard plenty about spoiled children growing up. The implication was that I had "spoiled" my daughter by giving her too much control over me and over her surroundings; this is a ridiculous notion. A newborn doesn't even know what she wants, so she could never put together the idea that screaming bloody murder was a great power play. Ida isn't crying to manipulate me, for goodness' sake. She's crying because she doesn't know who I am other than Mommy, or that her loud crying is scary and frustrating for other people. I'm sure that, on some level, she knows she needs something. Her cries are loud, long, and impossibly strong. No one, not even a baby, would choose to scream like this. It has to hurt her tiny lungs. But the only thing that consistently stops her tears is nursing, and even then, she stops only because she has milk in her mouth.

At the moment, my mom has been singing the same Christmas song for almost ten minutes straight. Although Ida stopped briefly at one point to stare at Grandma's face, eyes wide like she was trying to stop an oncoming car via telekinesis, she is still crying now and clearly wearing herself out, too. But Ida perseveres, determined to deliver her own Christmas carol, the longest and loudest in the history of the world.

I don't think I've ever been confronted with a terrifying situation like this that I have no means of stopping. Ida isn't terrifying; she's sweet and beautiful, but my inability to calm her 90% of the time is terrifying, and I can't run from it. Every cell in my body is telling me that I'm in danger, and these crying jags cut down every splinter of hope in the broad, optimistic vision I had for the future. Eric and I had been talking about Psalm 127:3-5, the "quiver full" passage. We'd imagined homeschooling a brood of happy, fun-loving children. We even postponed my second postpartum appointment at the birth center because we knew they'd want to know our plans for birth control. But Eric isn't doing this, not all of this, every day for 24 hours. Don't get me wrong, he's doing his share and then some, but he's at work for six hours every day—and he's still running most days, too—while I'm at home making my lunch with one hand and holding Ida with the other so I can keep her asleep long enough to eat. I'm not mad at him for being a guy, I promise. I'm just...mad. And tired.

Oh, and we're moving again. As if it wasn't enough to give birth and drive four hours each way to visit our families for both Thanksgiving and Christmas, we're also going to move over New Year's. Mom and Dad are coming to Maryland next week to help us move out of our tiny basement apartment into a two-bedroom rental home. The idea was to have more space, including a baby nursery. We committed to this house only a day or two before Ida was born. But at this point, Ida hasn't slept in her crib for longer than five minutes. But more living space is good.

"It's the Most Wonderful Time of the Year," Andy Williams

I'm just awake enough to realize I'm awake, but I don't know what woke me. Ida is still fast asleep on the bed next to me, and I myself fell asleep so quickly that I never even pulled my shirt back down over the exposed breast she was nursing from. Then I hear it again and realize that someone is knocking on my back door, persistently.

I heave my huge, seven-months-pregnant self out of bed to make my way to the door, frustrated that whoever is knocking has interrupted my own nap, and knowing that Ida's will likely end pretty soon, too. If she hears me in another room, she'll get up and come find me.

As I lumber down the narrow hallway filled with excess groceries and heavy winter coats—some hung on hangers, some on the floor, and some dangling off a hanger or a pile of stuff in between the rack and the floor—I notice the hammer sitting on top of my clothes dryer. *Dang it,* I think. *I still haven't finished hanging those pictures in the living room,* and I think of the half-done gallery wall I'm trying to create by the TV, the one I never seem to have the energy to finish. I'm so tired and lazy that I can't hammer a darn nail into a wall and hang a picture.

My thoughts are still wandering, but I try to refocus on answering the door. Through the window on the door, I can see a black woman with short hair and an ID badge on a chain around her neck. Great, it's another overdue bill. I can't understand why Eric keeps letting that happen.

When I open the door, she tells me that her name is Danielle, and she is here from the Anne Arundel County Department of Child Protective Services, and can she come in. Still only half awake, I'm not really looking at her but at her giant SUV parked at the curb nearby. There is a car seat in the back, but no child. *Well, if she's a mom, at least she understands why it took me so long to get my giant pregnant self to the door.*

I happily let her in when she says she is here because she was told I could use some help with Ida. Talking quietly, I tell her that Ida is asleep on my bed in the next room and that yes, I could use some help. Assuming that my therapist at the Naval Academy clinic called her, I am thankful she's here. I know that my depression and anxiety are only barely under control and that because I had to stop taking depression medication with the pregnancy, I am in bad shape mentally. To top it all off, I had to make a change to my medical insurance so that I could be seen for this pregnancy at the same birth center where Ida had been born. This baby will only be 15 months younger than Ida, and with everything going on, neither of us had the energy to find another facility or even consider trying a different style of birth or a different birth center or hospital. No, things hadn't gone the way I really wanted them to with Ida's birth, but at least I knew the people there. I couldn't do all the research again. So, I am back to paying copays for my medical treatments, which means that obstetrics is all we can afford. We don't have enough money for me to see a therapist on top of that. But I'm so stressed and tired and frustrated that I can't be a good mother to Ida, so I did go to therapy last week, anyway. I saw someone at a medical center about 15 minutes away, in the fancier town of Columbia, Maryland, and I'd also decided to start taking a partially used bottle of Wellbutrin that was still sitting in my cabinet. I know the pills could harm the baby, but if I kill myself, he or she would be harmed even more. I've been taking them once a day for about a week now, and I am definitely feeling a little better. Just a little.

I'm glad Danielle's here because I have no one to talk to. I talk to Ida, but she doesn't understand me, of course, and often, she doesn't even turn her head or look at me when I'm talking. I talk to Eric when he gets home from work, but after he rushes around to clean up any messes I didn't get cleaned up during the day, he sits down and falls asleep almost immediately. For the past two months, he's been arriving at work earlier and staying later to prepare for an upcoming Christmas event—plus, he has a good hour commute both ways on the MARC train. He also goes for a run almost every day, and he sometimes brings work home, too. He does most of the cooking, too, although mostly we're both too tired to use more than the microwave. I know he has to be so angry and resentful that I don't keep the house clean or cook dinner for him. I don't do the grocery shopping, either, because I'm so scared of what people think when Ida starts screaming and I can't get her to stop.

I'm a terrible wife and a terrible mother, and I know it, and anyone who sees me knows it. I can't control my baby, who is unhappy any time we leave the house, yet here I am, big and pregnant with another one. I am a walking advertisement for birth control, and I'm ashamed of that. I'm sure Eric is ashamed of me, too, since he never wants to talk to me, or spend any quality time together, or go anywhere.

I tell Danielle all of this. I tell her that I saw the therapist last week and that I started taking the Wellbutrin, which will probably hurt the baby. When Ida wakes up, I take her into the living room, turn on *Baby Einstein* on repeat play, and go back to the kitchen to talk with Danielle. I'm ashamed of that, too, I tell her. I have a baby DVD of some sort playing most of the day because when I try to play with Ida, she doesn't seem interested, and when I encourage her to play on her own, she doesn't seem to know what to do with her toys. The DVDs are the only thing that really keeps her occupied, and watching them is the only thing that seems to make her happy.

To make things even worse, I tell Danielle, Ida's pediatrician has been having me bring Ida in every week now for the last two months because Ida is underweight. She's 13 months old but only weighs about 14 pounds. Danielle asks what the doctor felt could have caused her to stop gaining weight, and I tell her how the pediatrician said that she was diagnosing Ida with "failure to thrive," that we had to figure out what was wrong with her immediately, and that to do so she would need to have what seemed like an enormous amount of blood drawn, all at once, to send out to a lab for an enormous number of tests. The problem is, though, that I know exactly why Ida isn't gaining weight: she isn't eating. I've been spending hours and hours every day sitting next to her in her high chair in front of Baby Einstein, shoving spoonful after spoonful, jar after jar of baby food into her mouth—but it seems like 90% of it comes right back out immediately and rolls down her chin, onto her bib. I have the stained bibs and baby clothes to prove it. I've tried using different spoons, combining foods she seems to not like with foods that she does; I've given her vitamin supplements, iron supplements, Pediasure—you name it. She spits almost all of it out as if she doesn't know how to swallow. The only time I know for sure that she's taking in anything at all is when she breastfeeds, which is why I'm still nursing her around the clock, even though I'm pregnant again. I can't understand why Ida would need all these painful blood tests when the cause of her stunted growth is so obvious.

Danielle sits next to me at the kitchen table and generously takes all of this in. I tell her my fears, anger, and resentment. I tell her how I question all the choices I've made over the last four years. Maybe I was too immature to jump into all this, but there is no way out. I tell her that I think about killing myself every single day, but I don't because I do love Ida, and she only has me. Not to mention the other baby as well, who makes his or her presence more and more heavy each day. I haven't had anyone to talk to like this in so long. I spoke to the therapist, but she only offered me 50 minutes, and Danielle… Danielle stays for hours, just listening. I feel reassured, and she tells me that Children's Services has options to help me and Ida, and that I don't have to feel this way anymore.

But then something changes. Danielle starts asking me about online message boards and webpages and wants me to tell her about my online activity. She tells me she's seen the website I use to post photos of the kids for our extended family, who we don't get to see very much. She has printouts from my website. Why did she print things off my website? She tells me that she knows I'm a member of a private message board group called Gentle Christian Mothers and that I talk a lot on there about how I'm feeling, too. I tell her that, yes, I do, because I have no one else to talk to—no friends here or anywhere else—and with Ida's high needs, leaving the house is too difficult most days. I tell her how helpful it's been to speak out to other mothers and just be real about what's happening inside my house and mind. Then Danielle asks another question.

"What about that message you posted when you said you were going to kill your daughter and then kill yourself?"

My heart stops for a moment, and my blood boils. How could she know about this? The Gentle Christian Mothers website is easy enough to find, but this was posted on a message board specifically for mothers suffering from postpartum depression, and it was supposed to be hidden from non-members. Has Danielle been *researching* me? *Spying* on me? Gathering some kind of evidence of something? The confusion rolls in. Could the military be recording phone calls between Eric and me when he's at work? I know Danielle is here to help me, but something about this isn't right, and I feel like I'm being raped, like my brain is being raped. I am violated.

Another knock on my door. Danielle answers it. *Why is she answering my door?* Another social worker, Stephanie, comes in and seems very young—younger than me. She can't possibly have kids or know what it's like to take care of a baby who cries more than she smiles. She introduces herself as Stephanie. If I saw her on the street, I'd think she was still in high school. She's smiling and pleasant. Too pleasant.

Danielle called her and asked her to come to my house because Danielle needed more help. She called her while I was in the bathroom. *What does she need more help with?*

Only then do I realize what's really happening. Danielle isn't here to help me. She's from *Child Protective Services*. She doesn't want to help me, and she only asked me all those questions and listened to my grief and hurt and frustration because she wants to help *Ida*. She believes, as does Child Protective Services, that Ida needs help—not *from* me but *because of* me.

The car seat in the back of Danielle's truck isn't for her child. It's for mine.

"The Way We Were," Barbra Streisand

I've never been to an outdoor funeral before, and it's damp and cold, with misty rain. Of course, sun and warmth don't seem appropriate today, but it would be nice to be comfortable.

We sit on metal folding chairs at round tables. We stare at each other quietly. She was my grandmother, but I don't know many of these people. Ida, who will turn five soon, feels heavy and wiggly in my lap. She doesn't understand what's going on, of course, and will likely have no memory of my grandmother. But she is wearing a pair of pink fuzzy pig slippers that were a gift from Grammy, chosen because both she and Grammy loved pigs. I put the slippers on Ida's feet to honor Grammy and to help Ida, in some way, understand who she was—that Grammy loved her.

But Ida doesn't really understand what's going on. She wiggles, climbing in and out of my lap, uttering a few repetitive words here and there. She can speak some full sentences now, even ones that express her own thoughts and needs, but she can't process this funeral. How do you explain to a child that someone she never had a chance to truly know, someone who loved her, has died?

Daniel sits on Eric's lap, behaving much the same way. They play with small toys on the table and eat granola bars together. Periodically, they say something to one of us, and we remind them to be quiet. I welcome the interruptions, though, because they keep me from putting together the enormity of all this in my mind. I think of the white box—the one that contains the ashes of my grandpa—and I wonder where it is now.

After the service of sorts concludes, an employee from my parents' farm drives us from my aunt's backyard to my parents' backyard, to the pond. It seems absurd, I realize, to climb onto this vehicle. It's an old school bus that my father purchased many years ago when it became clear that the older tractors on the farm were struggling in muddy patches. He needed vehicles to take customers to pick their own fruit out in the fields, but in eastern Pennsylvania, mud is an inevitable part of life, so he needed something that could get through a big mud patch. So my dad bought two old school buses, but wanting to make them more tractor-like, he cut the tops off of them, starting at the bottoms of the windows, and removed the traditional seats in favor of benches. Even when he did this when I was a kid, I found it amusingly ridiculous, but most customers seemed to find it novel, so the idea stuck around. But now we're on one, in the rain, and in funeral clothes. That said, Grammy would have gotten a kick out of this idea.

We get out and sit on more wooden benches set out in rows on the side of the pond closest to the orchard. The children are really getting riled up at this point, and there is whining and crying and the need to run around in the wet grass. They are in nice clothes, and Ida is in slippers that are already wet, but fighting to hang onto them would be a losing battle. So they meander around in the grass, their sweet voices occasionally disrupting the somber mood.

And then the time comes, as I knew it would. I've been anticipating it throughout the entire service, just as I have been since I was six. Someone presses play on a portable CD player. Barbra Steisand's smooth voice emerges, its tone fitting perfectly with the ugly weather. My father, my uncle, and my aunt stand together at the pond's edge, open a box, and cast my grandparents' ashes out onto the water. My dad seems a little confused and is mumbling in a way that doesn't fit the moment—a fact that breaks my heart even more than the moment itself already has. The curse continues, no matter how much it hurts.

We each approach slowly, taking our own handfuls of the ashes, of Grammy and Grandpa, in our hands and casting them out onto the water. The ashes feel dirty and smooth in my hand, and I am surprised that there are small, hard pieces among them—the remains of their bones.

I'm frustrated now as I drag my whining children, whose diapers are, no doubt, very wet, through the equally wet grass toward my parents' farmhouse. I'm frustrated with the children, of course, for ruining the aesthetic of the day, for not allowing me to focus all my energy on the sorrow and the anger and the ache of it all. It's easy to blame them for being children, but I know they are not the source of my pain. The source of my pain is the disease. Alzheimer's Disease. Old Timers' Disease. It took my grandfather before I could really know him, and now it's taken my grandmother, too, because her anger and hurt over the loss of her husband had been reflected in almost everything she did and said. She had rejected God and put space in her relationships, even with her own children and grandchildren. She was sweet and caring, but I could always see the pain she held onto. This disease took her, too. Collateral damage.

And now, my father is the one fated to carry it on into yet a third generation. My great-grandfather, who first purchased the farm that my parents now own, was lost to this disease before it even had a name. My grandfather was lost to it before it had a treatment. And now my dad is lost to it, because while there are pills to help his symptoms, three generations of research have not yet found a cure. Soon, I will lose my dad, too.

Walking through the grass and carrying/dragging the children, I let it all come in—not just the pain but the fear of it all. I've been only moderately successful at holding back the fear inside me—not just at the funeral, but since the day my grandfather died. The fear, that feels so much like knowledge, that this disease would devour my father's mind, too. And it is; that fear, the curse, is real. I've known it all along.

I also know that it's coming for me.

"The Christmas Song,"
Nat King Cole

The first thing Stephanie says after hello is, "Why do you have a hammer sitting on top of your washing machine?"

This is ridiculous. If she thinks that hammer has anything to do with my ability to take care of Ida, I'm going to lose my daughter tonight.

"I was hanging pictures in the living room yesterday. It belongs in the shed, but I'm not done with it yet, so I put it there so Ida wouldn't be able to get ahold of it." But Stephanie doesn't respond. Her opinion of me was already set before she got here, so now she's spinning that around in her head, imagining the worst possible scenarios of child abuse.

Danielle shifts my attention back to her interview, but there's little else for me to say. In desperation, I tell her that I've already seen a therapist last week and that I started taking the Wellbutrin two weeks ago, but she says nothing. So I begin telling her I want help. I tell her how I have no friends and can't really make any friends because Ida cries so much whenever we leave the house. *Don't all babies cry?* No, not like this. Ida seems terrified when she cries. And when she is terrified of something, I am terrified of her. I don't know how to stop her from feeling this way and crying this way other than staying home.

I tell Danielle that I *want* to go to a support group, or have a mother's helper come by a few times a week, or for Eric to be able to take off work a day or two each week to give me a chance to sleep. I'm trying to make her see that I will do anything, *anything,* to keep my baby because, for as many times as I've wished I hadn't had a baby, the imminent threat of losing her because of my own inability to be a good mom is terrifying me.

Baby McDonald drones on in the other room. Ida wanders out to me, nurses, then wanders around the house and back to the TV. I feel a pain in my head so heavy that I can barely hold it up, so, realizing I have nothing left to lose now, I lay my head on the table. I am hungry, and it's dark now, past dinnertime, but I have no energy to even lift my head, let alone make myself a meal. I called Eric hours ago and told him he needed to come home immediately. Where is he? I need him. I need my knight to come and save me.

Out of the corner of my eye, I see Stephanie pick the hammer up off the washing machine and move it to a high shelf, hiding it under some coats. I hear Danielle call her son's daycare center to tell them that she cannot leave "work" and doesn't know when she will be able to pick him up. *Your child is growing up in a daycare center while you're here, accusing me of being a bad mother. I spend all day and night with this baby. It's your son who needs help, not my daughter.* The anger over it all boils within me, but all I can do is sit at the kitchen table with my eyes shut, peaking at Ida every few minutes. I want to go to her, hold her, nurse her, and feel her in my arms because this might be the last night I have her—the last night I'm her mother. But I am too scared to move from this spot, too worried that every move I make will be interpreted as abusive.

Danielle makes phone calls from her cell phone and shuffles papers in her briefcase. She pulls out a form and begins writing on it. Stephanie asks me why Ida is so skinny, and I tell her that she only eats a very small amount of baby food, explaining for what seems like the millionth time that I spend many of my daytime hours trying to get her to eat but she can't seem to swallow anything unless it's liquid. "Does she eat anything other than baby food?" I tell her that I give her little things like Cheerios sometimes, but I've never seen her swallow one.

She does like yogurt, but I'm worried that dairy products could cause indigestion. "Does she feed any food to herself?" I look at Stephanie, not sure what she is expecting with this question. I tell her, "She doesn't know how to hold a spoon." *Should she know how to use a spoon?*

Suddenly the back door swings open hard, and again, I grow worried about who might be coming in—the police, maybe—but it's Eric, and he is angry, more angry than I've ever seen him before. He's still in his dress blues. He tosses his things roughly onto the kitchen counter. Stephanie begins asking him where he's been, why he didn't come as soon as he was called, and how it could possibly have taken him more than two hours to get home. Danielle starts cutting in with a very innocent-sounding explanation of why they are here, but Eric isn't listening to her, and neither is Stephanie. Eric is staring at Stephanie like an animal about to attack its prey. "I work in D.C. I commute there every day. You called me in the middle of the afternoon, on the single busiest day of the year for me. I take the MARC train to work, so I have to take it back home, too. Then I have to drive home from the station. This is how long it takes." His voice is quiet, but his tone is threatening. He usually changes into sweatpants before coming home, so I recognize that the uniform is intentional. He's trying to take control of the situation.

When Stephanie has no response, Danielle finally manages to speak up. Her words are one small step short of a memorized speech, and she directs them toward Eric. "I know you're very concerned about your daughter and your wife. We are here because we were contacted by Fleet and Family Services on behalf of your daughter's pediatrician and by an anonymous reporter. Two unrelated individuals, both concerned for Ida's wellbeing. Both are concerned that your wife isn't taking proper care of your daughter. Ida's pediatrician indicated that Ida's weight has been consistently below the normal range for her age for the last several months but that your wife refuses to bring her in for the blood tests that were ordered. The anonymous caller stated that your wife made a threat against her daughter online. I have been here interviewing your wife for the last few hours, and she has confirmed both of these accusations. Your wife wants to kill your daughter and commit suicide..."

She goes on and on, telling him things he already knows, assuming that he is completely unaware of anything that involves me or Ida. Assuming I'm hiding all this, somehow, from the one person who actually does understand, sort of. But Eric doesn't respond and just continues staring at Danielle with daggers in his eyes, his muscles tense like he could throw a punch at any minute. I feel thankful that he's here, that he will vindicate me, and despite his ferocity, I feel like some small amount of weight has come off my shoulders just by him coming in the door. Danielle says, "Melanie, is there anything else you'd like to tell your husband about what's happening here?"

She is speaking to me as if I am a toddler who has been caught stealing an extra cookie. I lay my arms limply on the table and then lay my head, face-down, on top of them. I feel so ill and so destroyed that I can't even physically hold my body upright.

"I told them everything," I say to Eric. "I told them why this is so hard. I told them I have depression. I just told them everything. I thought that would help." My words, spoken through my forearms and into the kitchen table, sound like a dying declaration. I feel as if they are. Eric touches me briefly on the shoulder, and I feel love and protection in his touch, but his outer demeanor hasn't changed. Then Stephanie butts in again.

"I can see that you're very angry with your wife right now. How have you handled it when she made you angry in the past? I saw a hammer setting on your washing machine..."

Eric doesn't let her finish. His voice booms, projecting like the professional singer he is, and I know that is exactly how he wants it to sound. "I'm not angry with her. She's done nothing wrong. I'm angry because you come in here with nothing more than a few unresearched accusations, one from a person we've never even met, and accuse her of intentionally starving our daughter..."

Danielle cuts him off. "Your wife also made a threat online, in a public forum, and said that she was going to kill Ida and commit suicide. We were able to see a copy of that message. Are you aware of that? Are you aware that your wife wants to kill Ida? Are you aware that she made the decision, without a doctor's input, to begin taking an antidepressant medication, and that antidepressants can harm your other, unborn child?"

"She is doing the best she can. She is a new mom with postpartum depression who is also pregnant. Ida is a difficult baby. She can't do much for herself. She can't walk. She screams when she can't see her mother. She doesn't like to eat, and she spits out her food," Eric is still forceful, but he's lowered his voice a bit. "What exactly do you expect my wife to do that she isn't already doing?"

Feeling some relief from Eric's support, I lift my head and join him in trying to, once again, explain our reasoning for not getting the blood tests done for Ida. The doctor and lab technicians told us plainly that the tests would be painful and would require them to take a large quantity of blood. Ida would be fine, they said, but it would likely make her ill for a day or so. It might be hard to catch her vein since she's so small, which could be painful, too. The doctor wanted to test for deadly diseases, many of which are extremely rare, and others that would require her to have a family history of disease that didn't exist. The doctor was mean about it, telling me that my breast milk could be causing the problem, that Ida wasn't developing mentally or physically, and that she might be developmentally disabled in some way. For a few brief minutes, I felt a tinge of empowerment. Eric is here, defending me, telling them that we made these decisions together, that I myself had chosen to find a therapist, and that I needed the medication.

Danielle says nothing.

The form that Danielle has filled in and set in front of me has several demands. I have to have a full psychiatric evaluation as soon as possible and make sure that her office receives a copy. I have to take Ida in and have the full set of blood drawn and tested first thing tomorrow morning. I have to attend private therapy sessions with a licensed therapist twice a week, and the therapist will need to submit as much information as possible to Danielle's office. And I have to be supervised by an approved adult during every moment I'm with Ida. I must agree to comply with all of these demands indefinitely, and a social worker will visit my house as often as possible, at any time without any notice, to confirm that I am in compliance. If I don't agree to all this, Danielle will drive away tonight with Ida in that empty car seat.

"She'll go straight into foster care immediately," Danielle says, "But I doubt she'll be in foster care for long. There are lots of mothers out there who'd love to be the mom of a baby girl like her."

It is a direct, intentional insult. She is taunting me and enjoying it. Why does she want to bring me down any lower? She has all the power over me and all the power over Ida. Ida, who screams in the very presence of strangers, would be raised by them.

This contract will mean that I have to prove myself worthy and able to raise my own daughter. They can come back at any time, require me to inform them if we move to another house, and they can track my mental and physical health by continuously following all my medical records. One slip, one moment of imperfection, and they will return to take her away from me.

"If you agree to these conditions, please sign the paper."

Eric says, "You make it sound like we have a choice."

My hand shakes as I sign my name.

"Mambo No. 5," Lou Bega

I will be okay without Eric. He's been on tour with the Sea Chanters for over two weeks and hasn't communicated with me at all, with one exception. He sent a group email out to family members and some friends from his past that was truly crazy. The email was a confession of sorts, but the things he confessed were from the past, including things going back ten years. And since there was no personal message to me attached, and I haven't been in regular contact with any of the other people who received it for several months, I have no clue what his motives were here. If he's depressed, that could be bad. I didn't get the impression he was before he dumped me or before he left on this tour, but I was also so depressed and scared of my now undetermined possible future with him that I needed all my emotional energy to take care of myself. I wasn't about to take care of his grief after he broke off our engagement.

The last two weeks have felt like two years, of course, because I am trying to grieve and imagine a future much different than what I've been planning. And then there's all the little stuff. What about all the nonrefundable deposits for tables and chairs and linens and caterers and photographers? Am I going to get stuck with those? Should I try to start a career around here? I haven't thought much about that yet since I was planning to move to Maryland after the wedding—where Eric's apartment is, along with my stuff. Do I need health insurance? How do you get health insurance? How do you pay for it?

I have been in limbo too long, I decide. While it might be okay to postpone making any major decisions, what I can do now is keep praying and doing the things I have to do and the things I want to do. It's April now, almost May, so the running weather in Pennsylvania is great.

So, I start bringing running clothes, shoes, and a water bottle when I head to Moravian for my classes. Not every day, but at least three days a week, I go for a run before I drive home from Bethlehem, the town where my college is. There is a pretty big running community around here, and because I'm doing my runs in an area that a lot of other runners use at a time when a lot of other runners run, I tend to pass the same people, depending on the day. Sometimes they wave. This is a community, and by running in it, I am starting to become a member. The cute guy from the gym keeps talking to me, too, and I try to figure out what nights he's there so I can line up my strength workouts for the same days and times. One evening, while I'm in the gym doing a speed workout on a treadmill, another cute guy comes in. I've seen him there before; he looks older, maybe a graduate or seminary student. But on that particular evening, he walked directly to my treadmill and talked to me. Turns out he's not a student at all. He is the coach of the college cross country team, and he asked if I'd be interested in joining.

I'm interested, but more in the coach than his team. That would be something to shove in Eric's face whenever he decides to come clean about what's going on with him. You're training for a marathon? Well, I'm running on a college cross country team and dating the coach. So shove it.

But as much fun as that particular payback would be, I turn down the offer. Knowing that the people I pass when I run outdoors are probably the team this coach is referring to, I would feel like a fool running with them. I am ridiculously slow and inexperienced by comparison, and the last thing I need right now is to feel even more ashamed because the truth is that I am completely desperate for Eric to change his mind. I can tell myself that I am attractive and smart and someone else will want to be with me, but I am in love with Eric, and I can't shake the feeling that we are *supposed* to be together. That it's God's will for us to be. And I'm so committed that no matter how bitter I feel about how he's treating me right now, I want him back.

That night when I get home, I climb in my single twin bed in my childhood bedroom, just as I have for my entire life. I reach for my jewelry box on a shelf nearby and pull my engagement ring out again. But I can't put it back on; it would be a lie. So I kiss it, and then I pray over it, pleading with God to help me either trust that Eric will give me some kind of answer, or that I will know the answer myself as soon as possible—one or the other. Then I put the ring back in the box, get out my Bible (*Melanie J Haas-Makovsky)* and read. And pray.

"Hey There Delilah,"
Plain White Ts

Child Protective Services may think that I'm a danger to my children, but frankly, I think it's them who are a danger to me, even physically, especially when I have to go to Walmart. Since I'm not on suicide/homicide watch anymore, I can finally do that, but as I put on the flannel baby sling, carefully slide Ida in onto my hip and adjust her left leg so it isn't poking into my eight-months-pregnant belly, and then put my coat on over it all, being alone isn't really feeling like a privilege. My body itself, with two babies attached, feels like an unbearable weight that only bears witness to the burden I carry in my mind and heart.

I pull out a cart from the stack at the front of the store, pull Ida out of the sling, and try to set her in the child seat in the cart, but she's not having it. She is almost 15 months old now, but she has not yet even attempted to walk on her own. She cruises quite well, hanging onto walls and furniture and whatever else she can find, but as the birth of her sibling (her brother, I think) approaches, she only clings to me more, wanting to sit with me more, sleep with me more, be held more, and breastfeed more. I am afraid that I am neglecting her (*"indicated child neglect"*) by even having this baby. She needs me so much now, and I can see that she is stuck. Even though the forced blood tests showed no results indicating that anything was physically wrong with her, as we knew would happen, she is not talking, not walking, and not sleeping through the night. She's not even trying to. How is it possible that she is becoming even more needy and even more like an infant only weeks before I will also be caring for a newborn?

But I can't waste energy thinking about it. I just need to get myself through this day, this moment. So I slide her back down into the sling, adjusting her left leg again so it sits on top of my baby belly rather than digging into it. As I make my way slowly into the store, I can feel her sliding her left foot up and down the front of me.

The baby seems to wake up from an in-utero nap and decides that now will be a great time to practice his karate. I feel the feet moving inside me, that indescribable sensation that makes me imagine I am not just carrying a baby but a swimming pool where he is working on his backstroke. Oddly, the feeling is rather comforting in this moment. Despite my fear of the mental and physical burden of raising two babies so close together when I have already been told I am failing, the little flutter of the swimming feet still feels like a bit of a miracle, albeit an unexpected one. I think of Mary, the mother of Jesus. She was only a teenager, not married, when the angel visited her to tell her she would have a baby boy, yet she responded with assurance and obedience, accepting that this was her calling. Being an unwed mother had the potential to bring shame to her and her family for the rest of their lives in her society, but she didn't get mad, and she didn't brood, and she didn't wallow in self-pity. These children—Ida and her brother—are *wanted,* are *blessings,* and I can do nothing but torment myself over them. But the little kicks remind me that they are miracles.

As I waddle through the aisles, the baby's kicks grow stronger until they feel like he might pop his tiny foot right through my skin. He is deliberately kicking in one spot, the same spot where Ida is painfully digging her left heel into my belly. He is kicking Ida's foot. I stop for a moment and notice that she is also looking down at her left foot as if she feels the kicking, too. Then the baby kicks so hard that I can see Ida's foot move a little, and Ida lets out a giggle as she sees it, too. Then she kicks back at the spot. And the baby kicks again, and Ida laughs again—and again. And I laugh, too. She is happy, and she is playing with her baby brother. I think of them, so close in age, growing up side by side, and I say a quick prayer that they will be friends. I realize that as they grow, they will develop their own relationship with each other, separate from me, and that they will be two different, unique people who will have their own lives, their own callings, and their own burdens someday. I laugh with Ida and realize that these babies are the children God promised me. They are *his,* just as I am.

"Here Without You,"
3 Doors Down

It's difficult to raise your hands to Jesus when you're holding a squirming five-month-old. I try to stand and sing praise with more than just my voice, but even five months after giving birth, my body is tired and sore most of the time. I had thought I would have recovered by now, but I hadn't considered the idea that I would get pregnant again during this time. But here I am, recovering from one baby while baking another. Eric and I are still the only ones who know about the new baby, and I'm still reeling from the shock.

So I sit, exhausted, and for a moment, I feel the slightest touch of shame for doing so, especially since the service just started. But then I remind myself that I am loved here. It's been less than two years since we found this church, but we dove right in when we did, and the dive was sort of literal. We went to one worship service and felt welcomed, but we were still surprised when we were invited to a church picnic and baptism at a private home the same day. And yet, we went, and we brought a casserole, and we talked to as many people as possible. And then, when the invitation to get baptized was extended to the congregation, we did, right there, in a small but deep pond on the property. The pastor said we were the first married couple he'd ever baptized together. And so, this church became our home even more than the rental house we're in now.

But I am sitting, and tired, and while I'm still fearful and a bit angry about a new baby coming along so quickly after Ida, and dealing with birth recovery and pregnancy at the same time, at this moment, I'm good.

Ida is wiggling and whining a bit, and it has been close to three hours since she last nursed, so I tilt her body toward me and carefully lift my shirt. I still have a big belly, so I am wearing a stretchy pregnancy tank under my flowy maternity shirt. My giant postpartum belly sticking out while I nurse is embarrassing, and I don't want people to notice me that way. And now I know that the belly will be sticking around for a long while.

I get Ida latched onto my breast, which is almost but not quite second nature now, and then I tuck my top shirt around my breast so that I am only exposing what I have to to keep Ida on my breast. After everything I've been through, all the unwanted attention my breasts got back in middle and high school, I don't need any more attention now. I'm not exactly sexy now that I'm more than 20 pounds overweight and gaining. I gently rock from side to side, watching Ida carefully for signs that she is finished and singing along quietly with the praise band. When our church completed construction on its brand new building, I had been excited for the day that I would get to use the "mother's room," a sound-proof room situated at the back of the sanctuary, with soft chairs and windows that allow us to see and participate in the service without needing to leave because of a crying baby. It's perfect.

Suddenly, my thankful thoughts are interrupted by the church administrator, a sweet older woman who has often admired Ida and encouraged me as well. She is standing in the room, though she wasn't a minute ago, and she has a gentle hand on my shoulder. "Come out to the lobby with me for a moment."

"She's almost done feeding. I'll be right there."

"No, now." I am being scolded.

I detach Ida, adjust my clothes, and follow her out of the sanctuary. Eric looks at me questioningly, but I tell him I'll be right back.

Standing in the narthex below the big welcome sign, she looks at me, and somehow, she seems both apologetic and stern at the same time. I'm baffled.

"You can't nurse the baby while you're in the sanctuary. Men can see you there. It's not modest behavior."

"What do you mean?" I answer, already feeling a lump in my throat and tears in my eyes. "I'm in the mother's room. I've been nursing her in there for five months now."

"You can't anymore. A man walking by could see you through the window. If she needs to nurse, you must leave and go to the baby nursery. There are only women there. That's the modest and appropriate thing for you to do."

I stare at her. She tries to go on, but she is stammering and can't find any further explanation for this sudden change in the rules, and I was unaware that there even were rules. We're at a stalemate, so she just walks away and leaves me there, rocking right and left to keep Ida calm while I burst into tears. Ida doesn't nurse on a schedule, in part because I was taught by other mothers and by the lactation consultant whom I speak with regularly that the baby will give certain specific clues to show when she is hungry and that, unless she went for more than four hours without feeding, I could simply watch for her signals and feed her on demand. Sometimes, she nurses for ten minutes, stops, and then acts hungry again a few minutes later, so I feed her a few minutes later. It's not misbehavior. If she's hungry, she's hungry, and breastmilk is all she has for nourishment and also the only surefire way to keep her calm when we're not at home.

But this new "rule" doesn't work. If I can only nurse her in the little baby nursery among the toddlers, then I will be in there the entire service, and what's the point of me waking up, dressing Ida and myself in our "Sunday best," and making the 30-minute drive here if I'm just going to sit in another room by myself? All of these thoughts are flooding through me too quickly, and I'm ugly-crying, and my eyes are blacking out. If I don't sit down, I'm going to faint and drop my baby.

I run quickly and quietly into the sanctuary and into the mother's room. I sit down next to Eric just long enough to catch my breath, clear the dizziness, and tell him, "We need to leave. I can't be here."

He takes Ida from my arms and we walk back out to the narthex together, and I tell him that I've been reprimanded. He is indignant and red-faced with anger. He is almost never angry; he usually chooses to acquiesce to whatever he's told and avoid everyone else's anger, even mine. He looks like a dog with his tail between his legs when he thinks he's in trouble. So this stiff-legged, red-faced anger feels good to me. He is my hero and my defender, and he will know what to do.

After a very brief period where we go back and forth about whether to complain about this treatment now or later, during which we determine that storming into the sanctuary and demanding retribution in the middle of the sermon would be inappropriate, so we leave. We could call or visit with the head pastor, and he would straighten this out. Why would he approve a building plan that included a mother's room if I wasn't allowed to feed a baby in it?

We leave quickly because I am shaking with panic and shame, and I don't want anyone to see me. Eric walks next to me, with his arm over my shoulder, as if we've been told that we can never come back. We don't.

"O Come, O Come Emmanuel"

As I open my eyes, I wish that I hadn't. This is another day, and I have to rise and face the accusations, the guilt, the anger, and the fear that the visit from Child Protective Services brought with it. I will need to care for Ida even while knowing that not only am I completely inadequate, but that if CPS determines that my inadequacy constitutes abuse or neglect, she will be taken from me and given to someone else. For a brief few seconds, I am filled with the thought that losing her would be a relief. I don't have a job or a social life to go back to if I lose my position as a mother, but simply having my body, my time, and my sleep back could give me a chance to become something other than the reproductive machine I often feel I am.

But of course, that's not true. There is no going back. I am a mother, and she is my daughter, and I have a baby waiting inside me to be her sibling. I can't go back from that, and I can't erase the changes that motherhood has brought me any more than I can erase the red stretch marks extending the length of my stomach and thighs. I can't erase my love for these babies despite knowing that my love isn't enough to make me the mother they need. And if they were taken from me, I would live with the guilt, the pain, and the loss, and it would change me even more in ways I don't want to think about.

The room is cold, and I am amazed that Ida is still asleep in her crib in another room. She has only recently been willing to sleep in it at all, and I suspect that my growing belly has left her feeling crowded out of our small bed. I remember now that it is Saturday and that the cold December snow outside is too much for our poor heating system and cheap, thin insulation.

I pull the blanket tighter around myself and roll onto my side, and as I do, Eric rolls to face me, also pulling the blanket tighter around us. He smiles in a dreamy, sleepy way, and closes his eyes again, holding me as closely as he can with the baby belly between us. I sigh and smile because this is why I'm here. The pain, the heartbreak, the sleepless nights with a crying baby, the anger, the arguments, and the complete awareness of my inability to do the very thing I need to do is overcome by the love I have for him and the immensity of knowing that these two children are here because our love for each other can't be contained in only the two of us.

Lying here, wrapped in Eric's arms and looking at the snow outside, my mind whispers.

God, if only you could hold me like this.

Seconds later, my heart hears his reply.

"I do. I just use his arms."

"Carol of the Bells"

Danielle and Stephanie—the CPS agent with the empty car seat and the young one who got so fixated on the hammer on top of my washing machine—are coming by again today to "check up on me." I have no idea what they're looking for this time other than to confirm that the babies and I aren't alone in the house, which we are not. My mom is here full-time now; she drove down six hours from Pennsylvania to Maryland in the middle of the night the same day that Danielle and Stephanie first showed up. I hated calling her late at night and asking her to do this, but I had no choice. Eric had to be at work, and the now-signed contract says I can't be alone at home with Ida. There are no reasons listed on paper for why I can't be alone with my baby in my own house, but verbally, they made it pretty clear: I needed to be supervised so that I wouldn't kill my daughter. They seemed to think it shouldn't be a problem, like I had some friend nearby who would come over and help, but I have no one. No one wants to be around me. No way am I calling up a person I met once or twice and saying, "Hey, can you come hang out at my house every day for an indefinite period of time and make sure I don't kill my daughter?" That probably isn't the best way to get to know someone. Now that we're not welcome to our church, either, I have no one.

Mom is planning on going home on the weekends, but otherwise, she will be here. Yesterday we spent the day cleaning the entire house until it shined and added about $100 worth of baby-proofing stuff—locks on the drawers and cabinets, covers over the door knobs, and plastic bumpers to prevent Ida from shutting a door on a finger. She can't walk, which limits her ability to do any of that, but I'm doing whatever I can to show that she's not in danger. They've only shown up unannounced once since the first visit, and I suppose that went fine. It was hell, but at least they didn't make more threats. They actually tried to give me an explanation for why their first visit had been so urgent—because supposedly, there was some other mom recently who told everyone that she and her kids were fine and then drowned them in a bathtub, and they needed to make sure I wasn't going to do something like that. All in Ida's and my best interest, of course.

I feel trapped. It seems like I can't do anything right, even though I thought I had been doing my best for Ida from the beginning—and the new baby. They threatened to take him or her, too. I don't know how this will all end, if it will ever end. I will always be the mother of these two babies, and I will always worry that I've failed them.

"You and Me," Lifehouse

I can't remember the last time I sat and watched a VHS movie with my mom. It was probably sometime while I was still in middle school. But it's a cold, dismal Friday in March, and the family of one of Eric's work friends brought us an entire bag full of VHS tapes that they don't watch anymore, hoping to keep me both upbeat and distracted from the continuing invasion of CPS into our lives. But I don't do well with distraction, and though I appreciate the gesture and having something to fill the awkward silence with my mom, I'm still miserable.

Last month—shortly after we got the letter that said I was convicted of indicated child neglect—we were informed that, because my case was closed, so to speak, I would begin a longer term of child welfare surveillance with a new social services worker, Lisa. Lisa would visit up to two times a week, and all her visits would be unscheduled so that she could catch me being a horrible mother, I guess. But in practice, Lisa has given me a few days' notice prior to most of her visits, and she treats me like the tired, struggling mother I am instead of treating me like a worthless piece of trash.

Once I was off of suicide watch, my mom went home to my dad and brother in Pennsylvania and stayed there for most of February, calling me a few times a week to see how I was coping with the grief and anger, not to mention the discomfort of my third trimester. She came back, though, a few days before Daniel was born, and she will be staying here for another two weeks to help me get used to parenting two babies with

162

different needs at the same time. I can't imagine that there even is a way to get used to that, but one day at a time. Daniel is two days old today, and so far it's been more like one hour at a time. I'm sore, exhausted, and unhappy, but I love my babies, and I love the way Ida likes to crawl up next to me while I'm holding her brother and kiss his head.

The movie plot is strange and boring, and Mom and I are both getting quite tired of it. It has more symbolism than it does plot. But we have nothing else to do, so we're half watching it and half sleeping on the big blue couch in the living room while Ida crawls around on the floor, the couch, and me. Eric has a few more days of paternity leave coming, so he is holding my skinny, big-headed, sleeping baby boy in the crook of his elbow and balancing his bum on the top of his thigh, all while working on an assignment for the online master's degree he signed up for through American Military University. It's a hell of a time for him to be working and taking classes, but it's tough to get promoted from Petty Officer to Chief in his unit, so he's pulling out all the stops. I don't want to live in this trailer park forever.

Ida crawls in my lap, sucking on the inside of her right hand and making a humming noise at the same time. This is how she tells me she wants to nurse. The La Leche League books I've read over the last few months helped prepare me for tandem nursing a toddler and a newborn, and normally, I would need to make sure that Daniel gets first dibs on my breast milk since his growth is critical in these first six months while my milk is his only nourishment. But with all the insanity over Ida being underweight, I'm not about to stop nursing her, especially since I'm still only able to get her to eat maybe four ounces of baby food a day. So I pull Ida close to me, unsnap my nursing bra, and hold her warm little body close to me. Then, as usual, she begins to doze off while she drinks, and the relaxing hormones hit me as my milk lets down, and pretty soon, I've dozed off as well.

But our nap only amounts to about 15 minutes, at which point Ida, my mom, and myself are all startled awake because Eric is yelling to us from the other room.

"What the heck is wrong?" I yell back, feeling irritated that I was woken so quickly from what could have been a decent nap.

"I need help with him." Daniel is crying pretty loud, but a crying baby hasn't been a problem for Eric before. "Why?" I yell back, still unwilling to stand up.

"He pooped, and it's on me," he says.

"Since when are you incapable of handling baby poop?" I moan to Eric. After all, this is his third child, and he's been changing diapers for a long time. Mom and Ida are both wide awake now, too, and Ida has a dribble of yellowish breast milk at the corner of her mouth.

"He pooped a lot. And it's all over me. And I'm wearing waterproof running pants."

Now I get it. Newborn baby poop is pretty much completely liquid, and it often comes out quite explosively for the first week or so.

Sure enough, as I walk into the other room, handing Ida over to my mom, I find Eric still sitting motionless in his office chair, with yellow mustard baby poop running down his windbreaker pants, pooling around the cuff at his right ankle, and dribbling onto the carpet. My anxiety level skyrockets to the ceiling as I grab my poop-covered son and tell Eric that I will take care of cleaning Daniel up so that he can change and clean up whatever portion of the mess is on him, his chair, and the carpet. Then, still holding a dribbling Daniel against my now yellow shirt, I quickly grab a clean diaper, a clean onesie, and a bath towel. Then I lay Daniel on top of the towel, right there on the carpet, and change him, wiping him down from head to toe while he wails continuously, overwhelmed by his own digestive output. I can't say I blame him.

Once Daniel is clean and redressed, I hand him over to Mom and then grab Daniel's poopy clothes, Eric's poopy clothes, and several poopy towels. It takes me a minute or two to decide how to handle this level of mess since my washing machine is full of clean, wet clothes that were washed this morning. But it doesn't take me long to figure out what to do.

I head into the master bathroom and begin filling the big, jacuzzi-style bathtub with warm water, and once I have a few inches of water in the tub, I throw all the poopy clothes and towels, plus my own poop-covered T-shirt, into the tub, and squirt in a bit of shower gel to combat the acrid smell. There, I think. I step back to admire my ingenuity. I am a poop-coated genius.

Daniel is still crying through all of this, so without bothering to throw on another shirt, I take him from my mother's arms and plop down on the couch, letting him nurse. While there is still a small part of me that feels awkward and somehow violated by answering a baby's screams with my breast, the wash of oxytocin—the brain chemical that creates feelings of both relaxation and love—flows over me, and I am as soothed as the nursing baby.

Mom sits beside me, and Eric comes out of the bedroom wearing poop-free clothes. There is a collective few seconds of silent relief, and then I tell Eric how funny and unexpected it was to hear him ask for help like that. Mom agrees and laughs, too, and Eric remarks that he will remember not to wear those pants while he's holding the baby. We share a laugh, then breathe another collective, cleansing breath together. And then we hear something else.

Ida's voice echoes from the bathroom, even louder than the sound of the water still flowing into the tub. She is yelling and giggling like crazy, more than her normal silliness, for sure. She is yelling one of the words she uses to play, "Bum!" over and over. This is the word she uses when she's pulling spoons out of a kitchen drawer or DVDs off a shelf, one at a time, but I can't for the life of me think of what she might be tossing in the bathroom. I detach Daniel and head to the bathroom, fully expecting to find my daughter splashing in the poop water.

But instead, praise God, I find a cleaner and much more amusing scene. As Mom and Eric follow my laughter into the bathroom with me, we find Ida standing next to the tub, holding a bag of menstrual pads I'd left next to the toilet. She is throwing them, one by one, into the murky, poop-filled tub of water. "Bum!"

With tears of laughter leaking from our eyes, we mark the moment. In a time when all of us are tired, weary, frightened, and angry, this single act of pure joy in the midst of the messes, both the legal mess and the bowel mess, has reminded me why we have children. Because these two children are people, and they are gifts to us from God. Because they will bring us pain, frustration, and anger, yes, but also joy, pride, and laughter. I look down into the smelly, yellow bathtub water, where clothes, towels, and now menstrual pads float like the worst soup ever made, and I have a rare moment of clarity in my tired mind. Someday, it will not be like this. Someday, they won't need me this much. Someday, I will again enjoy a full night's sleep, more smiles, and less laundry. We have been given the gift of loving and caring for new people, a girl and a boy, made in the image of God, and it will not always be a hardship. This will not be the last time they make us all laugh, or cry, or smile.

As I turn off the tub's faucet and lay down on the mattress on my bedroom floor, I am full of joy. Child Protective Services only sees my struggle because that's all they're looking for. They're skimming this chapter in my life, looking for a few catchphrases that stand out, that show I am a bad mother, so they can prove their worth and keep their jobs. They don't claim I wanted to hurt my daughter because they really think I did; they claim it because that is the picture that puts them in the hero's role, the one that could mean a raise or a promotion. But they did not "save" my daughter because there wasn't anything to save her from.

If I wasn't going through this fight—in life and in my mind—to prove that I am worthy and capable of being their mother, would I appreciate this silly, lovely moment? Would I realize that even though this mess made my nerves go into panic mode and will mean multiple loads of laundry tomorrow, it is also part of the cement that makes us a family?

As I drift off to sleep on the mattress, I ask God to solidify this moment in my mind. I can't afford to let a moment of joy slip through my hands right now. The only way I can love these babies the way they need me to is to build an altar for each moment of discovery, each time the joy breaks through the monotony to show me that this is only one page in a very long book whose ending is many years away. This is the book I get to live.

"Get the Party Started," Pink

So the decision is made. I am 20, I am pretty, and after some experimental flirting with a guy at the gym and an old boyfriend on AOL IM, I've determined that not getting married in July could quite possibly be the better choice on my part. It's wrong and cruel of Eric to string me along for two years and then intentionally act like a jerk to push me away so that he doesn't have to admit he doesn't love me anymore. He's trying to make this broken engagement something I want so that he doesn't have to be the guilty one. Fine, whatever. He wins. So if he calls me at all before he returns from the tour, I'm going to tell him it's over, that he has successfully forced me out of love with him.

I'm angry, obviously, but that doesn't mean I stopped loving him. It only means that I know I'll survive, that life will go on, and that I don't want to marry someone who changes his mind like this—as in, changing his mind and then trying to get me to do the hard part of ending the relationship. My engagement ring is still in my jewelry box, and I will give it back to him when he gets back to Pennsylvania, and then it will be over and done.

My phone is ringing. It's him.

Oh my gosh, what do I do?

I'm ready to do this, but not, like, *right now.* So I let it ring until it stops.

167

And two seconds after it stops, it starts ringing again. And it's still him. So I guess this is it. Go time.

And… it's done. And I'm smiling. Bouncing on my bed, actually.

Because he proposed again.

This is how it went:

1. He said hi. I said hi.
2. He asked me how I was. I said that depended on why he was calling.
3. He said, "I'm calling to ask you to marry me. Again." I said, "I was planning to call you and tell you that I want to move on."
4. Silence on both lines. The longest minute and a half I've ever experienced.
5. I said, "What made you change your mind?"

He told me that Mary, another member of the Sea Chanters, had a new baby, and because of that, her husband and baby joined them on the tour, driving city to city alongside the tour vehicles and staying in hotels because she was breastfeeding the baby. Eric said that yesterday, he was sitting down eating the hotel's continental breakfast when Mary, her husband, and the baby joined him at the table. Eric started making faces at the baby, and the baby would grin and giggle and laugh, which made him grin and giggle and laugh in turn.

He said, "I want to have that. I want to have that with you."

Holy crap. I am still completely in love with him.

So I said, "I want to have that with you, too." And that was basically it.

We talked about the potential of having to delay the wedding since our wedding date is only seven weeks away, and all the planning has been put on hold for the time being. But he said he would make some calls and see what it would take to pull everything off as originally planned.

I am truly crazy and truly madly in love with him. Again. I feel as happy as I did the day he proposed the first time.

I can't remember the name of that guy at the gym, and I don't want to.

"I've Got The Joy, Joy, Joy, Joy Down in my Heart," Wonder Kids

I am literally shaking at the library. I'm only here because I have to be because the therapist I'm seeing, who I don't really like anyway, said that I need to get out with other moms at least three times a week. I resent her for saying that and for a number of other reasons. I don't want to be out with other moms three times a week. I'm more tired than I ever imagined possible, but I've discovered that I can do quite a lot on four hours of broken sleep. Sometimes less. The problem is that I don't want to do things when I've only had four hours of sleep; I want to stay home and do as little as possible—just keep Ida and myself alive until the next opportunity for sleep arises. I never know when that's coming, though. Ida is 14 months old now, but she hasn't figured out the walking thing yet, so she just climbs. And this baby inside me is due in less than two months.

I most definitely do not want to be standing here in the library lobby at 9:00 a.m., holding Ida in the sling carrier with her leg kicking my enormous belly. She's kicking her sister or brother, but she doesn't know that of course; she only knows that the baby bump is in her way. But I have to be here, because I see the therapist again next week, and she will ask me if I went out of the house and met new people. And if I tell her I didn't, she will tell Child Protective Services that I am "noncompliant," which will be enough to bring them back to my door with the empty car seat.

I feel like a fugitive disguised as a sweet young mother. As I see other moms with babies and toddlers come in, I wonder if they will think I'm just like them or if they will see through this façade I can barely maintain. I'm not like them. They are good mothers with babies that sleep at night and nap during the day and stay asleep even if they don't lay right next to them. They are good moms who knew to use birth control so they wouldn't get pregnant again five months after giving birth. And they don't have to keep looking over their shoulders, wondering when the people with the ID badges around their necks will come back to take their babies and make more demands that they can't fulfill. I am not like them. They are good moms, and I am a child abuser in danger of losing not only the baby on my hip but the one in my uterus as well.

I'm still shaking as I quietly follow them into a tiny room no larger than a long hallway closet. There are way too many of us to fit in this space because, with the exception of one woman still pregnant with her first child, we all have a baby or toddler along. The room is too small for chairs, so we sit cross-legged on the floor, struggling to keep our babies in our laps. This is especially hard for me because I don't have a lap. Ida starts moving around and across the other women and children, alternately crawling and "cruising." She uses their bodies as if they were simply obstacles to move over or around. She doesn't respond when the other moms greet her or when the other toddlers pull on her or cry. She just moves across the laps and diaper bags methodically, circling the room over and over. But when I try to pick her up and hold her still, another mom with a little boy and a baby in a carrier tells me it's okay. No one minds if she climbs all over everything. She says all the babies do. When the meeting begins, she introduces herself as Monique, a mother of two and a trained La Leche League leader. Courtney, the other leader, has two small girls with her as well.

Going around the tightly wrapped pile of women and babies, each mother introduces herself and her children. Even this seems like more than I can bear. If I say my name, they will know me, and I will be exposed, and they will be able to tell anyone who asks exactly how they see me treating my child and anything that I might say in the meeting. But I surprise myself when my turn comes. I tell them that I am Melanie, and she is Ida, and I even introduce my baby bump as Lydia or Daniel. We are asked to share one thing we are doing as mothers now that we didn't think we would do before our babies were born.

Hold my baby down while the pediatrician forcibly draws her blood through three different veins and cuts her ankle open with a scalpel to get more.

I tell them that Ida is underweight, and her doctor is concerned, so I am feeding her baby food with egg yolk as an added ingredient. I tell them that I will "do anything" to help her gain weight and that I'm dealing with postpartum depression even now, while I am again "partum." As it comes out of my mouth, I worry that I will regret it. That I will regret telling anyone these things, that I will regret being here, that I will regret not having killed myself before I managed to end up pregnant again. Any one of these women could call CPS immediately and report me, just like the mom on the message board did— and she hadn't even met me in person. Then Danielle will be back at my door to take Ida. She may even show up at the birth of the new baby, only to take him or her right out of my arms. I can't allow anyone here to know that I'm an abusive parent, but I feel like it's written on my face.

When the meeting ends, I force myself through some small talk with the other moms. I tell them that Ida is still waking up every two or three hours to nurse, that she doesn't talk, doesn't walk, and isn't really trying to, and that I'm *so tired.* Of course, they're all *so tired,* too. Their babies don't sleep, either, I learn. Then, I make sure to introduce myself to both Monique and Courtney. To my pleasant surprise, the meeting wasn't so bad, mostly because they were so calm, friendly, and yet so *real.* I feel a churning inside me, a need to connect with someone, to have a friend. I just want to tell someone what's happening to me and have them look at me and say, "This shouldn't have happened. You're a good mom." But that seems like a long shot. For now, though, Monique and Courtney seem nice enough, and I realize that I haven't had a woman friend, or even someone to talk to, in a long, long time. Since they don't know I'm a terrible mother *(not yet),* I can talk to them, and the therapist will be happy and not scold me for giving her problems.

But later that week, when I finally gather the courage to call Courtney, I tell her everything. Telling her—or anyone—was exactly what I didn't want to do, but somehow, listening to someone who had two babies of her own but was happy to listen to me without filling me with unwanted advice made me want to unload the burden of the turmoil I've been through for the past month. Telling her felt good, like setting down a heavy backpack after an arduous hike. As I laid it all out and told her my whole story about Danielle and Stephanie and the empty car seat and the forced therapy and psychiatric evaluations and the horrible blood tests they put Ida through, it felt relieving, but I was also scared. The words and the story just poured out of me, and I didn't have enough control over them to think before they came. I told her everything, though I'd only met her once and knew so little about her, and when I finally hung up the phone, my anxiety was through the roof. Telling felt good, but telling, *oversharing*, was what got me into this mess in the first place. But now it was too late, and once again, I would have to accept the consequences, knowing that I have no idea how to measure another person's trustworthiness. *It's my own fault now, and anything more that happens will be, too. My verbal diarrhea will end up killing me and the babies. And I don't know how to stop.*

"Drops of Jupiter," Train

Mom and I have assumed the usual positions, as have the kids. Ida is moving between the big blue couch and the carpet, singing and dancing to a *Baby Einstein* DVD. Mom is on one end of the big blue couch, and I'm on the other. We are both fighting the urge to fall asleep, but I'm the only one doing so with my shirt pulled up and my bra pulled down. Daniel, too, is dozing off as he nurses.

My eyes pop open when I hear the back door bump open, and Eric comes in, carrying groceries and the mail. I am relieved to see him, mostly because any time that door opens, I'm afraid. Lisa from Child Protective Services only comes about once a month now, but I know they're still tracking me. If they wanted to, they could come in that door at any moment and take away both of my children. So I breathe a sigh of relief that I didn't know I was holding in.

Eric drops the groceries on the counter, puts the cold ones away in the refrigerator, and opens an envelope he got out of the mailbox. Bills, probably. Most of the time, we can pay them. But as he's reading this first one, he walks into the living room next to the big blue couch and suddenly pounds a fist against the wall.

Mom and I are immediately startled from our weary dazes, Ida turns away from the TV, and even Daniel pops off my breast and looks up at me, brown eyes as big as quarters. Daddy almost never seems angry. The relief I'd felt 30 seconds ago is gone. What is CPS, or someone else, accusing me of now?

"What is it? What is that? Who's it from? What does it say?"

He leans against the wall, still staring at the letter, for a long time; then he closes his eyes, breathing deeply.

"The Naval Academy Chapel is firing us."

Eric has been working a side job at the Naval Academy on Sunday mornings for a couple of years now. He provides leadership and a strong voice to the tenor section of the Protestant choir during Sunday services. This past June, when the soprano section also needed a leader, they hired me as well.

"What?! Why? What does it say? They can't fire us; we're independent contractors." All the disbelief, anger, and fear seems to pour out of me at once. Eric sighs, and I know there's going to be a longer explanation.

"A couple of weeks ago, I went to rehearsal and explained that you were still recuperating from Daniel's birth. Well, at the end of the rehearsal, Martin pulled me aside and said that a number of the more significant attendees—I assume that means the admirals and whoever else—have complained about you nursing Ida in the service."

"What?! The admirals all sit in the front. How would they even know I'm nursing when the choir loft is behind them, in the back, and two stories up?"

"I know. I've been drafting a letter to Martin to explain that breastfeeding is biblical and necessary for Ida's health—and Daniel's, now, too. He told me about the concern and said we should pray about it and let him know. Apparently, that meant nothing, though. They had no intention of letting us stay on."

The tears come on, rushing over me like a flash flood. I'm not especially attached to the position at the chapel; I hadn't really wanted to do it at all, but it was work, *professional* work, and it seemed to legitimize my music degree. It was fulfilling to contribute, to lead and sing real music in a beautiful space, and we needed the money.

"What do we do?" As I say it, and the tears pour down my breasts and onto tiny Daniel's cheeks, my mom gets up and sits next to me, putting her arm around my perpetually tense shoulders.

"We can fight it," Eric says. "I know there's an Equal Opportunity office on the base somewhere."

At this suggestion, my despair turns to self-righteous anger. This is the second time in less than a year that we've been asked to stop feeding our babies the way God designed them to be fed or leave a church we were previously welcomed into. Darn right, we're going to fight. But even as I imagine the potential positive outcomes for us—the honor of taking a stance on an issue that is of the utmost importance to us, the potential money we could earn from a lawsuit—I know that this will be a fallout tragedy, the final sip of a poisoned potion first served on the night Child Protective Services came in the same door that also brought in this letter. And, as the mother of two breastfeeding babies, any poison I drink will invade their lives, too.

After Eric picks Daniel up and Mom takes Ida into another room to see if she will eat dinner, I stare back at that door, tucked so discreetly at the end of the hall next to the washing machine and the propane heater.

I hate that door.

"Bubbly," Colbie Caillat

We almost never get a babysitter, but it's worth it tonight. Babysitters are expensive, so it will have to be quick, but it feels amazing to be somewhere with Eric where the kids aren't. And I really need a beer and a buffalo burger tonight because it's been a long winter, and spring isn't looking much better at this point.

So we're here in a booth at Ted's Montana Grill drinking sodas with cool paper straws, saving the beer for when the burgers arrive, when Eric drops a bomb by saying he has *something to tell me*. This must be big because he avoids planned talks as much as possible. When I've tried initiating them in the past—and I have many times—he sat there like a scared little kid who's about to get a spanking, or worse, like a pissed-off monster about to strike. One makes me feel guilty; the other makes me scared. But this time, he only looks nervous.

Immediately, I'm catastrophizing, managing to believe that he is cheating on me despite the total lack of evidence. That's always my worst-case scenario. He has a girlfriend, or several, and kids with other women—other than the one he actually does have. He's been having affairs for the entire eight years we've been together, and he only married me to maintain his image. It's all been one big con. He doesn't love me. It's been less than 60 seconds since he started talking, and I'm dizzy and hyperventilating.

But no, it's about Angie, Abigail's mom. Of course it is. If it's not about Child Protective Services, or people thinking I'm a whore for breastfeeding, or Ida having autism, or my dad having Alzheimer's—it's about Angie. Angie is really the only heavy discussion topic that doesn't involve me being a bad mom.

For the past year or so, Angie, Abigail, and Abigail's little brother have been living in an old farmhouse they rent from an Amish farmer. The problem, though, is that Angie has no source of income other than the child support Eric pays her, which isn't much. Actually, I don't really know how much it is, or when he pays it, or how. Money is an off-limits topic with Eric. But that's a whole other problem.

Eric explains that he found out Angie had received a few reimbursement checks for dental work Abigail had done that our medical insurance had covered after the treatment was paid for. The checks were made out in Eric's name but went to Angie's address, but instead of turning them over, Angie forged Eric's signature and kept the money—more than $500 total.

Of course, I'm livid. That's not *her* money; it's *ours*. She should be glad we even keep Abigail on our medical insurance at all. But the bigger issue is that we have been having problems with Angie taking advantage of us for months. I've thought that she's a gold digger from the beginning. Eric lets her call all the shots—not just about child support money, but about when we can visit Abigail, what we do when we visit her, all of it. And Eric is *my* husband, not hers, and he never was hers. He *married* me, and we have *two* kids that came along *after* our wedding. I'm the legitimate wife here, and she doesn't get to control my husband or our family.

And this isn't the first installment of this particular conversation, either; it's just the newest one, the final straw on the camel's back. Because Abigail's been telling us stories about the farmhouse that Angie is "renting." She says she can hear rats at night when she's trying to sleep and that she's cold because there's no heat. And, just to confirm that Abigail was right, Eric and I went to the house last time we were up in Pennsylvania, and it was awful. There weren't even locks on the doors, and anyone could just walk in—like we did.

I've been bugging Eric for years to get a lawyer and a formal child custody agreement set up with Angie, and now, he says, he has finally contacted one. Thank you, God; he's finally using his head on this. When Angie takes advantage of him, when she wants his time and his money and to call the shots about when we see Abigail, she is taking time and money from *my* kids.

And so our date night becomes a long tirade about Angie, about having to regularly go up to Pennsylvania to see Abigail when our lives are in D.C. and we are dealing with Ida getting diagnosed and Daniel being underweight and the whole lawsuit against the Naval Academy for firing us and my dad having Alzheimer's and Eric not really liking his work much anymore. This crap should not be taking up our time and energy, too.

By the end of the night (less than three hours later), we decided it wasn't enough to make Angie pay the money back and adhere to our schedule for when we would visit Abigail. We decided that Abigail would be better off with us, and we would fight for custody. We would move Abigail in, and she could share a room with Ida, and we would get to call the shots about when Angie could see her. After all, we (or Eric, rather) are the ones with a stable income and a secure home with heat and without rodents.

It felt like a huge win, at least for a battle we had only just decided to start. CPS had tried to take *my* kids away, but now, less than two years later, *I* would get custody of someone else's. Who's the neglectful mom now? Ha. Who's the one who gets to have a husband who supports her and fights for her now? Ha. Who's the one who gets to add another kid to her house and another responsibility she has no clue how to handle? Hmm.

"Lifesong," Casting Crowns

I'm learning that babies are good icebreakers. When the therapist I was required to see in the aftermath of the visit from Child Protective Services suggested (or, rather, commanded) that I find social opportunities, playgroups, book clubs, something social to do that would force me out of the house, I was angry and appalled. She'd made it sound like it was easy, like it was obvious, like I was actively avoiding such things, but I wasn't. I'd never been invited. I didn't know anyone who would invite me to something. Ida is scared of new people, big rooms, new environments, even bright lights and crowd noise. I can't make friends when my daughter is screaming in terror. The idea was ridiculous. And now that I have Daniel, too, I can't even comfort her the way she'd like. Ida is starting to toddle a bit, for a step or two anyway, but Daniel is still this wobbly tiny thing that needs full body support. He's all head and barely any body; it's quite funny, actually. He looks like one of those bobblehead figures people put on their dashboards. So when Ida is scared and screaming, I literally have my arms too full to help her without an appropriate seat to put Daniel in. Plus, at least when she's really scared, what she wants to do, and what works the fastest and the easiest, is for her to nurse. And that has a whole other set of problems that have nothing to do with my babies and everything to do with all the other people in the room who can see me. For the first six months or so with Ida, I was pretty proud to breastfeed in public; I wanted everyone to see that I was doing this great thing for my baby.

But now I know that no one else sees it that way, that I am, at best, an eyesore while I'm nursing and, at worst, a slut.

The first parent playgroup I tried was awful. It was a good half-hour drive to get to the town where they met, and I didn't feel comfortable with anyone there, which I later learned was a mutual feeling. The first group playdate I went to before Daniel was born was a lot of kids with a wide range of ages and temperaments—not to mention screaming abilities—in a huge empty room. Ida screamed, climbed in my lap, and hid her face, and frankly, I wished I could hide, too. Chaos is not a good environment for socialization. But I was too scared to tell the therapist that I wouldn't go to these events because I know that she is sending all her notes and anything I tell her to CPS so they can monitor. (My therapist complains about how difficult I've made things for her every time I see her.) If I refuse to follow her advice and continue attending social events for at-home parents, it would be considered noncompliance, which has the potential to bring Danielle and her empty car seat back to my house.

Thank God I recalled hearing something about an organization called MOPS on the Christian radio station. Mothers Of PreSchoolers. They meet at churches. I didn't look them up right away, but shortly after Daniel was born, a mother from the loud, crazy playgroup called me, kind of out of nowhere, and asked if I wanted to come to her house for a playdate, just her kids and mine, so I went.

I wasn't quite sure how Eileen knew I needed a smaller, quieter situation to be able to make any social connections without talking over Ida's screams, but when I got there, she explained that she couldn't go to the huge playgroup events either. Her son, who is just over two, has special needs, and he also can't handle that sort of situation. He has autism, and that type of situation scares him as much as it scares Ida. And this is the first and only playdate Ida has ever had in which she actually played. That is, she played with Shawn's toys on one side of the room while Shawn played with other toys on another side of the room, and *Baby Einstein* droned in the background. Shawn's mom, Eileen, said that he wanted to watch *Baby Einstein* DVDs almost constantly and that, for her as well, it is one of the only things that keeps him calm.

Eileen invited me to a MOPS group, and I was thankful to hear that there was one nearby. Well, sort of thankful. I don't actually want to go anywhere to socialize. I don't have the energy or mental stamina to deal with adults when I am dealing with these babies; they take every ounce of compassion I have. But anything to keep CPS away.

The good news, though, is that this particular group meets once a week in the evening, and for the moms, it's a night out alone. They don't bring their kids. At first, I immediately dismissed this as impossible in my situation. I couldn't go to something like that because Daniel is too new and needs to nurse at least every two hours. It was a convenient way to get out of an invitation, of course, but it wouldn't satisfy Danielle or anyone else at CPS.

"Never mind that," Eileen said, "no one will mind if you bring him along as long as you don't mind."

Tonight I'll be at my third MOPS meeting, and the first one I'm truly looking forward to. Coming here, even with Daniel, feels like an escape. Eric was completely willing to watch Ida for one evening a week, and no one here has complained about a baby coming along or batted an eye when I nursed him. I had forgotten what it was like to talk—to actually converse—with other women about life and faith and the exhausting, debilitating monotony of taking care of babies. I poured my heart out the first night because I felt welcome, and these women understood the loneliness that comes when you're too tired for relationships.

This group, these women, I realize, are giving me back my faith. For the last few months, my faith has been challenged, at best, and much of the time absent. I am doing everything I thought God had called me to do in my marriage, childbearing, and mothering, yet I have been persecuted by outsiders the whole way. CPS aren't the only ones telling me I'm a bad mother and a bad person. But these women make me feel known and tell me that this persecution isn't coming from God. I know this because they love God, and they aren't persecuting me.

Since Daniel isn't much of a crier, attending MOPS with only him has enabled me to be more myself. It isn't easy because sometimes I feel afraid and different. I am not the only one who brought her baby with her, but I am the only one who seems to be struggling and the only one lifting my shirt to nurse two or three times during every meeting. But no one seems bothered, and they all seem to enjoy Daniel's bobblehead and his big, toothless smile almost as much as I do. Though I haven't met their children, several women have already told me that they also have a toddler who screams, doesn't speak more than a few words, and seems afraid of anything remotely new. I am welcome here, just as I am, and I smile here. God is here.

"We Belong Together,"
Mariah Carey

It's been almost five months since Danielle showed up at my door with her empty car seat, pretending she wanted to help me when she was really there to tell me what a terrible mother I am. Mom is still here, and she's been here every weekday since the day it all began, making the four-hour drive back home every Friday night to spend the weekend with my dad and brother while Eric is off from work. How many lives have I ruined now? How many people are displaced because I can't handle my own daughter? I've never felt so ashamed as I do now. Even through the sexual harassment and groping in junior high, the whispers and taunts once the news came out about my dad's misdeeds, the sharp increase in their ferocity when he was sent to jail, the embarrassing way I couldn't hold back tears when I got dumped more than once in high school—that all seems like water under the bridge now. This is much, much bigger. This is me losing everything I have.

But Eric and Mom are by my side. Eric is still angry, the same way I am, but loving, and at least once a day, he reminds me that I've done nothing wrong. I don't know if that's true, but I'm glad he thinks it is. Personally, I'm not sure if I've done nothing wrong or everything wrong, but it has to be one or the other. And Mom is here when I need her, as she's always said she would be, even when I didn't want her around. It's not necessarily easy to have her here with me constantly in this tiny house, sleeping in the spare bedroom with an electric space heater since the heat never manages to make it in there. There are a lot of moments when she drives me crazy. But I need her, and I have no other choice. The good part—the great part—is that she's someone, and she's here, and she defends me, too. And I can talk to her. For more than two years, I've had no one to talk to for eight hours a day, five days a week; now that she's here, she listens, we share memories, and we laugh.

Three weeks ago, Mom asked me to give her a wish list for Christmas gifts for Ida, Eric and I, and the new baby. I have no idea what she wants to get or spend, but in a rare moment of optimism, I decided to shoot for the moon. I typed up and printed out a two-page Word document with my ideas. I didn't expect her to get all of it, of course, but I wanted her to have choices. I was a little worried she'd think I was demanding, though. But when I gave her the list, she laughed a little and said in a silly voice, "Whoa. This is quite a list. Santa will have to do his ho-ho-ho-ching." I laughed harder at that than I have laughed in months.

It's Saturday now, and Mom's back at home for a few days while Eric takes some Christmas-time leave from work, and we're packing Ida into her fluffy brown one-piece snowsuit that leaves her looking like a brown paper bag with a little head on top. We call it her "sack of 'tatoes." It takes a good ten minutes to get her into the car seat with the straps adjusted securely, so while Eric takes care of that, I walk slowly to the bank of locked mail boxes in the middle of our mobile home complex. It's been several days since I've checked the mail, even though it's not far from our house. You'd be surprised how hard it is to wrap a heavy baby in a thick blanket, put on a heavy coat, and then carry said baby on your hip in a way that also allows you to walk with a giant pregnant belly. It's more effort than I usually have energy for.

When I open the box, the pleasant, count-my-blessings feeling I've had for the last week or so drains out of me. Amongst the bills and late Christmas cards is an envelope addressed to me—*Anne Arundel County Department of Child Protective Services*. Every time I think this is almost over, it isn't. Every time I fulfill their demands, they tell me to do more. There is nothing good in this.

Eric already has Ida buckled in and the car running when I get back to our parking pad. I climb in, show him the letter, and fasten my seatbelt. As he backs out, I'm already shaking and holding back tears.

At this time, the formal investigation of the crimes against the minor child, Ida Makovsky, is complete. The Anne Arundel County Department of Child Protective Services has determined that these crimes, committed against Ida Makovsky by Melanie Makovsky (mother), are prosecutable. As the result of our findings, you are hereby convicted of **Indicated Child Neglect.** *As a result of this finding, your name and the names of each of your family members (Eric Makovsky, Melanie Makovsky, Abigail Makovsky, Ida Makovsky) are now registered in the Child Protective Services Registry, with the convicted individual,* **Melanie Makovsky,** *marked as the perpetrator of these crimes. This marker will indicate the perpetrator for seven years, after which the marker will be removed. The record of names is recorded indefinitely. Please complete the attached form if you wish to appeal this decision. This case is now closed.*

That's it. One letter, one page, and it's done. I am a perpetrator, a criminal, and I've been given a punishment, a sentence. Actually, if the whole family, including poor Abigail who doesn't even live here, is listed, then the whole family gets to serve this sentence with me. How appropriate. Like father, like daughter, as I've always thought things would go. And, similarly, I am *marked.* A criminal. *Indicated Child Neglect.* And the rest of the family will bear this marking, this scarlet letter, forever—just as I do. We are all punished together, including my tiny victim, my sack of 'tatoes girl. And this is the way it should be because that's what happens when you are a criminal. Even when there is only one criminal and one person being hurt, everyone around is hurt in the fallout, marked permanently with scars—visible and invisible—like the sign of the beast.

The rest of the day, and really the rest of the whole weekend, is spent crying, fighting over, debating, raging, and mourning this letter. Eric is most upset that there is no right to a trial, a jury of my peers; in fact, there was no notice that any such thing had ever taken place. There is no use of jurisprudence. (Only Eric would even remember terms like *jurisprudence* at a time like this.) I am simply confronted, run through a series of humiliating tasks and punishments that serve no clear purpose, and convicted. Iesus Nazarenus, Rex Iudaeorum. INRI.

But how like me to compare myself to Christ, to claim the innocence or glory of a martyr, when I am, in fact, guilty. The finding isn't even complete. I may have neglected Ida, but certainly she has been abused, as well. Having a mother so ignorant and incapable is abuse in itself. Of course, they wanted to take her away from me. Maybe they should have since I am such a failure.

"We'll appeal it," Eric says. "I'll find a lawyer. This is D.C.; there are plenty of lawyers."

With whose money? I wonder. We can barely pay the bills, as far as I can tell. But I don't argue with him; he has no more answers than I do. He has married a natural-born criminal, a woman who is marked for failure, unable to control her words or behavior, only capable of the most menial of tasks, and not worthy of consideration as anything more than a quiet housewife. He has married a woman who has ruined his family's future with a few misplaced words and a few impulsive choices. She's just like her dad.

"Don't Know Why,"
Norah Jones

Eric will be home soon, and even though he never complains about the house being messy and never even implies that I don't do enough while he's gone, I am kind of desperate to get the dishes done. I've observed enough over the last four years to know that dirty dishes in the sink bug him a lot, and even though I know he won't complain about doing them himself, I don't want him to have to.

At least, I think he'll be home soon. It's already past the time I usually expect him, and I'm starting to worry. Would he call me and tell me if he had to stay late at work? No, probably not. Would he find a way to contact me if the train broke down or his car didn't start when he got back to the station parking lot? Again, probably not. So basically, my thought that he'll be home soon is nothing more than a wild guess. But it's early March, and this isn't an especially busy time for the Public Affairs Department of the Navy Band.

I'm always ready for him to come home because I can breathe a sigh of relief when there is someone else around to take care of the babies, and in Eric's case, he doesn't expect anything from me in return. Not that he should. He's as much their parent as I am, but I must remember that his work is a job, too, and not necessarily an easier one than mine. Even though it seems like it is.

Just as I start seeing the first hints of the coming sunset through the sink window, the phone rings. I pick it up, drying my hands on the slightly damp dishtowel, but it isn't Eric.

My mom has been back home for the last year, and even though I can't thank her enough for the sacrifice she made to stay with me all day, five days a week, throughout the CPS ordeal, I still feel a sense of dread when she calls. I always assume she either wants me to do something or has bad news. I hit the button to answer the call and pick Daniel up from the floor—time to feed him.

"Hi, Mom."

"Hi honey, how are you?" Her voice trails down in pitch at the end of the question. So it's bad news.

"I'm okay. What's up?"

"Well, as you know, Dad saw the neurologist a few weeks ago, and they weren't sure if he has Alzheimer's or frontal lobe dementia. So, they took a sample and sent it out for a genetic analysis since Grandpa had Alzheimer's and got it around the same age that Dad is now."

"Yes." I am frozen. I could stop the conversation right now because I know what's coming, and I've always known it was coming, but I never knew *when* it was coming. Today's the day.

"Dad's blood test came back positive for a genetic mutation known to cause Alzheimer's. But there's medication for it now; it's not like when Grandpa had it. There was nothing they could do for Grandpa. So don't worry. You have nothing to worry about."

She couldn't be more wrong.

"But Mom, even if there's medicine to help, it's not going to mean he stops having Alzheimer's or he gets his memory back."

"No."

Silence. What else is there to say? The thoughts racing through my head won't change anything, and they might start an argument with her. That much information is enough. I can't hear about anything else, and I didn't want to talk, either.

She tells me a bit more about the doctor, the hospital, and my dad's next appointment. I ask how he's taking it, knowing full well that he, like me, won't have much to say about it yet. When you start talking about some new horrible thing, you never say anything that matters, and blathering on about how you're feeling when no words make any sense is just wasted effort. Then, she apologizes for having to give me bad news——which seems weird, too. What else is she going to say? What else am I going to say? There isn't anything to say.

I hang up and have a good, hard cry. I'm not ready for any of this. It's all I can do to get five hours of cumulative sleep at night, and with the commute from D.C. being what it is, Eric leaves before dawn and comes home after dark. Despite being declared a neglectful parent, I'm the only parent available 95% of the time, and there isn't a single person I trust to babysit or even help me. Even if there were, we have no money to pay them. Baby Daniel will turn one next week, but he's still sleeping with Eric and me because the only bedroom space we have for him is on the opposite side of the house, and the heating system doesn't work in that room. We don't have the money to fix it. And it's late and I'm hungry and I can't figure out what I could put together for dinner even for myself, and I'm so stupid because I don't know how to cook and now Ida is crying and Daniel has rolled off the couch again, and…

When Eric gets home, he finds me sitting at the kitchen table in the same chair I'd been in the night that Danielle came with the empty car seat, in the same position, with my head cradled in my forearms and my forehead on the tabletop. But this time, I'm not quite as scared. I refuse to project too far into the future. I refuse to think about my dad forgetting who I am, forgetting the kids' names, going to a nursing home, and dying. The grief I have right now is plenty. I'm definitely not thinking about myself, about how genetics work.

Eric has his own news: that his sister has ended a relationship with someone she'd been living with since before Eric and I ever met. It doesn't feel like big news in comparison, but I have enough cognitive, logical thinking to realize that it really is a big deal.

When we've both said our piece, Eric gets a beer from the shelf behind our winter coats and pops it open. He never drinks alcohol on weeknights. I get one, too. A few hours later, our new, good friend Jerry comes over, not realizing that he's walking into a storm the size of Baltimore. But he stays and has a beer, listens, then has another. He stays and listens, gets us both laughing a little and drinking more beer, and then he goes home.

The beer has mellowed me, and I realize that this is what life really is. Our life isn't any worse than anyone else's. Another thing has started; another page in our life book is dog-eared. Another moment has come and gone, one that will set a marker for what came before and what comes after. It is well after midnight, and Ida and Daniel have fallen asleep on the couch and in the sling, respectively. We wake them in the dark house long enough to change their diapers, and by some very welcome miracle, Ida falls right back to sleep in her bed, and Daniel does the same in ours. Eric and I fall asleep on the mattress, being sure to stay close enough to touch.

"Here Comes Peter Cottontail," Gene Autry

It's finally getting warm enough outside for the babies and me to sit on our giant blue couch without wearing two layers of clothes. This is our usual position. There is plenty of space for us in the house, but typically, we're here, on the blue couch, watching *Baby Einstein*, or Ida is in her highchair, and I'm feeding her and helping her use a spoon while watching *Baby Einstein*, or I'm on the couch nursing Daniel with my giant breastfeeding support pillow tucked around my waist. For the first half of each morning, we are in the big bed together, which is Eric's and my full mattress on the bedroom floor without the bed frame, plus a twin mattress pushed against it to create a family-sized bed. Daniel, of course, is still nursing every two hours around the clock, and we're both simply too tired to get up and go to the crib to retrieve him that often, so he sleeps next to Eric and me on the big bed every night. Ida is finally happy to sleep in her crib, some nights without even waking up at all. So, for the first few hours of the morning, after Eric leaves for work, I am snuggled next to my two babies, using my breastmilk to keep them asleep—or at least still—until I've either accumulated enough sleep time to survive the day or have given up and decided to move on with the day. After that, we typically move to the big blue couch.

There is a knock at the back door, and the immense adrenaline rush of fear fills me, as it always does now, ever since Danielle arrived with her accusations and her contract and her empty car seat. For a few brief seconds, I wonder if this is it, if they are here now, if they've decided I'm not good enough for them, that they're such cute babies that another mother deserves them, and they are going to come in and take them away. But then I remember that Lisa, our follow-up social worker, told me she was coming this morning.

I tolerate Lisa, maybe even like her. Although Danielle and Stephanie came to my house to accuse me and punish me for being a bad mom, Lisa comes here and asks me how I'm doing, if I'm still seeing my therapist regularly and taking my medication, and how much sleep I've been able to get. The others were here to take my children away, but Lisa is here to make sure I can keep them. So I tolerate her, which is the best I'll let her believe because, of course, what I really want Lisa and CPS to do is go away and leave us alone.

Lisa follows me in and sits beside me on the big blue couch. Daniel has fallen asleep on top of the nursing pillow but wakes up when he feels my movement and hears our voices, so I begin nursing him again, mostly just to keep him from crying. I need Lisa to see that these babies are happy.

As we sit, Lisa asks me how Daniel is. Is he growing at the appropriate rate? Is he nursing often enough? How many wet and dirty diapers does he have in a day? She asks about Ida, if she is doing any talking or walking yet, and if I've taken her out to play with other kids. All the answers for Daniel are yes, but all the answers for Ida are no. But Lisa doesn't blame me for that.

We hit a lull in our conversation when Lisa finishes asking me all the necessary questions, and for a few minutes she just observes the babies doing their thing, and me doing mine. Then she asks, "What are you doing for yourself right now?"

I am dumbfounded. Even if I knew of something to do for my body and mind that would make me happier, I wouldn't have time for it, let alone the money. Who would watch the babies if I left the house?

I spend a good ten minutes defending my position to Lisa, telling her that I can't do things for myself because the babies need me constantly, and both scream and cry if I put them down, even if it's only for a few minutes. The very idea of doing things for myself is absurd. What would I do other than eat and sleep?

After I explain this, Lisa sighs. It seems like there's something I'm not getting here.

"Do you read books?"

"Yes!" I tell her with some excitement. "I'm never not reading a book. As soon as I finish one book, I start the next one. I even go to the library." After this, I think, "I went to the library *once,*" but I don't add this.

She asks me what I'm reading right now, and I get up excitedly and bring the book to her. I know she will be happy and proud of me for this because I'm reading Dr. Sears' *The Fussy Baby Book* (again). How could I possibly be an unfit mother if I am spending time reading this?

But she sighs again. "When I asked you if you read books, I meant do you read them for yourself?"

Yes… What am I missing here?

Lisa looks me directly in the eye and says, "You need to read a novel."

I appreciate her opinion, but this is ridiculous. These children, both of them, need me 24 hours a day. How could I possibly start reading books?

But after she leaves, I keep thinking about the question.

When was the last time I read a novel? Before Ida was born? Before we got married? High school? It does sound like fun.

So that afternoon, I go back to the library.

Blues Clues theme song

It's echoing through my head as I stand at the sink, rinsing the never-ending line of dirty dishes. This particular DVD is the most annoying. *I've been watching Blues Clues with one kid or another for seven years now,* I think. I don't want to think about this resentment that's building in me, a resentment aimed at the very people and the very dream that we'd had. That we'd laid in bed and talked about like it would be a fairy tale. We have the fairy tale now: the house, two babies—a boy and a girl—Eric off to work at a good job that he can keep forever, me at home, Susie Homemaker, reading Bible stories to the babies.

And I hate it. With every part of my being, I hate my life.

I am overwhelmed and scared and painfully, frighteningly inadequate. Ida and Daniel need me constantly, every minute of every day and every night. I am not a mother; I am a slave. I feel inhuman in a lot of ways. For two years now, I have nursed them at my breasts, both of them at once sometimes. Ida is almost three years old now but continues to nurse, sometimes two or three times a day. She eats regular food, but only if it meets her exact specifications. The problem is, though, that I don't always know what her specifications are. She still doesn't really talk. She says words, but she doesn't communicate anything. When I was 12, an old friend had a rudimentary computer program that showed a digitized parrot. When we spoke into the microphone, the parrot repeated whatever we said in its own parrot voice. We said hello; the parrot said hello. We said go to hell, and the parrot said go to hell.

This is how Ida talks. She repeats things but seems lost as to the meaning of her utterances. Like the computer parrot, she just repeats things as she hears them, and much of the time, her words tell me nothing. I can read her emotions because she smiles and laughs when she's happy and screams bloody murder when she's upset. Sometimes she uses the phrases in a way that makes sense. Once, she peeked at me through the slats on the back of a kitchen chair and said, "Ah-see oo!" I see you. My words repeated exactly as they came to her ears while playing peek-a-boo.

It's entirely my fault that Ida doesn't talk. I know this because I have committed Indicated Child Neglect. I realize that many moms with young children feel inadequate; people tell me that all the time. Older women whose children are in school, carrying conversations and sleeping through the night, tell me that they felt inadequate when their children were babies but that it was such a wonderful thing to raise a child and that they grow up so fast. I will miss this someday, they say. But would they still say that if they were feeling my feelings? If they could only sleep in fits and starts, broken moments of unconscious nightmares interspersed with demanding screams? No—how could they? No one would.

This is what I think about when my hands are in the sink or in the laundry, desperately trying to remove stains from onesies. The stains are impossible to get out, but I try anyway. Both Ida and Daniel need iron supplements and nutritional supplements because they are too thin. But they don't like most foods, and there was a time when they liked no food at all except my milk. We struggle to get them to swallow the supplements, so every onesie is stained with brown "chocolate milk" marks that don't come out no matter what I try. Their clothes are stained, too; it took me a few tries to realize that I should take their clothes off when I have to force feed them the supplement. Most of their clothes are stained in some way. I am too tired to soak or pretreat their laundry, so they wear stained clothes. Indicated Child Neglect.

Ida comes into the kitchen where I am. She is wearing a little thrift shop dress and pigtails and holding a piece of plastic play food. "Purple, like grapes! Purple, like grapes!" she announces happily, her characteristic gorgeous smile spreading across her face. I can't help but smile when she does. She is truly beautiful, and that smile is her best feature. Too bad she is a victim of neglect and can't really talk.

"Purple, like grapes!" I realize that the play food item she is holding is, in fact, purple grapes. She knows the color purple and what grapes look like, I realize. She is showing me that she knows this.

"That's the color purple, like grapes," says the fluffy white dog puppet on the TV. She has watched this a million times on repeat.

"Purple, like grapes!" she says again, staring at me, both anxious and excited.

"You're right," I say, "those are purple grapes."

"Purple, like grapes!" She doesn't seem to understand that I've already told her that she correctly identified them. "Purple, like grapes, purple, like grapes, purple, like grapes!" She is angry now, or frustrated. She wants something from me—always, but I'm never sure what.

"Yes, purple, like grapes," I say to her, finally. The mood-lifting smile returns for a moment, then she happily runs back to the TV. She only wanted me to repeat her words. She couldn't understand mine.

Indicated Child Neglect, with pigtails and a heart-breaking smile.

"Lose Control," Missy Elliot

It is hot as hell out here, but somehow, it feels good because the conference room is so cold. I hate that about summer. It's not comfortable anywhere unless you're in just the right mood—which I'm not.

I'm holding Daniel, his tiny body like jiggly, warm rubber against me in the sling carrier. Mom and Eric are walking with me on the beautiful, summer-busy sidewalks in Annapolis. But even though I'm sweating, my mind and thoughts are shaking like a leaf, and simultaneously, I want to scream devilishly. I briefly imagine myself handing Daniel to Eric and then running, postpartum fat rolls and all, straight to the bay, jumping in, and drowning myself right here in front of the tourists. Wouldn't that be a fitting end to my drama? But I won't do it because I know my natural instincts would kick in pretty quickly; I do know how to swim.

We're on our way back to my trial. Today, with the help of a lawyer who I barely know, I am (kind of) defending myself against the Indicated Child Neglect finding that CPS has put on me. Thankfully, this conviction hasn't been published in the paper or posted on the internet for the world to see, like Dad's was, but, just like Dad, I'm on a registry now, too. I will never be able to work with children because if a church or a parent looking for a babysitter or anyone else requests a background check on me, it will indicate that I was convicted. And that's all it would indicate. Just my name, my family's names,

197

and "Indicated Child Neglect." It won't tell anyone *why* I have this on my record, so anyone who reads it won't know that I happened to have a skinny baby and postpartum depression at the same time. They could just as easily assume that I left my child alone to starve to death. They tell me that the "marker" that's placed next to my name as the perpetrator will be removed after seven or eight years, so no one who checks would know that I'm the evil one on the list. But doesn't that just mean that they'll always be able to follow us, to track us down, and that anyone who accesses this will see that this group of five names is on a list of criminals? I think what I'm really doing at this trial is wasting valuable time and money. We'll be in debt to this lawyer for years, even if I lose.

When we get back to the building where my trial is being held, I sit down on the one tiny bench available in the lobby and begin to nurse Daniel. Despite being four months old, Daniel is not allowed in the room during the trial, so my mom and Eric have been taking turns with him while I'm in there. The only support person I'm allowed to have present through the whole thing is my lawyer. But Daniel has only been nursing for five minutes when they tell me it's time to start again. And so, once again, Eric and I are arguing with these officials who are working under the assumption that I have no intention of being a good mother while also preventing me from being one. They graciously grant me five more minutes with my tiny son, and though he needs at least ten, I hand him, whimpering, over to my mom, who takes my place on the tiny bench. They're calling Eric in too, as a witness.

Eric has to sit across the conference table from me and my lawyer. I can tell he's nervous, but I'm the only one who can. I can feel his nervousness as if it is my own. I am worried, too—wondering what he will say but worried about what he will be asked. My lawyer begins.

"Please state your name."

"Eric Makovsky."

"And what is your relationship to my client?"

"She is my wife. We've been married for three years."

"Have you ever had a reason to believe that Melanie wasn't or isn't capable of adequately caring for your children?"

"Never."

"Is your wife a good mother?"

"Yes."

"And how do you yourself feel about your wife?"

"I love her something awful."

He looks across the table, directly into my eyes, and smiles. It isn't an act. He is smiling the same smile I remember from the first time he kissed me almost six years ago. I suppose he could be doing it for show; I haven't been easy to love for years now. But his smile does to me what it always does, and I smile, too. Right here—in this conference room that is pretending to be a courtroom today, after six months of being judged, degraded, accused, and convicted—with this man, at least, I am still loved. My husband still loves me, still defends me, and still wants me to be the mother of his children. He just testified that. Under oath. So help me God.

And the thing is, although I can only see Eric's smile, I can feel God's. God is right here. My attorney is sitting on my right at the shiny, ugly conference table, but in the empty chair on my left, God is sitting. I mean, I can't see him, of course. But I can feel his love from that place just as well as I can feel Eric's love in that smile, beaming itself across the table to me. And, for a few seconds, I know that, once again, I am right where I am supposed to be—even though I don't belong in this conference room, this trial.

For the rest of the day, until well past 7:00 p.m., I stay warm inside, filled with the love of God and of those who love me in the middle of this terrible circumstance. I feel the icy cold of the conference room air conditioner on my skin, the anxiety and shame of the proceedings, and the ache in my breasts. I have not nursed Daniel in five hours, and it's been 12 since I nursed Ida, who is waiting for me at home under the care of my brother.

But finally, this day ends. They won't even give me an answer about the judge's findings today because, despite more than 12 hours of talking, there wasn't enough time for the attorneys to present their final statements. I will get another letter within two weeks. But I don't care. I need to pee, and I need to nurse, and I need to go to sleep at home. I need to lie in my bed, with my husband, mother, and brother all there in the same house with me. With the exception of my dad, everyone I love most will surround me there because they love me, too. For today, that's enough.

I'm no longer drowning. I can make it to the surface.

"My Day," Veggie Tales

Even though it's impossible to really get personal time—or personal space, for that matter—when you have two active babies who can both walk pretty well, I need that space. This is what I recite in my mind; it is my litany for these times of exhausting, overwhelming parenting responsibility. These two toddlers are smart and capable enough to get into things that I never would have thought they'd take any interest in, but nonsensical enough to hurt themselves pretty badly in the process. In truth, though, even with CPS out of my life (hopefully for good now), I am still fully expecting that at some point or another, I will do something or not do something that will bring them back. As much as these little crazies can make me laugh, they can equally frighten me, but I am less frightened that they will hurt themselves badly than I am that they will hurt themselves enough for me to be reported for neglect again.

But I simply need some space. I love their incessant baby kisses the best, I think. Daniel, who has only recently gone from a few shaky steps across the carpet to running so fast he trips over the furniture, still likes to give me the slobbery, open-mouth baby kisses, giving me affection in the same way he drinks from my breast. Ida, in her cute but unnervingly repetitive behavior, gives cheek kisses to Eric and me the same way she gives top-of-the-giant-bald-head kisses to baby Daniel. She places her (closed) lips against our foreheads or the tops of our heads, and, instead of actually kissing us, she makes a sound like "Mwwaaahh," the sound of a kiss if it was turned into a word. I taught her to do this dramatic reenactment of affection while I was pregnant with Daniel, concerned that she might try to hurt her newborn brother out of jealousy for my attention. (She never did, not once. But I'd read that older siblings may get jealous of the attention a new baby receives and try to hurt the baby if the mother doesn't actively prevent it and teach the toddler to treat the baby with love.) So now Ida seems to have generalized this to mean that this is what a kiss is: you put your mouth on someone and make that noise. Or put your mouth on some*thing*. She also kisses her *Baby Einstein* DVDs and sometimes the carpet.

I'm browsing through the internet one room over from the kids because even just that much physical space from them feels like revival. I have nothing to do on the internet, as I have steered completely clear of message boards now, and the number of emails I got from Yahoo Groups was way too overwhelming, so I've removed myself from those, too. So, instead, I'm just following links at random, with my only object being to keep myself out of trouble and to keep the kids from looking for me or killing themselves while I'm taking a 20-minute break.

Right now, Ida is in the bathtub. A half hour ago, I filled the tub, stripped them both down, and bathed them together, dumping in about ten dollar-store bathtub toys. As per Ida and Daniel's protocol, after being bathed, one wanted to get out of the tub right away, and the other one didn't. This time, it was Daniel who wanted out and Ida who wanted to stay in. It's pretty chilly today for mid-October in Maryland, so I dried him off well and immediately put him in a diaper, a pair of cotton pants, and a blue sweater. This house has never consistently held the heat in. It's a common problem in mobile homes, and on winter evenings, we often resort to lying on the couch with multiple blankets and layers of clothing.

As I wander aimlessly through the interwebs, I can hear Daniel's tiny feet running back and forth on the carpet, and Ida, still in the tub, laughing her head off. Ida's laugh fills me with joy. It always has, but since the CPS problems resolved, and as I've gradually become more confident that I won't be getting any more visits as long as we lay low and stay off their radar, I find that hearing her laugh and knowing she's happy and loved and cared for is a brand new kind of pride and joy.

So, sitting there in the swivel chair in front of the Dell desktop, I am smiling ear to ear, and I praise God for this unassuming moment of thankfulness. But it's also been going on for quite a while, so at the risk of breaking up a good baby party, I walk into the living room to check on what's actually going on.

The first thing I see is Daniel running around on the carpet. One of his socks is half off his foot, and he's gripping a Dollar Store couch pillow in each little fist. He runs in a circle around the living room a couple of times and then pell-mell into the bathroom, where Ida is still sitting in the tub, making little splashing sounds. And then, Daniel runs back out of the bathroom without the pillows and Ida laughs again. Oh boy.

I'm concerned, of course, but still smiling. I can't help it. Ida's laugh, Daniel's tiny feet and giant bald head, and whatever game they've managed to come up with are just too much to resist. But when I walk into the bathroom, I stop laughing.

But only for a minute.

Ida stops laughing as I walk in, apparently feeling the need to explain herself. She is still sitting in the tub, and the tub is still full. But what the tub is full of is dark blue water... and Dollar Store couch pillows. Seeing me staring at her, she grabs one of the sopping-wet pillows from the water, grips what she can of its outer lining, and pulls it up a few inches from the water. And then she looks up at me with her giant, beaming smile and says, "Piwwhoas!"

Immediately, I hear Daniel's tiny, clomping footsteps as he runs into the bathroom as well. He finds me sitting there on the toilet lid, and after a few deep breaths, I am laughing so hard that I can barely breathe.

I can't be angry about the pillows. They are cheap and ugly and were only purchased to give me some level of satisfaction that I was a halfway decent housekeeper. They are only symbols of my need to feel like I am a good wife who takes care of her home, and they've even failed at that. And now that they are in the tub, they have failed quite spectacularly.

The tub water is only at room temperature, so I lift Ida out, dry her, and dress her. Then, I pull the drain plug, pick up a plastic bin, and toss the hopelessly drenched pillows into it. Then, so I don't have to risk a neighbor seeing me outside of the house while the babies are inside, I dump the pillows-turned-sponges onto the small deck on the side of our house. By dark, the wet pillows have collected a layer of ice, and when Eric arrives home and walks in, he says, "Why are the couch pillows icy and lying on the porch?" And I just laugh.

"Crazy," Gnarls Barkley

Don't hit me. Don't hit me. Don't hit me.

I'm praying, but more to the cars passing me on the highway than to God, I suppose. I'm alone, and the shoulder is narrow, and it's a four-lane expressway, but I can't figure out any other way to make sure I get my ten-mile-long run done today. And it's hot as hell—way too hot to be running on the blacktop off the side of the highway in the middle of the day, but I do what I have to do. And what I have to do is this long run because I have to keep off the weight I finally lost, all 80 pounds of it. And we're going to Ruby Tuesday tonight, so I need to get myself to negative calories now.

We're on vacation in Solomon's Island, Maryland, with the babies, of course, but also with Abigail and my mom and dad. It's been… interesting, I guess. Mostly good. Yesterday, I got a compliment—or rather, my mom got one for me from another woman who talked to her at the pool. Mom reported that the lady told her I looked great for someone with a baby so young, and I will definitely feel good about that for a long time. Daniel is, after all, only 16 months old, and I'm thinner now than I was when I got pregnant with Ida.

Mom and Dad came with us on this trip because we figured it would be low-key enough to not make my dad nervous or anything, and that they could potentially hang out with the kids so Eric and I could get some time alone. That hasn't happened yet, but that's okay. Today's my mom's birthday, too, and she's certainly had a hell of a year with my dad getting diagnosed in March. We all have. So we're going to Ruby Tuesday for dinner tonight, and Eric has already called ahead and asked them to surprise my mom with a birthday cake at the table.

I finally finish the awful, long run, and I'm so sweaty that it feels like I'm going to melt into the blacktop, starting with my sneakers. I walk onto the military vacation center base, flash my ID from out of my elastic belt that holds my water bottles, and climb the stairs into the old, resort-style hotel rooms with cheap carpeting, old beds with old mattresses, and wide, creaky porches. Praise the Lord for lukewarm summer showers and shampoo that smells like flowers.

Once I'm out of the shower and into my bathing suit, we all head down to the beach together. "Beach" isn't an entirely accurate term in this case because it's only a small sandbar that juts up against the ocean water as it flows into an inlet. But it's ideal for the babies since Ida can walk now. By the time we have blankets and towels spread on the sand, Daniel is fast asleep on a blanket under a canopy, Abigail is in the water, Eric is asleep on the blanket next to Daniel, and Mom and Dad are knee-deep in the water, too. Abigail runs back up to me briefly, telling me that all the other kids in the water are telling her there are jellyfish all over the place and they're stinging people, but I tell her they're probably just trying to scare her. It's an inlet; the water here isn't even 100% salt water. She presses me about it, claiming she saw one, but I tell her not to worry about it. She looks frustrated with me but goes back to the water to hang out with my Mom and Dad. I go back to my lunch and my book.

A little while later, Dad walks back up on his own and sits down in a folding chair next to me, then asks if Eric is cooking dinner tonight again. I tell him that he has to keep it a secret for now, but we are going to go to Ruby Tuesday because it's Mom's birthday, and that Eric has already purchased a cake and delivered it to the restaurant to surprise her. I'm glad to get a chance to talk to him alone. It's been four months since his diagnosis now, and I was worried about coming on this trip only to witness him forgetting everything and needing help. As much as I realize that Alzheimer's is his reality now, I wasn't ready to see it firsthand. But, thankfully, I haven't. He doesn't seem to have any symptoms at all. Gene mutation or not, he's the same as he's been for years now.

Ida toddles down toward the water, so I get up and follow her, and my mom walks from the water toward Ida as well. I wade in until I'm about ankle-deep, and as Mom approaches, I tell her about Abigail's claim that there are jellyfish in the water. To my surprise, Mom confirms it. She says they're pretty little, but they're everywhere, and they're stinging. I feel a little guilty for not believing it when Abigail told me, but if my mom and dad felt them and the sting didn't hurt, it can't be a big deal. So I talk to Mom for a few minutes while I keep an eye on Ida, who is walking through knee-level water (for her) and babbling to herself. She's good. So I turn around and make my way back to the beach blanket. Time for another Coke Zero. I earned it.

And then Ida screams bloody murder.

I spin around and bolt toward her, barefoot on the hot sand, not even noticing my tired quad muscles that thought they were done working for the day. Ida is standing with the water up to her knees, still screaming. A lifeguard is walking quickly toward her, but I make it first, and there it is. A blob the size of my fist that looks like thick, transparent jello has adhered itself to her left thigh, and long, leafy-looking tentacles have coiled themselves around her leg down to her foot. It would be pretty if it weren't attempting to kill and eat my kid. So, I grab the blob part with my left hand, put my right hand around the tentacles on her thigh, and, with an Amazon-style war whoop, and while feeling a sting on my own hand, I yank the thing off her leg and throw it further out in the water.

I've had quite enough of people and things trying to hurt her. Die, brainless jello.

We had planned the dinner and cake at Ruby Tuesday because it is Mom's birthday, and by the time we dealt with jellyfish stings on both Abigail and Ida, and on my parents' feet, we'd all earned our burgers and salad bar. I order the biggest bacon cheeseburger they have, make a couple of trips to the salad bar, mainly so I could say I ate something healthy, and prepare for dessert. The waiter checks on us, takes ice cream orders for the three kids, heads back to the kitchen, and returns carrying the ice cream, with another staff member behind him carrying the cake we'd dropped off, including lit candles. We sing "Happy Birthday," and a few people from surrounding tables join in. Unlike many others, my mom isn't embarrassed a bit by the presentation. She blows out the candles, and Eric slices the cake.

"Wow," my dad says, "one of these guys must have told them it was your birthday. I sure didn't." He looks at Eric and then at me.

"Eric brought the cake here and asked them to do this earlier this afternoon, remember?" I say. "I told you earlier."

Dad just stares at me. "Well, I didn't know that."

I look at Eric, who is already looking at me. Dad had forgotten.

I wait until we're in the car before I start crying.

"Boulevard of Broken Dreams," Green Day

Suffice it to say that the intervention of Child Protective Services has only made things harder for me. It's definitely over at this point, with the final finding being that I was, indeed, guilty of child neglect, which means I am also guilty of putting us in more debt, paying for the lawyer we hired who didn't succeed in having the finding removed. I'm trying to move on, and I did find a psychiatrist and begin taking medication again, but... I'm still me, I'm still alone for a good 12 hours a day with the babies, I still don't have anyone who can babysit or help me when Eric is at work, and I'm still the abusive and neglectful mother they accused me of being. Oh, and I have a record and a hugely traumatic experience to try to recover from.

And at the moment, Eric and I are arguing again. Loudly. Like, "I hope the neighbors don't call the police because they'll take my kids" loud. We've been arguing at some volume or another for over an hour now, and this has been the standard for the last six months. Mostly, it goes like this:

I have to do everything without help. There is no one to help me. You're never home, and when you are, you fall asleep immediately.

I can't help that the trains are always full. And I get up at 4:00 a.m., even on the nights when the kids are up all night, and go to work as early as I can so I can get home to help you. What else do you want from me?

I want you to give me a break once in a while. Didn't you get the message when the government tried to take our kids? I'm an unfit, suicidal mother, and you're leaving your children with me 24/7.

You're not an unfit mother. You are their mother. And I don't understand what you expect from me. I have to work. I have to pay the bills. I have to be there for a certain number of hours each day. The Navy doesn't call them suggestions.

From there, it usually progresses to me telling him that I don't have a choice either, and his job doesn't involve wiping bottoms and listening to screaming kids all day. It's a pointless conversation, and we both know it. Neither of us can change our situations, though we both want to. It's just that I need someone to get mad at, to yell at.

Today, I say this: "Why don't you just friggin' leave me? Take the kids! I'm a neglectful mother! I'm inadequate! I'm sure you'd love to shack up with one of the new girls in the Sea Chanters!"

"I will not. You are my wife. God calls me to be your husband. He will not allow me to leave you."

And then I surprise myself:

"You say that like you still believe that crap! Do you? Because I don't."

The surprise I feel after that statement isn't about the words themselves or even the truth behind them. The surprise is that I said it out loud. It seems more final, more devastating, as it echoes through our double-wide mobile home with the punch-stained carpets. I said it loud enough for the neighbors to hear, and I wonder if someone will call the police. That would be bad.

"I do still believe it. I will not leave you. I made that commitment to God, not just you," he says.

I have nothing left in me; the burst of energy that always arrives with my rage has run out of me. I turn, run into our bedroom, and slam the door. The entire house shakes, as it always does when I slam a door. The house shakes again as I throw myself down onto the mattress and begin my own wailing, angry cry. But later, I relent, telling Eric that I will go to church with him, but only if he can assure me that we can keep the kids with us and no one is going to make me leave when one of them needs to breastfeed.

A week later, after I had forgotten that I'd relented on this, he tells me that he spoke with a pastor on the phone. I am incredulous, but Eric is claiming that this pastor said he doesn't think anyone in the congregation will mind if we keep the kids with us, including when they need to nurse. But I needed more than that. I asked if the pastor understood that these were not tiny, newborn twins but toddlers, that the two-year-old may also want to nurse, and that I won't be putting a blanket over them when they do it.

"I explained to him that both Ida and Daniel still nurse and that they don't cooperate when you try to cover them in public."

Okay… though I'm not sure I believe it. "What if they make noise? Ida's screechy thing she does when someone approaches her?"

"He said there is at least one other person with an older child with special needs who sometimes makes noise during the service. It's a little church, only like 20 people at the most."

Hmm. That could be good or bad, but it does explain a lot.

"He also said, 'Bring a blanket and some of their toys and snacks, and you can just sit with them on the floor and do what you need to do. Whatever you need to do in order to be here is fine.'"

I cautiously agree to go to another church.

Fugue in G Minor,
J.S. Bach, BWV 542

"No, you can't say that because she's my *wife!*"

Eric is arguing with Angie over the phone. We are in the midst of packing up to move into base housing in D.C., and Ida just started school for the first time in a special ed. classroom. She's barely four. There is so much stress right now that we don't need Angie giving us any more, yet here we are.

I'm not entirely sure what they're fighting about, but apparently, it's something to do with me. What did I do to make Angie mad recently? I really don't know. The only thing I can remember is that the last time we were up at my parents' house in Pennsylvania to visit Abigail, Eric had taken Abigail to see *The Incredibles,* and I had wanted to go, too, but Eric insisted I stay home. So maybe he wanted to tell Abigail something I wouldn't want her to know about me, or maybe he had to set Angie straight about something about me. I sincerely *hate* knowing that I'm being discussed by other people for negative reasons. Just talk to me about it; don't talk around me.

Eric hangs up the phone and slams it on a side table in the living room. Slamming a phone down was much more effective when phones weren't tiny and fragile, but he communicated his frustration nonetheless.

"As soon as we're settled in the base house, I'm going to get custody. I just can't deal with this anymore. She is keeping Abigail in a house with an active rodent infestation. But we're the ones who have CPS problems."

We've tossed the idea of getting custody of Abigail back and forth briefly before, but with the CPS intervention a few years ago, I'd given up on the idea. I wasn't about to do anything that would attract their attention again. But Abigail says she sees mice in her room at night, and there are bugs in her bed. But, honestly, I can't handle another kid right now, either. So I'll just have to hope that Eric and I can calm down about Angie's living situation, pray that Angie finds a way to get out of that house, and pray that I can remain off the CPS radar. I have a busy two-year-old and a disabled four-year-old. I don't need to raise any others right now.

"Anytime You Need a Friend,"
Mariah Carey

This is the second week in a row we've attended this church. So far, so good. As promised, no one complained about the couple with the baby who nursed twice during a one-hour service and the toddler who wouldn't sit still. Ida is still crawling more than toddling, but now, at 18 months, she seems to at least be a bit more interested in walking. Today, the pastor and his family are hosting a cookout at their house in the afternoon, so I made brownies—the one baked good I have learned to make from scratch.

Since the other people here have been attending for a while, Eric and I talk with the pastor and his wife, sitting down on their porch with paper plates and warm grilled cheeseburgers. As it turns out, Pastor John doesn't have a seminary degree, but he's working on one. He has a full-time job, but they decided to start the church in a casual way after determining that none of the other local churches were a good fit for their family. I told them about our last few church experiences— the repeated rejection and scorn we felt from being asked to leave the sanctuary to feed Ida. It was a cathartic emotional dump on my part that more than likely made all of us uncomfortable, but they assured me that we were safe here.

It's hard to express the comfort I feel in knowing that we are welcome here as we are. Everything over the last ten years has happened so quickly that I've always felt three steps behind. When Eric and I got engaged, I was so confident—prideful, really—because my life was moving faster than everyone else's. I knew I was in over my head with school and Eric and Abigail and even the idea of getting married and being independent, but I really thought I could handle it. I wanted to handle it. I should have been able to handle it. So why couldn't I?

"Chasing Cars," Snow Patrol

I just got off the phone with Monique, my La Leche League leader. She calls to check on me periodically ever since I told her about the CPS situation with Ida. But even after that came to an end last year, Monique still calls, and she's made LLL a wonderful breastfeeding support group—and for me, anyway, she's extended that into a friendship. I wish I had a way to repay her, but I'm still learning how adult friendships work, and I have no idea if I'm a good friend to anyone right now. I had believed that the women on the Gentle Christian Mothers message board were my friends, too.

Last week, I told Monique about my MOPS group friends as well and how anytime someone tells a story about their child, it seems like their child is much older than Ida. Abigail was talking in short but full sentences when she was three, but when Ida talks, she only repeats sentences and phrases verbatim. She also copies the tone of voice of the characters on her DVDs. Basically, she talks, but only by mimicking, and I have no idea what she's thinking, even with simple things like whether she wants buttered toast or buttered noodles for dinner. Monique knows about and has seen Ida's picky eating, too—and Deidre, Monique's two-year-old, eats better and talks in a normal two-year-old way.

According to a medical website Monique found, Ida is indeed quite behind in development, but according to a separate article on the same website, Ida is exhibiting almost all of the symptoms of autism. I'm floored by this news, but oddly relieved, too, because if Ida has autism, it would explain why she's not reaching the right milestones for both her behavior and her physical size. I've met other kids with autism, and she does seem kind of similar.

Finishing the phone call, I find myself at a loss for how to feel about this. My initial reaction was relief, but that was a selfish thought, as if a disease with a name would exonerate me from the guilt of "indicated child neglect." Certainly, this explains her eating and speaking issues better than simply poor mothering. But this selfish desire for vindication, this "I told you so," was a childish idea and useless now; I've already been convicted.

But what do I do? Why is this information coming to me from friends and websites while doctors are busy judging me instead of evaluating Ida? This idea that she may have autism is ripe like a peach off of one of the trees at Strawberry Acres. It is tender and bruises more easily than the idea that I was simply an inept and self-absorbed mother, focused only on my own mental torment, spinning the wheels and reliving every scene that presented my failure. Worse, autism would require more doctors, more evaluations, and more dramatic testing of Ida's blood and Ida's brain.

But now that I understand this, now that the odd development milestones and nonexistent communication are so abundantly and obviously explained, choosing to ignore that information, to ignore her symptoms, would be neglectful. If I get accused of neglect again, CPS will take her and Daniel from me. Once again, I'm presented with what looks like options and personal choices in my parenting when, in fact, I have none. If I ever make a plan for my children that someone—a social worker, a doctor, anyone—thinks is the wrong choice, I risk turning over my children to someone else.

I watch Ida, walking in her happy, bouncy walk and tilting each ear toward her shoulders in beat with her steps. Right now, she's into hats. It took some time and frustration for both of us, but I have convinced her to exchange her warm winter hat shaped like a penguin for a bucket hat with a picture of Dorothy the Dinosaur and the Wiggles.

I know that we will need to take this risk, to seek out a doctor to tell us whether or not she has autism. I will not raise my children in the shadows of my fears.

"Unwritten,"
Natasha Bedingfield

How many hard and terrible things can a person get through in a span of five years, or ten years, or a lifetime? Maybe someday, that will be a question I can answer, assuming my life won't always be this hard. But maybe it will. Maybe life really is this hard, this draining, for everyone. Does everyone face trial after trial, metaphorically, around every corner and with every change? Most of my friends from high school are beginning careers, dating, going to graduate school, or just plain working, according to the stories my mom hears back in Pennsylvania. A few have gotten married. Some are still finishing college.

This is where I am, in the car at 6:00 a.m., with Eric driving and Ida and Daniel in their car seats behind us—quiet for once, and probably more than a little confused since the sun isn't even up yet. We're all quiet—tired, mostly, but also nervous and worried, and in some ways, glad this strange day has come. We are on our way to the Children's National Medical Center to have a pediatric developmental psychologist evaluate Ida. We think she has autism.

At the time the referral came back approved by Tricare, the wait list for a diagnostic appointment with this doctor—the only one anywhere near us who specializes in diagnosing developmental disorders—was nine months long, but an opening came up last week, and they called me to reschedule. The person whose child had had this appointment had moved out of the area before their turn came up. I hope they'll get seen quickly somewhere else.

The clinic is tiny, too small for much of anything. There are public bathrooms bigger than the reception and waiting area, and when we are ushered to the room where Ida will be examined, it's twice the size but completely empty, save for a small desk, two chairs, a mirror, and paper towel and soap dispensers. There are two cardboard boxes with lids behind the desk, as well. We give Ida and Daniel freedom to walk around the room; there is nothing they could destroy here. Images of *Law & Order* police interrogation rooms come to mind, but I let go of the anxiety that wants to pop up. After all, I was interrogated in my own kitchen.

But the appointment does indeed begin with an interview. A young woman, "not the doctor," she says, reads off the information I provided when the appointment was made and asks me if any of it has changed since then and to further describe how Ida is different from other three-year-olds I've met, periodically interjecting to ask for more details about something I've mentioned. I talk for what seems like hours before I catch myself. I've done it again; I've poured everything out at once, including all my feelings about it, a therapeutic information dump better suited for my own mental health sessions. When I recognize this, I backpedal, making excuses for myself—"I just want to make sure I don't leave out something important."

When she asks about pediatricians and preschool, I realize that if I don't tell her at least a portion of the problems we've had with CPS, it will look bad for me since she may already have that information from someone else. But even two years later, I can't entirely control my own narrative about this. So the tears, the anger, and all the gory details are laid out on the table yet again, my naked confessions of every flaw, a manifesto of failure.

"This kind of stuff happens to parents of kids with developmental delays," she says. My self-righteous anger flares again. This is happening to other women, other parents, too. If a child struggles, it must mean that their mother is inadequate, and the solution is to punish them both by separating them. But my husband, always the voice of wisdom and discernment when I'm out of control, steers the conversation back to Ida's needs.

"So, the way she only wants to eat a handful of different foods and spits out anything else we try to feed her, and how she repeats long phrases but doesn't seem to know how to respond to a question—all of those things are autism symptoms?"

She briefly explains that autism is a pretty specific diagnosis, so the day will continue with herself and the doctor working with Ida to see where and how autism, or something else, is evident. "Autism is just one name for these sorts of symptoms, but the criteria listed for autism in the DSM-IV are very specific. There are a few other disorders similar to autism, so she could fit better into one of those categories, or she may not fit any of them." But she assures us that there is most certainly a delay in Ida's development and that they will be able to determine a plan of action for us today.

And so, for the first time in her life, Ida takes tests that don't involve blood and is evaluated by a doctor for longer than ten minutes, without being manipulated or even touched, for the most part. At one point, everyone had to take a 20-minute break when Eric pulled a wipe from a dispenser to change Daniel's diaper, only to realize too late that it was not a baby wipe but an antibacterial one. Poor little guy screamed bloody murder. The doctors left the room at that point until Eric managed to wash him off and eventually get him to sleep in the sling.

The doctor determined that the best diagnosis to apply for Ida was Pervasive Developmental Disorder Not Otherwise Specified, or PDD-NOS. She has many autism symptoms, but not quite enough for that specific diagnosis as it's written in the DSM-IV. They reassured us that picky eating and speech delays are very common ASD symptoms and that none of these symptoms were caused by us. This is simply a part of Ida, not a reflection of our ability to care for her. Our next step is to have her evaluated by our local school district because they have therapeutic programs for preschoolers on the spectrum.

On the escalator leading back to the parking garage, I cry and become lightheaded, almost swooning. When I right myself, I am surprised to see the sun through some windows along the hospital's high ceiling. We had arrived in the dark and are now even more exhausted than when we came in. Surely, the day should have come and gone, and we should be emerging into another night. So much has happened since the time we came in. But when we start the car, the clock on the dashboard says 3:15. It's only the weight of the unknown future that's depleting me.

April 4, 1994

I am outside watching the sunset. I'm sitting on the old well. The cat is next to me. This is my favorite spot to sit because I can look out over the pond and see the sun go down behind the peach trees. I can see bubbles in the water, which means the fish have woken up. It all makes me so happy to be who I am.

I rode my bike up to Grandpa's memorial stone at the church. I sang him two songs and talked to him a little bit. Someday, I want people to know I made a difference.

"Say," John Mayer

Despite the six-month wait before our appointment with the neuropsychiatrist who affirmed that Ida has an autism spectrum disorder, Ida can't get help from our local school district until their people do their own evaluation. The good news, praise God, is that they were able to schedule it only two weeks after we saw the doctor.

The "office," if you could call it that, is located in an old temporary classroom building, like the ones that are really just fancy shipping containers. I'm thankful I brought a coat; those classrooms didn't have reliable heating when I was in school, and this one doesn't either.

The two-person staff inside work in different areas of the space, segmented by cubicles. Just inside the door is a designated "play area," but in this case, the "play" is really an evaluation of the child's needs. One woman sits with Eric and Ida in this area while another young woman asks me questions about Ida—physical health things, like how much and how well she eats and if she can walk well, but the questions are open-ended, and she uses this to learn the specifics of Ida's autism symptoms. The whole thing is frightening. It's frightening to know Ida has autism, that she will need special education classes, and that she may never be an independent adult. I've spent the last four years reassuring myself by thinking of Ida as a little girl who will grow up and eventually no longer need me. That childhood is temporary. I made mine as temporary as I could. But now I need to accept, or maybe grieve, the possibility that Ida may still be a little girl, even when she's 17.

Throughout the interview, I detect no sense that I am being recorded, no sneaky CPS workers listening in, and no searching questions like the kind I fell for before. The questions are about Ida, I remind myself, and these government employees are the ones who actually work to help people like Ida—which, in turn, helps me. But I keep reminding myself to avoid showing emotion other than love for Ida. It's because Ida is autistic, I think, that she had trouble eating and learning to talk, not because I was an inadequate mom. This reassurance is one that I repeat to myself several times a day, and I try to believe it's the truth.

The school district evaluators readily conclude that Ida will be allowed to attend an existing special education preschool at our local elementary school. The class is specifically for kids ages three through six with symptoms of autism. Somehow, this information manages to simultaneously be a relief and a gut punch. I had never truly given up the idea of homeschooling Ida and Daniel. What we've experienced in these last few years was more than adequate to teach us to stay out of the public school system and out of the eyes of social services. But Eric's enlistment, and now Ida's autism, ensure that we will remain tethered to social services—maybe forever. Am I willing to continue living in fear of another unscheduled CPS visit? If that's what it takes for Ida to go to the right school and for me to know that no one is coming to my door to take my babies away, I gladly submit.

Lord, if it is within your will for me, make me into the mother my children need. Amen.

"Love Song," Sara Bareilles

I spoke with Ida's teacher today. Next week, we move to the base housing in D.C., and it's been less than a month since Ida's first day of special ed. It feels wrong to uproot her again when she just started adjusting to school.

When we applied for a three or four-bedroom house on Joint Base Anacostia-Bolling at least a year ago, we had no idea when we'd get the phone call that a house was opening up for us. We only knew that the wait lists for most military base family housing units are long and that a three-bedroom is more in demand than a two-bedroom. So, after we applied, we kind of forgot about it. We've been living one day at a time ever since the CPS stuff, and with different parts of the mobile home breaking down, paying bills, and the constant needs Ida and Daniel still have, neither Eric nor I have the mental-emotional energy for a future beyond tomorrow.

The good thing is Ida's teacher told me that even though D.C. public schools are very culturally different from Ida's current school, her time during these few months here has taught her a lot about what school is, what the routines are, and how to be a student. And the teacher is right. The miracle for me is that she wants to be there at all, and knowing that within a few weeks she decided that she loves school means that she knows school is a good place to be.

Eric hired movers this time. With all we've been through in this house, we need this move to be easy.

It's startling how different our way of life here is compared to our lives in the town we grew up in. In four years of marriage, this will be our fourth move, but only Eric's initial move to the D.C. area and our first apartment in Maryland were required as part of his Navy career. First, we wanted a bigger apartment, and then the next year, we needed a place with an extra bedroom that would become a nursery, although I could probably count on one hand the number of times Ida slept in it. And now, having seen that the time I spend alone caring for Ida and Daniel should be minimized since I am apparently an unfit mother, we need to live closer to Eric's work. And on the base, we'll be so close that he could run or bike his commute.

But Ida having autism and needing to go to school intervention programs at age three adds to the complexity. That's another hurdle for us. We will need to start and maintain communication with the school district, its special education department, and the staff of any school she goes to. We could reject a school or a teacher of a program or any aspect of her Individualized Education Plan (IEP), but doing that will always be a risk. Without having signed our agreement to the final version of Ida's IEP care plan from the district, she could be removed from special ed. altogether until we have an IEP that we are willing to sign.

Moving in April, closer to the end of the school year than the beginning, complicates all of this even more. When Eric and I talked with the special education department of D.C. Public Schools, they had a placement in a class with other kids with autism symptoms, but not until next school year. The only appropriate placement for the next two months will be at a school on the opposite side of the city, in a building that is so dilapidated that it will be torn down after the school year ends in June. There are only two functional bathrooms in the whole building. Oddly enough, that part isn't a problem at all because Ida isn't potty trained. That's not usually something that the parent of a preschooler would call fortunate, but here we are. Now we can put off potty training a little longer.

These last few years have felt like I was playing pretend. Before having kids, I guess I assumed that some sort of biological instinct would enable me to properly take care of my baby. I didn't have to learn new skills to get pregnant, and although we did take natural childbirth classes, it was only in order to avoid any medical interventions that weren't necessary for Ida and me to survive. Even after Ida and Daniel were born, I didn't have to learn how to feed them. I learned breastfeeding techniques and how to ensure that the baby ate well while also avoiding any discomfort for me, but my breasts knew how to make milk, and the babies instinctively knew how to get it. I didn't realize how much of parenting happened through improvisation or that an infant could engage an adult in a battle of wits.

There's no parenting book to tell you that if your kid won't eat, it could be that she's still using an infant's tongue-thrust reflex, even though she's two. I don't know for sure that that's what was going on with Ida, but it seems that way. They expected her to be eating solid food, but she wasn't, so there had to be something wrong with me. I went to therapists and psychiatrists, but no one ever considered that maybe Ida was the disabled one.

All of that is over—and has been for two years. But the pain and fear is still very much a reality. Any sideways glance, questions from strangers about why she doesn't answer their questions or won't give them a hug, the fact that I ate the lollipop the cashier at Trader Joe's gave her—not because I'm a mom who won't let her kid have candy, but because my kid doesn't like candy. She likes noodles, toast, butter, yogurt, and cheese. That's about it.

"Anti-Hero," Taylor Swift

Peeking at my own face in the mirror on the car's sun visor, I'm embarrassed by what I see. My face is usually the only part of my body that I find remotely attractive, but this morning, my face looks ashen. Lack of sleep does that to me. Ida and Daniel certainly sleep through the night now, but to get Ida to her school on the opposite side of the city, we all need to be up before dawn. Before I had kids, there were nights when I went to bed at this hour. But today, it's 6:00 a.m., and I've already fed and dressed myself and my two children and driven to the Metro station.

Of course, I will do this every day so that Ida can be in an appropriate school setting for her needs. But before I had kids, when I heard about moms who accomplished huge feats to help save their children, I assumed that said moms were emboldened by their love for their kids throughout the entire act. Not me. I'm frustrated, weary, and just plain exhausted. When I was a kid, my parents had backup plans for their backup plans. If a parent couldn't drive us somewhere, there were three different grandparents, plus aunts and uncles and even friends who could step in, willing to help not out of obligation or for payment but because it's just what friends and family did for each other. But I don't have any other family members here, and even if I did, to ask someone for help for something with my kids could be misconstrued as a sign that I'm incapable of caring for them, and if I want to keep CPS away from me, I have to at least look like I've got everything—especially myself—under control.

Some of the older subway systems screech loudly, but thankfully the Metro doesn't. A gust of stale, dirty air greets us before the train stops. I roll Daniel, sitting in the umbrella stroller, and Ida, in the baby sling on my left hip, onto the train. Normally, one of them would walk, and I'd leave the stroller at home, but it's way too early for me to direct them without yelling. Ida is four now, and usually she's in the stroller and Daniel's in the sling because he's lighter, but today, I am taking Ida to school. It will be her first official day at the run-down, soon-to-be-a-pile-of-dirt school in the northwest quadrant of the city. I still can't fathom how it's come to this.

I did not cause Ida's autism. I often find myself rehearsing that sentence in my head. I suppose I think this so often because I need to be able to say it with confidence because it's the truth, and some people really do think that autism is something caused by frigid mothers who neglect and mistreat their children. Although the word autism didn't come up at all during my conversations with the CPS workers, they built their case around the belief that Ida's development was delayed because I was neglecting her and that I was neglecting her because I didn't want her, or because I was a depressed nutcase. I don't deny the depressed nutcase part, but I couldn't have caused her to have autism.

Autism isn't a weapon wielded against a child by a frigid mother. I think of all the mothers 80 or 100 years ago who were accused the way I was, who may have loved their child and longed to help them learn and talk and be more independent, for her sake as much as theirs. I want to become a competent mother of an autistic child, but even more so, I want to be confident that Ida is autistic because God designed her that way. She is fearfully and wonderfully made, just as she is right now. I want to be able to say that with assurance when people ask me why my four-year-old is still in diapers, and I want her to believe that herself ten years from now—although I certainly hope she won't still be in diapers when she's 14. But if I'm going to teach her and the people around her to believe this, I have to believe it first. And I don't, yet.

The drop-off at the school did involve good, loud crying, but Ida wasn't alone in that. Ida cried when I left her, and Daniel cried when we left the building, but I cried the whole time. Not because I'll miss Ida and not because Ida cried for me. I cried when I couldn't remember how to get from the Metro stop to the school. I cried sitting on a random curb because I wanted better for my baby girl than a loud classroom in a partially flooded school building and because I may never be able to stop worrying that maybe I really am a bad mom. Mostly, I cried because I am just so, so tired.

I thought I'd done all the things right as a mom. I breastfed and played music and moved her around to the beat. I held her when she wanted to be held and taught her how to play with toys when I saw that she didn't seem to know how. Yet I screwed up; I didn't take care of my mental health, and I didn't bring her to the doctor when I saw that she was developmentally behind. But I know better than to blame myself for Ida having autism; autism isn't an illness or a deformity, and really, it isn't even a problem because we know how to help her through the world of neurotypical people. Even if I had done everything wrong, Ida would be Ida. I take a deep breath and exhale slowly. God is in control of Ida's life, and for today, and until God leads us in another direction, Ida is where she needs to be. My ways are not his ways. So, by implication, I am where I need to be, too.

The sun emerges from behind the clouds as Daniel and I walk back to the Metro station.

"Running on Empty,"
Jackson Browne

It's an ugly feeling to be jealous of your own husband, especially when I know other people can tell I'm jealous. No one's ever actually accused me of this; when I talk to anyone about his accomplishments, I always emphasize how proud I am of him and mention that he's a wonderful husband and father. It's totally possible to simultaneously feel pride, anger, love, and frustration about a single person continuously.

So right now, we're in Cincinnati. We drove here from Maryland because flights are expensive, and Eric wants to hang onto every nickel and dime he can. By "hang onto," I mean that he collects and distributes his nickels and dimes on every available flat surface in the house. I've decided to consider this one of those quirky habits that geniuses always seem to have. That said, I end up collecting loose change around the house like a beggar on a street corner.

Anyway, we drove, with our two babies, to Cincinnati so that Eric could run another marathon. Boston's done, but Eric's not, I guess. He's even got a coach now to help him get faster. And since I still have a little bit of leftover pregnancy weight to get rid of, I trained for and ran a 10K here this morning. The marathon isn't until tomorrow, but we're in the city park that hosts the race because Ida and Daniel have races today. Ida is signed up for a 50-foot distance toddler race, and Daniel is signed up for the "Diaper Dash," an event where crawling or toddling babies get to run, walk, toddle, scoot, or crawl—whatever it takes—across a six-foot-long gym mat laying on the ground.

The whole area is chaotic; most race sign-ups are, but most race participants don't cry, throw dirt, or poop their pants before the start of the race. Nevertheless, I pick Ida up, pin her race number bib to her shirt, and head to the start line for her run, which is wider than the race is long, since toddlers aren't accustomed to moving in one direction or in a straight line. As I have been for the last three years, I'm exercising mental caution about how Ida's experience with this race will unfold. She may scream or cry, become overwhelmed by the crowd or the movement or the huge open space of the park. She may refuse to move from her spot at the start line, cling onto my leg, or scream in terror. I've learned to accept any of these possibilities. Her way of thinking and decoding the world and any given environment she enters is broad and unconventional. This isn't something she chose, to interpret a grassy hill or a talking toy as something to fear. It sounds terribly cliché, but this is how God made her. These challenges, which are really only challenges for us as her neurotypical parents, are unique qualities we need to learn to navigate ourselves in real time as she confronts them. We have to do our best to see things her way and then find ways to adapt our thinking. Sometimes, that means helping her adapt her own thinking, but a lot of the time, it doesn't.

Anyway, the clustering mob of parents and small children at the start line gets continuously bigger until the lady with the bullhorn tells us they're going to start the race. My legs are still sore from the 10K this morning, and I'm getting cold as the sweat from this morning evaporates off of my skin. But finally, the bullhorn lady says, "Go," and everyone goes. The effect is like watching birds scatter after a loud noise. So I hold Ida back for a few moments and then loosen my grip as the crowd spreads out a bit. To my pleasant surprise, Ida moves straight forward, happy as I've ever seen her, walking on her tiptoes and tapping her ears toward her shoulders on alternate sides. This is her fun, happy walk. I follow her as she meanders, but she definitely seems to understand what and where the finish line is. When she gets to it, I take a picture of Eric holding her on his hip, and she even smiles and poses, holding her little finisher's medal up over her head.

And later, when Daniel does his Diaper Dash, he also puts on an adorable show. Eric sets him carefully on his feet at the end of the four-foot-long mat that is the baby/toddler race course, and Daniel immediately walks steadily, with his little belly jutted out in front like a peacock, to the end of the mat, where he stops to smile and clap for himself.

Back in our hotel room, we try desperately to get them—and ourselves—to nap. In a quiet voice, Eric says to me, "You know, the way Ida walks on her toes like she does, her calves are gonna be super strong someday. She'll make a great runner if she keeps walking like that."

The Boston Marathon is only a beginning, I suppose.

"Big Girls Don't Cry," Fergie

"Mom! Turn on the waterfall!"

I'm in the process of potty-training both Ida and Daniel, but it's complicated. Ida is at school for about six hours every day, but Daniel is only two, so, of course, he's at home. Both of them have a ways to go, and I can't even remember if this is the second or third time we've tried to work on this particular developmental skill. Right now, Daniel has peed in the potty exactly once, but he is obsessed with washing his hands and making soap bubbles.

This isn't the best homeschooling setup, but it will do for now. I'm only a few feet from Daniel in the bathroom, crammed into a tight space at the kitchen table, looking over Abigail's home/online school curriculum.

She's only been living with us for about six weeks, but it feels like it's been six years. Our base housing here is good, but outside the base is the roughest, poorest part of D.C., and the local public schools reflect that. She started school at a private charter school on the opposite side of the city, with Eric dropping her off before he went to work and picking her up after his late afternoon run. But by the second week of school, Abigail started saying that her teacher was doing things like making the students walk around and around one city block in the middle of the day in 90-degree weather or redo entire assignments if even one answer was wrong. We looked into other charter schools

233

briefly, but the solution we landed on was to put her in an online public charter school.

The school has its own curriculum, much of it online, and Abigail has a teacher who really only sends emails and grades online tests. It's basically homeschooling. I have to make sure she does the assignments, set up science labs and do them with her, check her work, and monitor her progress. So, I do most of the hardest parts of a typical teacher's job. With Daniel here, too, plus Abigail's two kittens, Onyx and Cheese, who moved in with her, this is not the best atmosphere for teaching fifth grade.

And that's only one part of the stress right now. A few weeks ago, Abigail had her tenth birthday party, a sleepover at my parents' house. I was super excited to host the party, but Abigail wasn't into it when I tried to make plans for games and food with her. I thought that if we collaborated and succeeded in working together to make a great party happen, she would trust me as a mom and allow herself to settle into her new living situation. She had lots of plans and ideas, but all of them seemed to require craft supplies and party decorations that we would never be able to afford. I'm trying to help her be happy here, but nothing is working, and my patience is wearing thin.

Anyway, when the sleepover finally happened, Angie was at my parents' house, too, and she came armed with food, gifts, and decorations. When I look at it all in hindsight, I realize now that Angie missed Abigail and that she's always liked hosting birthday parties, so I have some sympathy, but that night was dark and ugly, and Eric spent the whole night "doing errands" away from the house.

"Turn on the waterfall! I went pee pee in the potty, but I can't reach it!" Daniel yells again. Reach what? There's no waterfall in my bathroom. Abigail, sitting behind me at the table, laughs. "I think he means the faucet on the sink," and of course, she's right. I'm just barely calm enough to laugh at my Little Man's ideas. We visited Niagara Falls last summer, so in his mind, he has determined that the bathroom sink faucet is also a waterfall since water falls from it. Daniel has some unique reasoning skills.

But things with Abigail and I are not going well. Like, at all. She's made it very clear that she doesn't want to be here. She's sullen, quiet, and even a bit snippy with Ida and Daniel. She has a cell phone now that's on Angie's account, and she's always on it texting and talking to Angie. When she's using the computer for her schoolwork, she waits for me to leave the room and switches over to emailing Angie and some friends from her previous school in Pennsylvania. Nothing is blocking me from reading these emails, so I do, and I get even more angry than I already am.

Abigail writes, "I hate it here. Ida cries at night and won't stay in her bed, and Mel's always trying to get her to sleep, so I can't sleep, and then Mel gets upset and cries and yells." Angie responds that this is Abigail's "cross to bear" right now, implying that I am somehow a deadly burden, a scourge, an instrument of torture. All I'm trying to do is give Abigail a two-parent, Christian home. I didn't realize that was going to include preteen attitude problems and two cats that keep pissing on the carpet.

It's only been about six weeks, but for me, at least, this arrangement isn't working. Abigail's seriously miserable. Ida loves her school and her bus rides, but I'm too overwhelmed to keep track of how she's really doing at school. Is she using the toilet, following along with the classroom routines, or saying anything that she didn't memorize from something else? Daniel, at least, is loud, talking pretty much normally, and generally happy. But I'll need to work on his potty training soon.

And on top of everything else, I keep getting bladder infections. Again. This happened when I was in college, too; for several months, I felt like I had to pee all the time, but I could only go a little, and it hurt to do even that. One time, it got so bad that my pee was full of blood, but thankfully, Eric was able to take me to an ER. I took so many antibiotics within a short period that I got chronic yeast infections. So this is the worst possible time for it to be happening again. But that's how things go for me; there's never just one problem. Is everyone's life like this—overwhelming and miserable and moving too fast? I have no way to know and no time to find out.

"River," Joni Mitchell

Wednesday has become my new favorite day of the week because I get to go to work. Last August, I went to a play group that the base housing office hosts once a week since so many families living here have little kids who aren't in school yet. It was always weird to explain that Daniel has an almost four-year-old sister who was at school to moms whose little kids were normal. Once, the housing office let someone come in recruiting for jobs at the Department of Transportation. They needed part-time people, even if they could only do one day each week. It pays $12 per hour. Working—or, more specifically, a day of doing something that doesn't require wiping tiny butts—sounded wonderful, and I applied right away. Eric was even able to do some of his work from home on Wednesdays. So, once a week for the last two months, I've been pretending to be a real person who does real things.

But on this particular Wednesday, I have mixed feelings about leaving for work. I even considered taking the day off. Last weekend, the crap hit the fan between me and Abigail. She left her diary open on her bed while Eric took her to soccer practice on the other side of the base. Soccer is the one thing she seems to enjoy here. But I had been under the impression that she was hiding the diary from me, so now that it was lying there, open and in the middle of her bed, it seemed like an invitation.

The first few pages weren't much—she had a crush on a boy on her soccer team, online school was stupid, I was always mean. But the very last thing she'd written cut deeply. "I wish that Dad and Mel would just die or go away."

To say I cried ugly tears would be an understatement; I lost all control of myself. I screamed and bit my forearm but didn't have the courage to make it bleed. I threw my body against every flat surface—every part of the couch, each chair, the floor. I stared in the mirror at my own fat, ashen, red, pock-marked face and hated it, hated myself, hated the world, my life, and every part of the last five years. I'd cried like this before when Eric dumped me before the wedding, when I found out he'd lied about my original engagement ring, and about a million times during the whole shameful CPS thing. And that was just it: Abigail living with us, I thought, would be my redemption after I'd failed so miserably with Ida and Daniel. I thought that, since Abigail was ten and hadn't endured life with me mom-ing her until now, I could do it better than Angie had and thereby prove to the world, to my family, to Eric, and to myself that I am a good, loving, caring, Christian mom. But, like the overly complicated science experiments in Abigail's online school curriculum, the results answer the question posed by the hypothesis. I'm a terrible mom.

As much as I understand that Ida has autism and that I didn't cause her to have autism, I resist the idea that none of it is my fault. Over and over, I revisit the events of her birth, my inability to help her sleep in the weeks and months after it, and I wonder where I messed it all up. I ate too many M&Ms—too much sugar in general—when I was pregnant. I went for short runs twice a week, well into my second trimester. I didn't let the midwife check my cervix often enough during her birth. Later, I couldn't get Ida to nurse enough, or maybe I nursed her too much. And I got pregnant again, robbing Ida of my undivided attention when she was only 15 months old.

With Abigail, I thought I had a head start. I could jump in as Mom where Angie left off and fill in the gaps I thought Angie had missed. I could figure out how to be a good mom by letting Abigail be my experiment, and then later, I'd do better with Ida and Daniel because

I'd had Abigail as my test subject. But Abigail has proven the original hypothesis that CPS had presented. I'm just a crappy parent.

On the day I found Abigail's diary while she and Eric were at soccer practice, I made quick work of telling Eric what I'd read in it. I asked Abigail to keep an eye on Ida and Daniel so he and I could talk. She did, but I could tell she was listening because she was hovering in the doorway. I used to do that when my parents argued. After I presented my evidence to Eric, I told him that I was out and could no longer homeschool her, nor could I drive her back and forth to any of the better schools in other parts of the city. I told him that I would prefer to send her home to Angie as soon as possible. Then I went upstairs to put Ida and Daniel to bed.

When my little "Irish twins" were settled and quiet, I sat on the staircase and listened to Eric's half of the phone conversation with Angie. Angie, I'm sure, knows everything that's been going on. She wasted no time in agreeing to drive the six hours to our home, pick up Abigail and all her stuff, and immediately leave again—which is happening this morning.

Right now, I'm the only one up, greeting the sun. I kiss a sleeping Eric after I dress for work. Downstairs, I find Abigail only lightly asleep on the couch, surrounded by three duffle bags and the big assortment of pillows and stuffed animals she'd arrived with in August. Everything is packed and waiting by the front door. Before I walk out into this dark, frosty morning, I sit down on the floor, pray for her and for us, and whisper, "I still love you. I hope we'll all be together again and happy someday." She nods silently and rolls over to sleep again.

"The Hustle," Van McCoy and the Soul City Symphony

When I'm really happy and smiling one of my eyelids squints a little more than the other one. It makes it hard to get a decent photo of myself because I always seem to look maniacal when I smile spontaneously, but when I try to do a different smile I look angry. But anyway, I'm walking back to the car with Eric, and I'm wearing my maniacal smile because we just did a big thing. We just bought a house.

We want to stay within Washington, D.C. boundaries now, because Ida loves school, her autism class, and her teacher. We even had a playdate with one of her classmates a couple of weeks ago. But the housing market is good and we got quoted for a great affordable mortgage, so as of ten minutes ago we are proud owners of a thirty year mortgage and a brand new townhome in Washington, D.C., Ward eight.

Eric and I walk out to the car and immediately I know I need celebration tunes, so I switch the radio from Eric's news station to the variety music station I like. But I start to laugh again because I have forgotten that it's "70's throwback weekend" on the radio. I am not a disco fan, but we happily bounce in our seats anyway.

We will be living in a brand new house in a neighborhood where caucasians are the ethnic minority. We were in this neighborhood while living on the military base, but the base is isolated from the outer

239

community by necessity for the security of the work being done there. In some ways I feel like an outsider in this part of the city.

We visited the house a few different times as we were looking into the financing, while it was still not entirely ready for residents. At one point last month when we did a walk-through, a utility truck was parked outside on the street while the driver was connecting the house to the power grid. As we watched, someone on the sidewalk stole the utility truck and drove off with it. The electrician tried to dissuade us from living there as the three of us watched the truck disappear after turning a corner, but we told him we were already planning to buy it. "I'll make sure I don't leave the keys in the car," Eric told him.

"Love Story," Taylor Swift

Leave it to me to get so excited for something that I have a total meltdown when someone else doesn't echo my exact feelings. I've been counting down the days until we move into this brand new, beautiful, big house, each day telling Eric and the kids how many days are left until moving day. Well, today is moving day, and I'm a wreck.

I don't really know what I expected—that we'd sing "Zippity Doo Dah" while loading up three of the vehicles with our belongings? That my three and four-year-olds would be over the moon about driving back and forth and dropping off boxes? It's Daniel's third birthday today, so I do feel sad that we're doing this instead of celebrating him and doing things he likes to do, and I guess that's a legitimate disappointment. But Daniel's not upset about it; he's too little to have too many expectations about what his birthday should look like. He just wants to open presents, and I took care of wrapping them a couple of days ago.

Eric is speaking to me curtly and moving the stuff, his body, and his words too fast. It has felt like he's been angry or irritated with me for the last few days, and I'm sure he is, even though he says he isn't. "I'm not mad at you; I'm just trying to get all this done so we have everything out and clean in the old house before the housing manager makes his final inspection." In other words, there's no time for kindness or hugs or feelings until we're sure we won't get charged for extra cleaning on the base house.

But that explanation for Eric's attitude does nothing to convince me that he isn't mad or frustrated about something with me specifically. His concern is about cleaning the house we're leaving, which is my job. I'm a stay-at-home mom, and in all honesty, I want house cleaning to be my job because we have two preschoolers and two kittens, and frankly, Eric himself makes more than his fair share of messes, too. Keeping our house in ship shape is truly a full-time job. I don't want him to think that I haven't done a good job, and right now, it sure sounds like he thinks that.

I let Eric, Mom, Scott, and his girlfriend, Amy, take the kids and the two trucks full of our stuff over to the new house without me, and as soon as they leave, I sit down in the corner of the almost empty room that was formerly Daniel's. When I know they're all out of earshot, I yell a few times and then resign myself to loud, ugly crying. It's the quietest moment I've experienced in a long time, but I'm filling it with hearty sobs. Then, Dad walks in the room. I didn't know he was still here. First, he just walks over to the window and stares outside, but after a good five minutes, he sits down on the floor next to me. "He's not acting that way because of you. He probably has no idea why you're upset. He's just getting stuff going." I sit still until my voice is calm enough to respond.

"He doesn't even have to try, and he gets everything right; I can't even keep the house clean, and we all know how useless I am. CPS proved that."

"Dinker, God doesn't measure us like that. He doesn't add or take away his love because we don't get something right. A good person doesn't do that either. Your mom didn't do that to me, and she could have."

A couple of hours later, we set ourselves up with mattresses on the floor. It's already after 9:00 PM, so I get Daniel's birthday presents and set them out on the hardwood floor on the middle main level of our new house. I dig out some of Daniel's favorite toys and show him his new room, and he plays up there for a little while. But when I call up the stairs to Daniel that he should come down to open his presents, he appears on the landing of the staircase naked with a hooded baby towel hooked on his head and Thomas the Tank Engine in his hand, making me chuckle. Discretion is not a concept Daniel understands yet. I ask, "Why did you get undressed? It's time to open your presents."

"But I want bath and night-night," he says in his sweet, squeaky voice. But when he sees quite a few wrapped presents on the floor, he changes his mind and opens them, still naked except for the towel. The photos still make me laugh.

The next morning, Eric goes to Home Depot and purchases a shed for our backyard—or rather, a flat box containing the shed in pieces. Eric and Dad spend the late morning and early afternoon assembling the shed together. Then, after Mom and Dad leave to make the six-hour drive back to Pennsylvania, I asked Eric about all the laughter I'd heard from them.

"You and Dad were having a good time out there."

"That thing was a bear to put together. I told your dad, 'I'm not sure if I'm prouder of the house I bought or the house I built.'"

In response, my dad had said, "Now you have a place to go when she pisses you off." I just laugh.

And so it goes.

"Three Little Birds,"
Bob Marley and the Wailers

I'm sitting at my new dining room table, working on a Beth Moore Bible study workbook while I wait for Ida's school bus to pull up out front. Daniel is napping, so it's quiet, and I'm cherishing the spring air coming in from the window. Our new house is beautiful.

After Ida's bus arrives, I walk her into the house from the front gate and ask her what she did at school today. "I drank milk," she tells me, With the same tone and inflection in her voice, with the same words she uses every day when I ask her that. She's working on speaking and having conversations, but transitioning from school to the bus and from the bus to home is a challenge for her right now, so this little speech routine that we repeat every day is comforting for her. It drives me crazy, but it's what she needs right now.

She walks out of the room briefly but returns after a few minutes carrying her Little People school bus and several plastic figurines. Then, she sits down and carefully maneuvers each of the figures, including a dinosaur, a toy wheelchair, and a plastic spoon, into the bus through its door. To most mothers with four-year-olds, this play is nothing to get excited about, but I'm overjoyed. Pretend play is a developmental skill that I've only seen her do a few times. The plastic bus with its motley assortment of "students" makes its way around the room, stopping periodically to let another student off. Ida is also singing while she's pushing the bus between stops, and it's a tune I recognize but can't quite place. The words of the song are unclear because Ida doesn't necessarily recognize them as words. This is her typical way of singing; it always sounds like she's performing the song with a big bite of food in her mouth.

"Bow ah-ee, beh eh-eh, ev-eh-eh-eh-eh, be ah why..."

I know this song, I realize, but with her quietness and the way she elides all the words, I'm baffled. But it's definitely a tune I know, that I've heard a few times but not often.

"Oh un-wee bow ah-ing..."

Suddenly, a switch flips in my brain, and I recognize the lyrics of her song. I try to quietly sing it with her, but she just looks up at me briefly and then goes back to the toys—and now I can hear Daniel's little footsteps, so I need to make sure he gets down the stairs safely. But the song is fully lodged in my mind.

"Don't worry...'bout a thing...every little thing...gonna be alright..."

March 1995

Yesterday, I finally lost it. The guys on the bus started talking to me about my boobs again. I told them they're not big, only 34B, and they should leave me alone. I thought that if I told them that, then they would leave me alone, but John tried to grab me, and I hit him, and now I'm afraid I'll get in trouble at school because I hit someone on the bus. Another guy from my math class keeps loudly asking me if my parents sell watermelons at the farm. I barely made it to the end of class and then I cried in the bathroom. Now, even one boy I thought was my friend is calling me "34B." A girl I sit with at lunch said I probably like it when they grab me. I'm losing a lot of weight.

"Firework," Katy Perry

After almost three school years in four different schools, today is Ida's last day as a preschooler and her last year in an exclusively special ed. classroom. Every teacher she's had has loved her, and although I know that my baby girl is certainly sweet and lovable, it is the teachers' love for these challenging, exasperating kids that has given me hope for Ida. She may still be learning to talk, but if she allows herself to love and be loved by good people who want the best for her, she'll get there.

Although I know what school she'll go to next year, and we have a general plan for what support systems will be in place for her according to her IEP, neither I nor anyone else can know whether she'll continue to improve and do well in a classroom. I don't know if she'll ever learn to read or take trigonometry or drive a car.

I tell her and everyone who asks that it doesn't matter to me if she ever does these things or if she never gets past kindergarten level. That's not entirely true, though. If she has to live her whole life dependent on me and Eric or someone else, she could miss out on the depth of beauty, or the ache of a broken heart, or the wonder of knowing that every person she meets has their own rich, complex inner world of thought and reasoning and love and hope. I want her to understand someday just how beautifully and wonderfully made she is, but I also want her to see the unique, beautiful, and wonderful in everyone else. To me, to love myself and to love God is to recognize from afar that there is depth and wonder that I will never know, but that it exists and reveals the vastness and intimacy of a God who created the world out of nothing and yet knows the mind and heart of every person and loves them all. Maybe, probably, Ida will have a wholly different understanding of that than mine, but if it's one that God reveals to her, it will only add greater awe and wonder.

That's not to say that I'm not still concerned for her future. There will be teachers who don't understand or honor her special needs and strangers and friends who blame her, her teachers, and most certainly us, her parents, for her intellectual differences. Some people choose not to accept that differences in physical or neurological development are not mistakes or the result of bad genetics or bad teachers. Or struggling parents. That's why Ida doesn't need to be fixed. She is not broken or deficient; she is custom-designed to be herself.

"Fallin' For You," Colbie Caillat

Between Eric, Ida, Daniel, and me, there always seems to be one person who is restless, and then that one person somehow always manages to get the rest of us restless, too, for our own unique reasons. Or maybe we are so unaccustomed to stability that whenever life gets good and comfortable, we all start stirring things up again in our own way. Is it possible to be uncomfortable with security?

Eric wants to find another job without leaving the Navy, and it's kind of freaking me out. The whole reason he's in the Navy is because he got in via his Sea Chanters audition. When they offered him the position along with the enlistment, it was a big deal because the position gives him a stable job that he can't really lose, along with the benefits that active duty sailors receive but without the moving around and deployments. Boot camp was the only serious hoop he had to jump through—that was the plan. And when he moved out of the Sea Chanters and started working for their public affairs office, that was even better. But now he wants to start a whole other career entirely, and he's excited about it, but I'm not. I am perfectly content with things as they are. His restlessness is flipping over my proverbial apple cart.

For the last few weeks, Eric has been telling me he wants to go to nursing school, and I've been not-so-subtly rolling my eyes. Susan, Eric's sister, made a career change and became a nurse a few years ago, and Eric has always said that when they were kids, he always wanted to do whatever she did. So now, not only is he following her lead by making a career change, but he's making the very same career change.

He brought it up the first time around Christmas, and I basically said no way. We just bought this house a year ago because we wanted to stay here, and going to school would cost money, and maybe even worse, it would take time, so he'd be away from home a lot longer each day. And we've also been dreaming about maybe having another baby, and why can't we ever just make one major life change at a time?

So, we took some time to think and pray about it. The first thing God showed me during the month or so we spent reading books about finding one's vocational calling and taking personal skills and spiritual gifts tests was that I am jealous of Eric. That on its own isn't new, but I'm realizing that I envy his all-around intelligence and his ability to learn new things in a fraction of the time it takes for me and everyone else. His ability to learn how to do anything and his capability of learning things on the fly is off the charts, and his IQ is higher than Einstein's. Not exaggerating; it really is. It's both the thing I love most about him and the reason I feel jealous and inferior to him in every way. Naturally, Eric found an obscure way to go to nursing school full-time, remain on active duty status and keep his current pay grade, and then commission as a naval officer and nurse upon graduation. Seriously.

Sometimes, I think that if Eric prayed for a car, a brand new Corvette would fall from the sky.

Of course, my bitterness is just jealousy because I've never even had one career—and no, being a mom doesn't count. Not to me, anyway. I want to excel at something and to use my brain for something other than housework and child care, and with Ida and Daniel in full-day school, now is my chance. But this plan is in conflict with the other calling that Eric and I are both experiencing equally and are fully confident about. We both want to have another baby.

On the second and fourth Tuesdays of every month, I go to MOPS at church, and I often end up getting questions about why my preschoolers aren't with me at the meetings like they used to be. Daniel's four, so I do still count as a mother of a preschooler. But the automatic next question I get when I tell anyone about my four and five-year-olds is,

"So, are you working, or are you planning to have another baby?" The answer is yes to both. But neither the job nor the baby has come to fruition yet. My restlessness is mostly just frustration that I honestly don't know what I want to do for a career or how to start something while still being available for Ida and Daniel and potentially another baby one day. I don't have the experience or expertise to offer in any specific industry or position; my skills and knowledge are all over the place because that's the kind of skills and knowledge I've needed so far. So I'm stuck.

Yet, as I write this, I recognize that Eric is stuck, too—but he's stuck because of me. He's stuck because I'm afraid to see him grow and change and because he's interested in a career that will put him around a lot of women. I need to be able to tell him that I trust him to hear God's call accurately and to remain faithful to me. I have no reason to think he wouldn't, but the ghosts of my past and his past hover, and I'm afraid of them.

"Alligator Pie,"
Dave Matthews Band

If my dorm room at Westminster Choir College had looked like this, I probably wouldn't have gotten that apartment during my third semester; in fact, I may have even stuck it out and earned my bachelor's there—but I could be romanticizing this. I haven't had an evening alone in a quiet room, let alone an entire week of evenings, since before Ida was born. But right now, I'm at Liberty University in Lynchburg, Virginia, and I'm doing my homework. I get this room to myself (it even has its own full bathroom, like a hotel room) for six whole days. It is slightly frustrating that I have hours of work to do on a collaborative project for the class I'm taking, but it's not so bad when I have all evening to do it without interruptions.

This is my first graduate course in ethnomusicology, and there are only three of us in the class. The other two have been in the program for at least a year. One works in the music department at LU, and the other has served as a missionary in China for years. And then there's me: a stay-at-home mom with no experience to speak of in any field of study at all. I'm not even entirely sure what ethnomusicology is, but here I am, beginning a career in it.

I don't know how we're affording this either. I got a scholarship from an organization that funds continuing education for the spouses of active duty soldiers and sailors, but I think it only covers a portion of my tuition costs. But I'm not asking questions. I finally have something brainy to do that is all my own.

Eric wants to do brainy stuff, too, but he *always* gets to be the one who is smart and experienced and seen as an actual person with actual work and actual accomplishments. I want it to be my turn this time. But even as I write that, I realize how childish it is. Eric and I are not in competition with each other for success. Why would I choose to deny my family and myself the income increase that comes with his officer commissioning?

In truth, I am just being obstinate, jealous of his consistent success, which is illogical and childish. The kids and I are the beneficiaries of his success. The gifts that God has given my husband, the callings God has placed on him during different seasons of our life together, are blessings for all of us. I love that Eric isn't afraid to dream, that he wasn't afraid to sit down across from me and throw out a pickup line during our awkward first meeting, wasn't afraid to go along with it when I wanted an out-of-the-hospital birth, wasn't deterred when I said I wanted a master's degree. I love him, and I love his sense of adventure and the roller coaster life we've had so far. So how can I deny him, or any of us, a new opportunity?

So I call him at midnight and tell him that I trust him, and thank him for giving me both dreams and opportunities to fulfill them, and tell him to go ahead and submit his application for the Medical Enlisted Commissioning Program (MECP). When I say it, I can hear his big, full-face smile, even over the phone. I can feel our baby moving in my womb, and I can imagine my own dreams. I can sense the presence of the Holy Spirit and hear His voice with my heart.

I have so much more for you.

"You & Me,"
Dave Matthews Band

Mom and Dad have been staying with us for three days already, and still no baby. It's over 90 degrees outside today, and between the heat, the humidity, and the exhaust fumes from the road, it isn't safe for me to even go outside anymore. It's not exactly deadly, of course, but I have the air conditioner down to 65 degrees in the house and I'm still sweating like a pig.

Baby number three isn't late just yet, but my belly is so stretched and my body is so heavy that the other night, I dreamt my belly just split open with a *pop,* and the baby birthed himself by spontaneous C-section. With a planned home birth and the level of discomfort I've been in for the last month, I started getting worried. So, since we hadn't had any ultrasounds at all, we got one for some reassurance that all is normal. When the scenographer confirmed that everything was fine, she also asked if we wanted to know the baby's gender, and Eric did something that was totally out of character for him. He blurted out, "I can see the gender already."

It's a boy. But we've still kept the gender secret to everyone else, even Ida and Daniel.

I'd really hoped the little man would let me sleep in as long as possible today, but between Braxton Hicks contractions and my very compressed bladder, that didn't happen. Yesterday, we all took Ida and

Daniel to a big playground and I waddled in circles around the whole place while they played, and my legs are sore now. Mom, Dad, Eric, Ida, and Daniel are all getting ready to go to the pool on the base, but I'm going to stay home in bed. The contractions hurt too much already.

I do manage to fall asleep watching reruns of *House M.D.* Eventually, I hear Eric, Mom, Dad, and the kids return, and a few minutes later, Mom comes to check on me. I'm definitely in labor now, but it's still early and the contractions aren't too painful. She tells me that Eric just left again to drive over to the base and get a few groceries, but he said it would be a quick trip. I close my eyes again. I'll be in labor overnight; might as well sleep while I can.

I open my eyes again when I feel a much stronger contraction. I'm alone and the room is dark. When a second contraction comes no more than five minutes later, I yell for Eric, but Mom appears instead. It's been almost two hours since Eric left, but he isn't back yet, and he's not answering his phone.

Mom stays with me, periodically leaving to check on Ida, Daniel, and Dad. She and I are feeling quite angry at Eric's AWOL status, but Mom has called the midwife to tell her the situation—which added another potential problem. The midwife is with another mother who is also in active labor and has been for 24 hours. Mother and baby are still okay, but the baby hasn't made her appearance yet. Can we make it another two hours or so? Eric walks in as I tell the midwife that, yes, I still have plenty of time, even though I know that isn't true. I'm in a phase of birth where the contractions are quite painful but I still have some ways to go before they become the pushing type of contractions. To distract me from the pain a bit, Eric is lying next to me, gently rubbing my back and telling me a story about how one time he had to do CPR on an older man who collapsed suddenly while on the base. "When did this happen? You never told me about that," I say, but my words are interrupted by little grunts that make me hold my breath for a short second. I'm going to need to start pushing soon.

"I never told you about this because it just happened today," Eric laughs.

"Today at the exchange? Like just now? You're saying you were just doing CPR on some guy an hour ago?"

"It's three hours ago now," he says. Eric had maybe watched a man die today, and now our son will be born on the same day.

The midwife arrives already exhausted but brings two apprentice midwives as well. With their encouragement, I spend a short time sitting in a warm bath.

"Ida and Daniel are good kids, right? They're doing fine now, right?"

I hear myself say this as if I am watching a movie starring myself. I think, *she needs to know she's a good mom because she almost lost her first two kids to CPS, and she doesn't want to risk it happening again.*

Eric tells me, "Yes, they're both doing great now. They're as excited for this baby as we are."

When a full, hard pushing contraction comes, Eric helps me out of the tub and dries me off, and the midwife walks me over to the bed. Another pushing contraction comes, but when it's over, the me who is on the outside watching me sees me do something so ridiculous, it's funny.

I sit down on the bottom end of the bed, cross my legs, and say firmly, "I'm not going to push."

Eric, the midwife, and the others share incredulous looks—smirking cartoon characters encountering someone too ridiculous to believe. But I hold my ground.

"I'm not pushing; I don't want to."

The midwife, exhausted and not enjoying my theatrics, squats to put herself at eye level with me.

"Melanie. You have to."

I crawl to the middle of the bed as if my moment of ridiculousness hadn't happened and try several different birthing positions, methodically, instinctually deciding how best to deliver the baby. I end up on my hands and knees and briefly acknowledge my thinking brain's reaction that this position is bestial and lewd before discarding the concern and pushing several times with only short catch breaths—the kind you take when you're singing a long, melodic phrase and don't want your inhale to interrupt the flow. As the baby's head crowns, I sense that one portion of the "ring of fire" needs a little more stretch, and I intuitively lift my right leg straight out to the side and hold it there like a yoga position.

Seconds later, I am sitting upright with my back propped on pillows and the midwife's assistants instructing me to wiggle around so they can put layers of Chux pads beneath me. The baby is round and big and active, and holding his fist at the level of his eyes, ready to either salute or punch someone. Later, one of the assistant midwives asks how—just at the time when they realized that the baby had his right hand up against the side of his head—did I know to lift and extend my right leg to provide a little extra space for the baby's tiny head and arm to come through at once. I told her I'd been feeling some fluttering, low movement around my cervix for the last few days and figured that he must have gotten his arm stuck there and couldn't move it, so he was wiggling his fingers.

Ida Carol.

Daniel Joseph.

Henry Terrence.

Weeks later, having sent both Ida and Daniel off to bed without too much protest, Eric and I sit on the couch, tired and contemplative. Henry is nursing, and the house is quiet. As Henry falls asleep, a drop of milk running down his chin, Eric takes him and leans him carefully against his chest. Several silent moments pass. Then one of us says quietly,

"We're done now, aren't we."

And the other responds, "Yes, we are."

Our family is complete.

"Song 2," Blur

As Abigail got older and started doing extracurricular stuff after school, her younger half-brother Max always had to come to all of her activities out of necessity. Ida and Daniel are so close together in age, though, that thus far, they've done almost every activity together. With Ida having autism and Daniel having *something*, they haven't done a lot of stuff yet, and we haven't been trying to find activities for them. It didn't seem necessary. But now, in the interest of social skills development, we decided to sign them up for U6 soccer in a tiny league that only includes kids who live on or near the closest military bases. We're already on this base quite a lot since it's only a couple of miles away, and we get our groceries tax-free at the commissary.

Playing in the base soccer league seemed to be one thing Abigail actually enjoyed during the time she lived with us, so it's soccer for Ida and Daniel, too, for the sake of keeping things simple. But of course, there's always some sort of complication in just about everything in our life, so Eric volunteered to coach the team. According to him, at the parent meeting last week, the youth center staff said, "We need one of the parents to step up and serve as head coach," and everyone but Eric took a step back. Of course, Eric never does anything halfway, so he's been researching soccer coaching and instruction for most of the last week, and he wrote up a practice plan that he is coaching the kids through right now. Henry and I are sitting on a blanket where he's kicking his legs and making cooing noises. I'm completely exhausted and would much rather be at home taking a nap. Henry is still waking up to nurse two or three times a night, which is normal for his age, but it means I'm constantly stealing myself to get some sleep so I can stay sane until the next nap opportunity comes around. But I don't have the same fear about it as I did with both Ida and Daniel. I know that it will only be like this for six months, tops. Six months feels and sounds like an eternity, of course, and I keep reminding myself that he will sleep through the night one day in the next few months. It isn't much consolation now, but I have enough experience to realize it's okay to just focus on surviving the first few months.

When I watch Ida and Daniel and remember how horrible and seemingly endless their first two or so years seemed to be, I can look at the evidence and see that those years did, in fact, end. Henry, I think, will benefit from having a mom who's able to see beyond the baby years. Ida and Daniel have certainly retained the unique (weird) characteristics they each had as toddlers. Daniel went from a baby who never stopped moving his limbs to a first grader who never stops moving his mouth. He talks constantly, but although he does use some repetitive, disconnected, memorized phrases like Ida's (*echolalia*, it's called), he can also tell a unique story and speak appropriately, even quite well at times. And Ida is finally talking in a communicative way— complete sentences, even. Four years ago, I had to learn to accept that she may never be able to carry a conversation. Now, she can answer questions and follow classroom rules, and she has short conversations with me almost every day.

Right now—both this stage of our family life and this moment, sitting in the grass, watching Eric become a soccer coach by evening and a nurse by day—is really good. We've turned a corner as a family.

Dear God, thank you for this moment, for this assurance. Let it be an altar in my mind, reminding me of your faithfulness.

"T.N.T.," ACDC

Eric, Henry, and I are at a college cross country race, laughing heartily about how old we are. When Eric went to his first few classes in nursing school, he talked with a professor and happened to mention that he's a runner. I still feel old, fat, and ugly, having a six-week-old baby in a sling across my chest and carrying about 100 pounds more body weight than is healthy. But in total contrast, Eric is feeling old because he's about to compete in his very first college cross country race at age 37. Already, one person assumed he was a coach.

"Hey Keisha," a girl yells across the grassy area where the students are warming up, "You're the same age as me, right? You were in fourth grade on 9/11?"

Eric and I hide our faces as we giggle.

We are just beginning to think about a future after parenting our kids. Of course, Ida and Daniel are still in elementary school, and Henry is a newborn, but now that we know our family is complete, we have also realized that they will grow up and very gradually become independent, and we may, at some point, have the freedom to explore our own interests. Although we did take steps to do this when Eric decided to become a nurse and I started graduate school, these beginning steps have led to visions of vacations alone, date nights without babysitters, family dinners that don't involve grilled cheese—and one day, maybe, a home without children in it.

Even thinking of it sets off emotional alarm bells in my head. I've read books and been in conversations with other moms who would probably be appalled that I'd give these sorts of plans any thought at all, because my children are still so young—especially Henry, of course. But it's not like we're looking at taking a month-long cruise. I get seasick when we drive through traffic circles, so that's definitely not happening. It's just that dreaming of and talking about just being Eric and Mel again reconnects us. It reminds us that we love each other, that love for each other came first, and it's still there for us to enjoy one day when we can. So, while we can't do anything big by ourselves right now, we can talk about it and dream. It's like preheating the oven.

Eric does great at the cross country meet, of course. It seems like running in competition with 18 to 21-year-olds is humbling for him, but he's having a good time with it.

"Red Red Red," Fiona Apple

There was a time when all this was everything I wanted. And there was a time before that when I wanted none of it. Now, I can't decide whether I was right the first time or the second time. Once upon a time, I wanted to be a rock star. And then, once upon another time, I wanted to be a wife whose husband was perpetually infatuated with her, and a mom with a whole litter of children who were all happy and polite, living in a new, fancy house, and homeschooling, all gathered at the kitchen table and enjoying every minute of it.

It's bitterly cold outside, and my third and final season of postpartum depression is in full swing. At least I know that's what it is now, and I know that the post-birth hormonal readjustment is what is messing with my head. The season isn't helping things either; January on the East Coast can be brutal. I expected that Washington, D.C. would at least be a little warmer than Pennsylvania when I made my final move here after our wedding, but I was wrong. It's just different. No colder in temperature, but less welcoming. Less friendly. Less like home—and yet it is. We've already been in this big house, with my own name on the mortgage papers, for almost two years, and we've been living in the D.C. area since our wedding—or even before that if you start counting at Eric's enlistment date. I'd thought this was it, that we'd be here forever, but now, with the start of nursing school, it looks like we'll be taking this freak show on the road at some point. Who knows where we'll end up, though I secretly wish to stay here.

I don't understand all this. I don't understand why he gave up a perfectly good career, and military benefits without the drawbacks, to go out and learn how to be a lacky for a healthcare system that has hurt us so many times. Hurt me and my babies. It's like betrayal. He's planning to work for the system and people that I hate.

But the worst part is the same, anyway: the loneliness. I felt alone in the basement apartment when I was 21 and had nothing to pass the hours but snacks and daytime television. I still felt alone two years later in the double-wide at the trailer park, laying my head on the high chair tray as I shoveled spoon after spoon into Ida's mouth, only to have her spit it back out, hour after hour. I was desperate, pleading with her to eat so she would gain weight, but even more desperate for sleep.

And now, I still feel alone. Ida and Daniel get up at dawn and ride a chartered bus full of strangers twice a day, but they're at the best elementary school that D.C. Public Schools could offer. It's on the other side of the city, but there's a sea of stop-and-go traffic and streets I could never learn to navigate between us, so it might as well be the other side of the world. And I'm here, in this huge house that we somehow bought for an amount of money that seems astronomical, staring teary-eyed at the computer screen while Henry smacks his gums around a piece of Italian bread.

There was a time when this was everything I wanted, everything we both wanted. But now I don't know what I want. There has to be more than this house that is beautiful but never quite warm enough, always fancy but never truly comfortable. I'm proud of it because it looks good. We are the people with the fancy three-story house, and we own it. No longer am I the angry pregnant lady with a baby on her hip in a trailer park. But I'm still angry.

Eric is at the beginning of the fulfillment of a dream, I suppose. He has not only arrived, he has the world in his hands. He's so smart, and so talented, and so gifted, and so perfect that he could take the risk of walking away from his cushy job sitting in front of a computer all day and editing documents while still receiving basic allowance for housing, and embark on a whole new career he has zero experience in. Not that it's the first time he's started a new career; he's worked every career I can think of, but all of those were to make money—just enough to get by. But now he's chasing his dreams and bringing the kids and me along for the ride.

And that's what I feel like, an extra piece of luggage. A super useful appliance that the movers will pack into a truck someday when we leave this big fancy house. The super appliance that does it all: cooks, cleans, does the laundry, changes the diapers, breastfeeds the babies. She also cries, yells, and sometimes smiles. She forgives, too.

He's happy. I'm happy, too. What's not to be happy about? All we ever wanted is right here. Three babies, two cats, and a mortgage on an enviously beautiful home. All that was left for him was to find the career of his dreams so that he could love the work he does and the money he earns from it. And so far, he does love it. There's plenty for him to complain about, with the problems in the college nursing department and the other students and even faculty chasing him down for help. But it's the work he loves, particularly his clinical time at the children's hospital. I'm glad he's happy, but I was also the first to point out that if he wanted to change diapers all day, he could just stay home.

But of course, no, that is my job. I am his help-meet, and he deserves one. He deserves a perfect woman to match his own perfection. He deserves a wife who is beautiful, modest, affectionate, capable, energetic, forgiving, good-humored, strong, kind, and graceful. I'm none of those things. I wonder how many of the other students, professors, and even patients that he meets would do a better job than I do at being his partner. I wonder how often that occurs to him, too. I particularly wonder about that this semester because he's working a clinical in a women's health department. Yesterday, I found a piece of paper on the kitchen table. It was a report on a woman's checkup. She was 21, and her breasts were of "normal palpitation." So he's palpitating girls' breasts now. And the Navy pays him for that, too.

I still have breasts, of course, but he's lost interest in them. He's too tired, never awake when he's home unless he's studying—and even then, he relies on me to keep him awake while also being grumpy around me when I wake him up after he falls asleep on a textbook. My breasts have been nothing more than milk machines for years, and I am so overweight that it's no wonder he's taking a job with so many female coworkers. I'm not much to look at.

So now I just sit here, staring at the computer screen in my dirty sweatpants and baggy shirt, listening to the same song on repeat so that I can examine every line and nuance, trying to figure out how this songwriter knew what it was like to be committed to someone so perfect. So perfect that I will never be worthy, that I will always be the one who is lucky to have him. Back when I was 17, I'd assumed it was *he* who'd gotten lucky when he found *me*. I had my whole life ahead of me and boys all around. I'd had my pick, and I'd chosen him.

But how long will he keep choosing me?

Sometimes I say I'm not happy, that I'm going to leave, or at least pack my duffel bag and walk out the back door in a huff, drive to a hotel, and spend a night alone watching television and eating snacks from a vending machine. It's a brilliant idea, but I never go through with it because that feels like giving up. Like walking away from responsibilities that I chose myself and from the one person who said that even if I left, he'd never let me go, never divorce me. "The only way you will get this wedding ring off of me is if you cut off my finger."

Some days that sounds like love. Right now it sounds like a trap.

"Crazy Love," Van Morrison

Someone Eric knows from nursing school gave him a workout DVD. We've got more than enough insanity in this house as it is, so I'm not sure why we ended up with it.

It's a set of home workout DVDs, and I've heard of it before, but really I'm just wondering why he accepted this gift. I've never once seen him follow a mass-produced workout plan; in fact, he rarely uses any plan at all other than the ones he designs for himself. And he only runs. He only does non-running workouts when they target something that will improve his running. A DVD workout, even one with a tough instructor, still brings back memories of Jane Fonda and leg warmers for both of us—although I've done my share of these since then, and I usually like them.

So we try *Insanity*, and it more than lives up to its name. There are a few exercises that I can't even figure out how to do slowly, let alone at the speed the people in the video do it, and others that I can't really justify doing because they're so over the top. Why would jumping high enough to kick my own heels into my own butt be something I need in my life? That's a sprained ankle waiting to happen.

This unexpected freedom in the late evenings is great. Henry does not yet sleep through the night every night, but he does most nights. He's what old ladies used to call a "good baby," as if a baby with minimal demands is somehow more valuable. These evenings together with Eric after the kids go to bed are a blessing. Most nights, we take about two or three hours to relax together. *Insanity* was the opposite of relaxing, but that was an exception. We spent a couple of months binge-watching every episode of *Law and Order SVU*. We played Monopoly one night. One other night, we pulled out a box of old VHS tapes, and Eric showed me a video of a performance he did with a boys' show choir in 1986. He still knew all the choreography, but when he tried to do those Russian squatting kick things, he fell on the floor instead.

Our other nighttime entertainment is listening to Henry babbling in his crib via the baby monitor. Some nights, Ida and Daniel get to hear this, too, before they go to bed. One night, Henry didn't want to go to bed, and instead of crying about it, he whined his own name for 15 minutes straight. "*Eh-weee. Eh-weee.*"

I sometimes wonder why Henry is so much easier to deal with than Ida and Daniel were at this age. An old voice still lives in my head that tells me it's my fault. I didn't take care of myself well enough when I was pregnant with Ida. I should have realized that her head wasn't where it should be before I went into labor so we could have been prepared, and she wouldn't have lost any oxygen. I should have taken her to a different pediatrician, one familiar with autism symptoms. I shouldn't have let her watch so much TV.

I know this voice is wrong, not just because these things aren't true, but because God is in control of her life and mind. I never allow myself to stumble over the questions I will never have answers to on this side of heaven. Did God design Ida to have autism, or was it caused by something else? Did God give this child, each of these children, to me in particular? Are their souls written in the Book of Life from their creation, or are they spiritual wild cards until they choose faith and salvation for themselves? I ask these questions fully expecting that they will go unanswered for now. Their stories will unfold while I watch, and though I may be able to influence them, their choices are always their own. Lord knows the life I've lived so far is one I never could have designed or imagined, and it will be the same for them.

Life is so much more fulfilling and wonderful when I allow myself to fully and honestly believe that the path God leads me on is best, even when it seems impossible or wrong or even too mundane. There's no natural reflex that even allows for that kind of faith; everything within my mind and heart wants safety, stability, familiarity, and ease. I want the still waters and green pastures and an open, clear, obvious path between one comfortable thing and the next. And, if I'm honest, I also want to wander away and out of God's view once in a while so I can do crazy, risky, sinful things while he's looking the other way. But I shouldn't, and I can't, because those kinds of things would never be worth the damage my actions could cause—breaking the covenant bond I made with Eric and then spreading destruction to my children and perhaps others as well. Sin is a viral epidemic that has implanted itself in the DNA of us all, and we innocently pass it on, unaware of the toll our own corruption takes on everyone else. How much sin and corruption did my words and actions cause in my own 31 years of life before I learned that there is a God who would transform me?

And how much since?

"Baby Baby," Amy Grant

Someone once told me that after you have your third child, you get to a point where you completely discard all the conflicting information and advice you received with the first and second child and just do whatever works and keeps you, the baby, and the family as stress-free as possible. Or maybe I told myself that. Either way, that's what I'm doing with Henry. I'm applying what worked with Ida and Daniel (like breastfeeding and using a sling carrier), giving anything that didn't work with Ida and Daniel a fair trial (starting baby food a little earlier worked, bottle feeding didn't), and otherwise doing whatever it takes to keep Henry and me comfortable, Ida and Daniel manageable and relatively happy, and Eric and I able to at least function on a basic level and remember each other's names. And this parenting method I've stumbled upon is *miraculous*. Why did I ever take the time to read all those books, analyze parenting styles, and decide that I would do the "right" one? I am not perfect at anything, so why should I even try to be? Why did I equate good, godly, motherly love and care and teaching with a specific method, or a combination of methods, that somehow formed a magic potion for perfect parent-child relationships? I meant well, really, but if making mothering as miserable as possible was an Olympic sport, I'd have the gold medal.

This semester is another first for me and Henry. I am taking two full-credit online classes simultaneously, and Henry is spending five to seven hours every day in daycare. Ten years ago, if you caught me on the day I rode the highest horse, I would have told you that putting a child in daycare when they could otherwise be home with a loving family member was sinful. But Henry is thriving there, and his teachers and tiny classmates love him. The teachers, Alicia and Felicia, have nicknamed him "O Henry," and he has begun calling both of them "Oh Weesha." When Eric dropped him off yesterday, several students inside chorused, "Oh Henry," when he entered. Eric said, "It was like he was Norm coming into the bar on *Cheers*." In a few months, he's gone from using a handful of single words to full communicative sentences. No autism evaluation for him. The other day I caught him rummaging through a kitchen cabinet, saying, "Aw, come on, where da keekees?" (Which meant, "Where are the cookies?")

I confess that Henry's intelligence and his ability to go with the flow is refreshing. I feel like I can let my guard down a little and stop wondering if I'm doing the right things as a mom. That someday I'll be able to let my kids see my weaknesses without worrying that knowing my flaws and my mistakes and even my sins will leave them feeling insecure. They can know that all I could ever do was figure it out as I went along. I want them to know that with all the good things happening right now, my heart—and I think Eric's, too—has softened on a lot of things. Realizing that raising children is much more about making it work than doing it right is a humbling idea when you've already spent many years doing it with the wrong attitude.

Inevitably, tossing our ideas about right and wrong in parenting had us wondering about Abigail. We haven't seen her since the day she and Angie returned to Pennsylvania after our failed experiment of being her custodial parents. We knew it was a failure by the time she left. Now I'm wondering if she still sees us the same way. I don't want these thoughts, though. I don't want to feel guilty about this because I was truly doing my best with her. I can't speak for Eric on this, but I know now that I don't want to spend the rest of my life wondering what happened to our "other daughter." So last night, I did what every other internet user does when she is up too late and wonders about that one person who has every reason to hate her. I Googled her name.

I found a few things but not much detail, which I guess is appropriate since she's only 15. But the difference between a 10-year-old and a 15-year-old is huge. She bought an alpaca that she enters into fairs and festivals where animals are shown, and she volunteers at the farm where it lives. She learned to sew in Girl Scouts. She competed in pole vaulting for school at one point. And one unexpected part of her life has stayed the same: she's still enrolled in the online charter school system she'd started attending with me. After a couple of nights of stalking one of my own kids on the internet, I told Eric what I'd found, and he admitted she'd been on his mind, too. He emailed Angie that same night, and Angie replied, saying only, "Give her a call. Her cell phone number is still the same as it was then."

The call was very short and incredibly awkward, and it should have been. We'd fought her mother in court because we needed to prove that we were better parents. When CPS and all of that terrible stuff had defeated me and left me broken, I retaliated, not by hurting my own attacker, but by attacking Angie—the only other friend and mother I knew who couldn't make it all at least *look* perfect. Eric and I are the offenders here. Neither Angie nor Abigail (who goes by Abi now) is obligated to forgive us. But that is what we need to ask for.

After making that short but awkward call to Abi, we arranged to meet her at one of about a thousand family diners in Pennsylvania Dutch country two days after Thanksgiving. I also opted to write my own email to Angie, telling her I had been so insecure about my own handling of motherhood that I'd wanted the chance to parent Abigail so I could prove to myself that I was a good mom. Both she and Abigail were collateral damage in my fight to redeem myself from CPS's labels. But, to my total bewilderment, Angie only responded to my initial question, "How are you?" by telling me where she, Abi, and Max are living, the status of other relatives, and asking about my parents and grandparents. She left only one short sentence in response to my long, tears-on-the-keyboard confession:

"As for the rest, all is grace."

"Teach You,"
Emily King and Sara Bareilles

I was nervous to meet Abi when she was two, but today, I find that I'm even more nervous—much more—to meet her again now that she's 15. If it weren't for Facebook, I wouldn't even be able to recognize her if I passed her in the street; that's one of the reasons I feel so much regret over all of this. Another reason is the nervous feeling in my stomach right now. Eric, the kids, and I are up in Pennsylvania for Thanksgiving weekend, and we've arranged to meet Abi at a restaurant and at least start getting reacquainted. No matter how we approached this reunion, it would be awkward, but if we avoided scheduling it and going through with it, we risked missing an opportunity to be a part of her life again. I'm not even sure I'll know it's her when I see her. There's a big difference between a girl at age ten and a girl at age 15.

But when the five of us pile into the busy dinner-time-on-Black-Friday diner, she's there—different, but recognizable. Her hair is longer, dyed an unnatural fruit punch red color that doesn't start until the level of her ears. Her natural strawberry blonde is visible on top, but it's more blonde than strawberry now. She wears silver-colored rings on most of her fingers, the kind I used to buy in Claire's at the mall when I was her age. I wonder if she bought hers in the exact same store I once went to for mine.

271

It's awkward, of course. We don't bring up the past. We tell her our updates on our new home and how Onyx is doing as the furry lady of the house, and Ida and Daniel are excited to tell her about school and their own perspectives on everything. Abi also tells us about school, the many activities she's doing, places she's gone with friends and youth groups and Girl Scouts. Henry, who has been moving back and forth between my lap and a restaurant booster seat, giggles like crazy when she makes silly faces at him and then reaches for me to lift him to the floor. Abi asks if she can hold him; I cautiously follow him as he toddles his way around the table, where she picks him up and sits him in her lap.

Seeing his little face, only a few months younger than Abi's at the time I met her, I'm taken aback. He looks more like Abi than he does Ida or Daniel, who both have the brown eyes and round cheeks I had as a child.

By the time everyone has finished eating, we've moved from very-awkward through slightly-less-awkward and arrived at awkward-but-at-least-not-hungry. Abi checks her phone, saying that Angie is waiting for her outside, but before we pay the bill and walk her out, she retrieves several hardened dough Christmas ornaments, each in a tiny gauze bag and labeled with our names. Smiling, I remember one she made for me more than ten years ago, a painted candy cane with Mel written on it with big block letters in her own kindergarten handwriting. Then, when we walk out with Abi to Angie's van in the parking lot, Angie gets out, talks with us for a while, then gives us each a hearty, genuine hug.

We forgive because we have been forgiven.

"I've Got a Feeling,"
Black-Eyed Peas

I have been blasting this song as often as I can for weeks, and today, I will need to hear it at least a few more times. This afternoon, Eric will be commissioned as a US Navy officer at our church in Alexandria, Virginia. He's completed his bachelor's in nursing with virtually perfect scores, passed the NCLEX nursing exam that's required prior to receiving his nursing license, and will complete seven weeks of Officers Development School in Rhode Island. Abi is here too for the occasion, and she seems to be comfortable and even kind of excited. She slept on our good ol' giant blue IKEA couch last night, and earlier this morning, she put a fresh coat of blood-red dye in her hair (and yes, it is, in fact, the exact same Kool-Aid color I used at her age). Right now she's teaching Daniel how to play Mario Kart on the Wii.

Honestly, I feel like this is my event and my honor as much as it is Eric's. Don't misunderstand; I'm intensely proud of him and continuously awed by both his intelligence and his ability to apply it. I told him a few weeks ago that the sexiest part of his body is his brain. But I am as giddy today as I was on our wedding day.

When the time finally comes for the ceremony, I'm just about ready to burst, and Eric's parents and sister seem a little annoyed with me. They often do, although no one's ever given me an explanation for that. My energy level is too high today to come down for a few cold shoulders. Heck, I'm balancing my two-and-a-half-year-old on my hip while wearing spiked heels. I'm tough like that.

At the opening of the ceremony, there is an honor guard presentation of the U.S. and U.S.N flags. This is usually done by active duty Navy sailors specially trained to do the job perfectly, but today's honor guard is eight first-grade boys with Daniel in the lead, followed by his Cub Scout unit. Eric has been leading their unit all year. The boys do their ceremonial work precisely and proudly, just as practiced. I never thought I'd see six six-year-old boys be reverent and honorable all at the same time, but today I do.

After the honor guard posts the colors, several speeches are given, which get long even for me, and I eventually go to the back of the sanctuary to talk to my friend who is keeping the Cub Scouts occupied. But as we quietly chat, Henry, who is once again perched on my hip, begins to wiggle around, so I put him down. I don't give it much thought; there is nothing dangerous he could get into, and I figure he'll just toddle around in the aisles. But he doesn't. He makes his way to the front of the room, climbs three stairs, and goes directly to Eric. "Hi, Daddy. What doin'?" My feet are a bit swollen at this point, but I move quickly to intercept Henry's halftime show. Eric picks him up, hugs him, kisses him on the forehead, and then hands him back to me.

When the ceremony ends, we offer light refreshments in a room downstairs from the sanctuary. One of the Cub Scout moms makes these incredible chocolate chip cookies, and she made some for the ceremony at Eric's request. Henry is happily walking around the room, smiling and charming everyone he meets, and, amusingly, so is Eric. I keep telling Eric that Henry is the most *his kid* out of all four of his kids.

I work the room with Eric for a while, playing the proud, supportive wife role, but darn it, I keep sneaking over to the dessert table to grab one of those cookies. Mom and Dad are back in that area, too, so I keep telling myself I'm going back to make sure they're comfortable, but really, I'm always just getting another cookie. Then, on my fifth or maybe sixth trip back to the cookies, the entire tray is missing. I ask Scott if all the cookies are gone already, and he cautiously points to another table. "Dad's been eating them nonstop. I moved it so he'd forget about them." I make my way to the new cookie table without telling Scott I've already had five myself. My dad is entering the later stages of Alzheimer's now. He's still able to walk and talk, but he walks with an odd, shuffling gait, and while he reacts to the energy and mood of the people around him, he can't follow conversations, and most of what he says doesn't make much sense. And according to my mom, he seems to have an imaginary friend he calls Manno.

After 45 minutes or so, Eric gets everyone's attention. A few of the guests have already had a few drinks, so it takes Eric several tries to get the group quiet, but then, when the room finally gives Eric their attention, he is interrupted again by Henry, who walks unevenly over to me in the almost-silent room and says loudly, "Hey Mom, I'm working on a poop." Henry has been having some problems with constipation, and I've been asking him about it a lot over the last few days to keep track of the issue in case I need to take him to the pediatrician. Of course, the room erupts in laughter, and Eric has to wait several more minutes to begin.

Eventually, Eric is able to proceed and presents a gift and a few honorable words about each of the four kids, and one for me as well. Before the ceremony had begun, I'd seen my koto teacher enter the room, and though I greeted her warmly, I couldn't understand how she and her husband came to be here. But when Eric asks Sensei Okamoto to follow him behind the stage curtain, I have a pretty good hunch about it.

I took koto lessons for the first time this past semester with Sensei Okamoto in her small apartment to fulfill a study requirement for my ethnomusicology program. I love the instrument; it's large but delicate, powerful, and versatile. My guess is that Eric purchased the practice koto I'd been using so I could keep it. But I'm wrong.

Sensei and Eric emerge from behind the curtain with a different koto, one of the nicer ones that Sensei owns, and I realize that Sensei has sold the koto to Eric to give to me. I'm overwhelmed yet again, and I hug Sensei by mistake for the second time in only a few hours. According to tradition, a student hugging her sensei is disrespectful, so I apologize again and she pardons me.

The after party at our house is, I think, even better than the ceremony. Most of our closest family members are there and we simply laugh and talk and eat. Our second-floor toilet overflows, which seems to happen every time we have guests, but we fix the clog and clean it up quickly. Someone jokingly accuses my sister-in-law Amy of being the toilet clogger, yelling, "It's Amy's fault, she poops too much!" The same guest would later look out the window and, seeing our back alley parked full of our guests' cars, remark, "Look at all those cars; someone must be having a party."

"Daylight," Maroon 5

There is a downside to Eric being commissioned as an officer. Actually, there's probably more than one, but this is the first one I'm encountering. Eric has to go to Officers Development School (ODS) in Rhode Island for six weeks. It's not really like boot camp because the living quarters are a bit more comfortable, it's more about studying leadership, less physical training, and more freedom to call me once a week. I have plenty to do to fill the time, though. Besides taking care of the kids, I'm also packing up all our stuff because we're moving to a rental house in Virginia Beach the day after he gets back. I think I've spaced out our preparations pretty well. Even before the commissioning, I had begun sorting stuff to pack.

Our D.C. house is big, far bigger than any me or Eric have ever lived in, and we've lived in it for five years—the longest we've ever lived in the same home as a couple. Even though Eric's been stationed in the D.C. Metro area since 2001, we found the need to move as our family expanded. I still love this house, and I regret having to rent it out, but with his commissioning done and our family complete, this is our opportunity to spend some time in new places. For me, the girl who lived her entire childhood in the same farmhouse where her father lived his entire childhood and still lives now, getting to not just visit but live somewhere new is a big deal.

And we're only stationed in Virginia for three years; after that, the Navy will decide to either keep us there for another three or move us somewhere else, somewhere that will also be new, and that pattern will continue for the rest of Eric's time in the Navy. We'll be old and gray with adult children and backaches by then. So my job while Eric's at ODS, other than keeping the kids alive, is to pack as much of this three-story house as I can. We already started before he left, but only about a fourth of our stuff is boxed or otherwise ready.

I'm trying very hard to not let myself get overwhelmed, but I have a few times, yelling at the kids and making them stay in their rooms—for Ida and Daniel, anyway, and I still have Henry to manage even then. But I'm trying really hard to let the kids know that we are all missing Daddy, which sometimes means that I'm tired and grumpy and worn out. I also made a paper chain to (get rid of the half-ton of construction paper we have and) use as a countdown calendar to the day Daddy comes home. Every day we tear off one ring, and the chain gets a little shorter, along with my patience. Lord, just get me through this.

"It Is Well With My Soul"

Henry is a simpler, more independent three-year-old than Ida and Daniel were at this age, but he's still a three-year-old. One challenge with him that's new for me is his relentless energy. Ida has always been the type to be happiest when she's unrushed; she's been known to literally tiptoe happily through the tulips. Daniel was a mile a minute with everything, especially his attention span. Henry, on the other hand, is blasting through every developmental milestone like childhood is a race. Well, except for potty training. He's three now, but I think the complication of Eric going to ODS for so long and then moving held things back a bit for him. But it's okay. If Ida could spend five years in diapers and still be doing fine now, Henry's got time.

I'm tired, so I am sitting on my glider bench in the front yard, enjoying the weather and the relative quiet of the neighborhood we've moved into in Virginia Beach. Sure, I can hear the traffic from the highway and some construction happening somewhere, too, but this ambiance is wonderful. At our house in D.C., the ambiance was sirens, cars, the stops and starts of the Metro bus, and often, people yelling, swearing, etc. One time, an old car exploded a few feet from our D.C. house, and another time, the police searched our backyard, looking in Ida and Daniel's playhouse for a shooting suspect. Good times.

Today, feeling whimsical on a warm fall afternoon in Virginia, I grab a rake out of the garage, rake up a little pile of leaves, pick up Henry, and sit him in it. Alongside all of his other exceptionalities, he's also photogenic. So I take some great pictures of him, including one I take straight down while standing over him. Plus, I see that if he is comfortably lying so still as he piles leaves, he is probably tired. Nap time.

I scoop him up, take him inside, change his diaper, and climb in next to him in mine and Eric's bed. Nap time for me, too. I send a quick text to a friend I've been texting with on and off all day to tell her I'm silencing my phone so Henry and I can nap. But ten minutes later, just as Henry and I have really settled in, my phone buzzes again, with the ringer-off, vibration-on sound. I don't move; Henry opens his eyes, but if I pretend I'm sleeping, maybe he will ignore the buzzing phone. It doesn't work, and when the phone buzzes again after a few seconds, I roll over and look at it.

My mom called. Twice. This is bad.

My dad has been in the hospital. He is in the late stages of Alzheimer's now, and at that point, even the functional, physical health components begin to break down. Back in the 80s, when Grandpa died, they couldn't list Alzheimer's as a cause of death on his death certificate.

As I return my mom's call, I can already feel the lump in my throat and the unwelcome surge of angry energy that does nothing to change what I'm about to hear.

Mom says, "Daddy just passed."

With all the hustle and bustle surrounding Eric's commissioning and being alone with the kids while also packing up and moving this summer, I hadn't seen him in a couple of months. I didn't know that the last time I hugged him goodbye would be the *last* last time, standing next to my packed minivan in the gravel driveway in front of the barn. He'd stuttered a bit but had said, "You're doing a good job." He'd said it to me several times during that visit, but only to me, his parting words.

Mom, who seems to be solemn and resolute at this moment, tells me that other than the visiting hospice nurse, I am the first to hear this news. News, I think to myself. In a week or so, his obituary will be in the paper—the same paper that also reported on his conviction 18 years ago.

"How Great Thou Art,"
Carl Boberg and Stuart K. Hine

The last time I was in this church, my dad walked me down this aisle. Today, my dad is in the box at the end of it, laid to rest at the same altar where Eric and I got married 12 years ago. An old friend of my mom's offered to hold Henry and sit with him during the service, but I refused. I want to hold him. I need someone to hold right now while Eric sits next to me. That's what I need.

We sit in the same part of the church where we sat for our wedding, but one pew back and a bit to the right. We sing "How Great Thou Art" because it is my grandmother Muz's favorite, and she is now my only living grandparent. Muz, my mom, and my brother are all I have left.

Something is off in the lyrics of this particular arrangement of the hymn. They are wrong. The words are all totally different, which isn't what I want, and I can only assume that Mom and Muz must have noticed, too. So I sing the traditional lyrics as fully and loudly as I can. I'm angry that, on this day of all days, some silly alternative lyrics could take away the confession of faith that this song is. For today only, I turn it into a protest song.

When the pastor finishes his portion and invites others to speak as well, I am honored by and in awe of the sheer number of people who have kind things to say about my dad. People who knew him as a child describe their memories. A new friend of my mother's remarks on his sweet demeanor, although she'd only met him a month or so ago. No one mentions prison, but a number of people recall the faith he found there.

Just as the pastor is about to begin the closing of the service, Eric stands up, saying that he would like the chance to speak, and so begins a moment when I fall even more deeply in love with my husband.

"Dan was probably the only person who never questioned why I would go out to run in the rain because he had to work out in the rain all the time. When it rained and I ran, he'd remind me, 'You can't get wetter than wet.'" Cue laughter.

"But on one particular day, I remember I came back from my run, and on my way down the road, I saw Dan sitting alone behind the fruit-packing house, and I sat down with him. It wasn't the first time I had done this; we did this pretty often for a while. On this day specifically—this was shortly after the 9/11 attacks—I was struggling with 'why' questions: why did God let this happen? And why, if the world is so evil, doesn't he just come back and save his people and bring them to his kingdom now? Dan took a minute, sighed, and then said, 'Son,'—he called me son, and that was big to me because Mel and I weren't married yet—'Son, he hasn't gathered all the sheep yet. He's still calling some of them, and he isn't going to leave them behind while he's taking care of the ones that are already in the pen.'

"That's what I think he'd say today if he were here. I think he'd tell you that you don't know the day or the hour God might gather his sheep, so now's the time to seek Christ for salvation."

I had to ask Eric later if any of this was even true. I had no idea that he'd had conversations about faith and salvation with my dad behind the pack house way back then. Eric assured me that it was true, and although he could only paraphrase the conversation during that particular discussion, that was my dad's answer.

When I've told people about my faith, I always say it started when my dad went to prison and found Jesus there. But Dad never insisted we believe as he did. Actually, he only talked about his faith if someone asked him about it. But I knew even then that my dad was a very different man when he came home. I wasn't ready to understand what true, devoted love for God entailed back then, but my dad and my mom waited and prayed and helped share the gospel with those who were ready. In the end, their patient faith was all the witness Eric and I needed, and now our children can choose to receive a salvation that they will grow to understand over their own lifetimes. A legacy.

"Baba O'Riley," The Who

I've decided to finally get back to my graduate ethnomusicology program now, because I've only been working at this darn thing since 2009, before I even conceived Henry, and now Henry's starting preschool. I still have no idea how I will ever really work in this field, but the longer I wait to finish my last few classes, the older I get.

I have three semesters' worth of work to go, with the final one being solely dedicated to researching and writing my thesis. I know, on some level, that I don't really want to keep going with this, yet I am too ashamed to quit after all the effort and money we've put into it. And now I actually own a koto, although I haven't gotten it out at all since we moved. Honestly, the only thing that keeps me moving on all of this is pride. I'm ashamed to admit that after all the classes and papers and lessons and projects, I've lost interest. And the number of uncomfortable social interactions that all of those steps and all of the thesis project steps entail is daunting. I don't really want to work with other people at all; the people who live in my house are already getting on my nerves. Yet, if I quit, I would waste every bit of the work I'd done along with Eric's financial investment in it, and I don't want that on my conscience either.

This semester, I have one class on Indian music and one class that will gradually walk me through writing my research proposal. The Indian music class has a lot of content that I need to learn and remember, but I'm used to that sort of work now. On the other hand, the proposal writing one is the first step toward my thesis and graduation, but it's hard and tedious.

Ida and Daniel are at school all day on the weekdays, but Henry is only at his preschool for four hours, and I have to drop him off and pick him up. I can get some work done while he plays and watches TV, but it's hard to concentrate, and he isn't taking naps anymore. I've been doing most of my work at night after everyone else is asleep and then sleeping while Henry's at preschool.

Now that I'm restarting this, I am learning that I don't enjoy the ethnomusicology subject nearly as much as I do writing all the papers. I'm writing A-worthy papers because I'm good at writing and I love writing. I get a kind of rush looking at a topic, writing down a thesis statement, and then filling every single sentence in the rest of the paper with information and details about why the thesis statement is true. I've been writing thesis papers since ninth grade, so maybe I'm only really enjoying this part because it's easy and familiar and doesn't drain me of brain cells quite as much. Maybe, for me, it's fun to write papers in the same way that it's fun to do a word search or color in a coloring book—it takes very little effort, but the final result is still impressive. It seems crazy to go on with all the work I have left to do in this program because of that, but if I stopped now, I wouldn't have a degree as proof of my hard work. It's backward thinking, I'm sure. But every time I write a good, solid research paper, I feel smart. I think that as a kid, I saw myself as a smart person, but I compared myself to classmates who were either just plain smarter than me or were smarter at subjects and projects that I was only average at. Like my seventh-grade math teacher, I believed that if I was smart, or "gifted," in one sort of subject or skill, I would be above average and smart in every other one, too. I thought I was either smart or I wasn't, and since I was bad at math, I wasn't smart, even if I aced English.

I got this idea, this theory that I, and probably thousands of others who'd been "gifted" kids, were actually gifted in specific subjects and work styles by watching Ida. When she was little, it seemed like she got frightened by almost anything new or out of her routine. But when she started in her autism class at age four, she was willing and able to learn, do, and say things that I had tried and failed to teach her. What the teacher did to teach her new things at school varied little from what I'd done at home, but learning those things with her classmates was motivating because her environment and her curiosity were more focused.

Even before I graduated from high school, I knew I had a number of topics I was interested in, not just music. But because I had a good singing voice and people affirmed my singing talent regularly, I thought I should nurture that uniqueness by studying music. And then, I got to college and realized within the first semester that wanting to sing and wanting to study music are two separate callings, and I only liked singing. And now here I am in grad school, studying music because it's familiar and I had to pick something. But all I really want to do is read, and write, and read about writing, and write about reading.

I'm glad I've finally learned this about myself, but it doesn't change anything at this point. I only have this one Indian music class to finish, and after that, all the work I have left before I earn my MA will be directly related to proposing, researching, and writing my thesis. I hate that I'm only now acknowledging this truth about myself because I'm not going back for a writing degree. I'm just going to write. I don't need a college degree for that, and I have plenty of pens.

Initially, my plan was to finish writing my ten-page paper for class, get it done by midnight or 1:00 a.m., and go to bed so I don't walk around like a zombie tomorrow. My natural inclination, though, has always been to stay up late and sleep through a good portion of the morning. I've gravitated back to that habit every time I've attempted to train myself to keep more normal sleeping patterns. My parents tried everything they could think of to get me to fall asleep faster; some of those methods became habits for me, like playing music from the radio, having the window open for all but the very coldest nights, and reading a book before bedtime, but none of those ever accomplished what my parents had hoped they would. I did all of these things but still only fell asleep around midnight, or sometimes quite a bit later. Of course, now I don't have my parents' guidance, but even with the greater challenge of getting my own kids up for school, I end up staying up too late and regretting it at 7:00 a.m. when I need to get them up and out to the school bus by 7:30. Nevertheless, I'm here now at 1:15 a.m., finishing my conclusion and reiterating the thesis statement, with the angel on my right shoulder saying, "Now be a good girl and say your prayers and go right to bed," and the devil on my left shoulder, telling me that, with Eric working as a nurse, one of only a few male nurses in the entire hospital and the only male nurse working in inpatient Pediatrics, his complete lack of interest in sex is really only a lack of interest in sex with me. No man turns down his wife's open, explicit invitation for months at a time unless his needs are being fulfilled by someone else.

This evil voice in my head whispers that he doesn't want to have sex because I'm crazy, because I spend too much money, because he is disgusted by my obese, plus-sized body. That since he is so clearly disgusted by me, and he won't acquiesce even when I cry and plead with him to show me he loves me, it can only mean that he has another means through which he is more satisfied. So now, after I upload my paper and email it to my professor, I start going through Eric's social media. There's little I can uncover, though. Every few months or so, I innocently bring up the idea of giving each other our email and social media passwords so that we can hold each other accountable for our sexual integrity, but he never wants to discuss it; he acts like he is focused on something else and hasn't really heard me. That's plenty of evidence that he's cheating right there. He's hiding his personal life and refusing to even give a reason for it. And frankly, men cheat because they can. That was always the warning for Christian wives and the excuse for Christian husbands. If a husband isn't interested in sex, it's because he's satisfying the urge with something, or more likely, someone else. They're hardwired to want sex more than women, and yet I'm the one crying.

The problem is that I've been conducting all the espionage I can for months now, and while I find plenty of evidence of him chatting with women in and outside of work, I have nothing I can truly call evidence. Hell, I even found one of those cheap burner phones in his backpack, but it was turned off and the battery was dead and I couldn't find a charger for it.

Eric knows that I've dug around his stuff like this. I try to make sure he thinks it's something I did in the past and stopped, but really, I do it all the time now. What scares me is that I'm kind of enjoying it, and not just because I'm being sneaky. I'm lonely, yet surrounded by kids and neighbors and busy all day long. Whether or not he's cheating isn't the real problem. My problem is that I can't believe he loves me if he doesn't want to have sex with me. He's a guy, so he's the one who should be wanting me, but he's not. And I've talked with at least three or four women at our church, and at least as many from the churches we've attended regularly in the past, and all of them have affirmed my fears—that if he is going upwards of six months at a time without sex and turning down even my direct requests for sex, he is involved with either another woman or pornography.

On all the late nights and early mornings that I lay around thinking about this, I always end up at the same conclusion. This is my fault. I have been a crazy, emotional mess since my dad died. As much as my dad was to blame for the affair he had all those years ago, maybe it wouldn't have happened if my mom hadn't kept starving herself with every new diet someone told her about, only to wave a white flag and put all the weight back on. And that's what I'm doing now. My food intake, weight, and pant size have gone up and down in the same pattern as Mom's, but over the last few years, the amount of time I've been able to maintain a decent diet has gone down sharply. Right now, I weigh 215 pounds—more than I did when I was nine months pregnant with Henry, who was my largest baby. Every night, I get to this point around 2:30 a.m. and end up lying on the couch or even on the floor crying and sometimes screaming into the cushions or the rug. No man could love me like this, and now, to make matters worse, I have at least a 50% chance of developing Alzheimer's by way of my dad's genetic mutation. Then, not only will Eric have an obese wife, but also one he has to feed and bathe and eventually diaper. I don't want to inflict that horror on my family. I'm told suicide is sinful, but what if my only other option is to become a burden to everyone else?

"You Gotta Be," Des'ree

I'm walking around the mall with a friend on our way to Torrid. I was just here three months ago when I spent $300 in one trip, but I'm fully prepared to do it again because the stuff I got in January is too small now. The bathroom scale read 185 before Christmas, but at this point, I'm well over 200 pounds. I keep wondering what percentage of my body mass is chocolate chip cookies.

My weight has always bounced around in direct correlation with my diet, and my diet with my mental health and life challenges. Before having kids, the highest weight I'd reached was around 155 pounds, but after I had Ida and Daniel, I got stuck around 180 for a while, then worked my way back to 125 the following year. The problem is that when I get my body where I want it to be and how I want it to look, I don't keep it there for long. Even when I'm careful, I inevitably come to a moment when I just want to eat something greasy and full of fat and wash it down with a large soda, followed by dessert. Most people can do that, right? They can decide every once in a while to eat a big, nutritionally vacant meal and then get right back on their healthy horse quickly enough that any damage done is negated. But I can't. When I stop indulging and overeating, I never stay stopped for long. A few times, I've managed to maintain a diet for a year or more, but I always hit a wall and binge eat again. I tell myself, "You can have one slice of cake; that won't hurt you," and then trade in my second piece of cake for an extra large value meal.

289

At Torrid, I try on size 18 pants in a different, less tailored design than the other pair of 18s I'm wearing now, but I still can't button them well. So, I end up getting one pair in a size 20 and another in a size 22 since I'll probably need those in the next couple of months. I know that some women are comfortable enough in overweight or even obese bodies, often because they've woven their physical appearance and their self-confidence together as a package and have chosen to love it, but I've been trying to make myself believe that for quite a while, and I just can't. On Valentine's Day this year, Eric and I went to a Thai restaurant; Thai is my favorite next to burgers and fries. I ordered a huge plate and a side and devoured it, but Eric ordered one plate-sized meal and only ate a little over half of it. When I looked up from my plate, I was so ashamed. To look at this amazing, brilliant, loving person—*my* person—the man who loves me, who cares for our kids alongside me, who held me when my dad died, supported me when CPS threatened our family, and worked hard to give our family great things on a single income—and what am I able to give him now? A wife who is an embarrassment, who can't go a day without yelling at the kids and eating a Reese's Fast Break. I am trash. Worthless.

"Are you sure you can love me like this?" I ask.

"What do you mean? "

He knows what I mean because we have this conversation regularly, but he's trying to gauge how many of my fears I've rolled into it this time—being fat, being angry, being miserable, being paranoid, being suicidally depressed.

"How can you love me when I'm enormous and angry and depressed all the time?" I clarify.

"I love you because you're you. Because you're my love-y wife." It's a rote response that he says at least once every week to answer the same question.

And then he says, "But,"

I look up quickly as the earth stops turning for a few seconds. There has never been a "but" in this conversation until now, and all the evil, paranoid delusions that spin through my head in the nighttime quiet do a speed run through my brain.

"… But I'm afraid that I could lose you to something you could have prevented if you'd kept yourself healthy. I love you, and I want you to be my love-y wife as long as possible."

I am rarely speechless, but his honesty and the risk that he was willing to take, the risk of me exploding in anger and rage, accusing him of something horrible in retaliation, has humbled me in the greatest of ways. I cry, asking for his forgiveness—not for my obesity, but for my angry verbal abuse, my inability to see how he makes efforts daily to ensure that I know I'm loved unconditionally. He has loved me in countless ways that I've completely disregarded, writing them off as an attempt to win brownie points or hold off my next rampage. I'd created a story with myself as the neglected, tragic heroine who must fight to prove her worth and stay alive.

I am not that heroine. I have a family, children, a few friends, and even a cat, who all love me. It had never crossed my mind that by believing they looked down on me, I was, in fact, looking down on them, refusing and denying the love they offered me unconditionally because I couldn't love myself.

Two weeks later, I went to my primary care clinic to ask for a referral for gastric bypass surgery. "I know I will still need to change my eating habits to prevent myself from gaining the weight back even after the surgery," I say, "but the surgery will give me a head start so that I can get to a healthy weight faster." The surgery referral was sent, but I'm required to work with a nutritionist for three months first.

Two weeks pass before I'm able to get a nutritionist appointment, and when I get to that appointment, she tells me I have to work with her for at least four months before she can refer me for surgery. I spend more than an hour looking at government-approved charts, diagrams, and statistics—all of which I know and have seen a thousand times before. After all, I wouldn't be here if I hadn't already learned how to lose weight and tried to follow all the rules. Experienced fat people know this: you don't wake up in the morning and decide to get major surgery on your digestive system; you have to be hopeless first.

At the end, she hands me a folder full of all the things I've known for years and tried before and a reminder card for another appointment in two weeks. The advice she'd offered was generalized and not in any way compatible with the types of food I like or the busyness of my life. I do not have time to make homemade soup or spend 45 minutes making a side dish for my lunch on a Thursday—or any day. She gave me advice like try to eat produce in all six colors of the rainbow every day. Make yourself a beautiful meal, relax, and eat it slowly. All of this is completely ridiculous for a mom with young children who's also going to graduate school.

At home, I thumb through the info in the folder over a peanut butter and jelly sandwich, potato chips, and chocolate. Nothing is helpful here either, but tucked in with the rest of it is a single-page, double-sided brochure card with a headline that reads, "Are you a compulsive eater?" Below the headline and continuing to the back of the card are 15 "yes" or "no" questions. I love a good quiz that reaffirms what I already know about myself. At the bottom of the back of the card, it says:

"Have you answered 'yes' to several of these questions? If so, it is possible that you have, or are well on your way to having, a compulsive eating or overeating problem." Uh, yeah. Duh.

At the bottom of the back page is a sticker, like the kind used for return address labels, with a website address. When I enter it into my laptop, I land on the home page for a support group for overeaters, and a little candlelight flame ignites somewhere within me. I knew there were groups for alcoholics and drug addicts and groups for their family members. I had no idea there was a group for people who can't stop eating.

The flame on the flickering candle inside me dances. *"This is a gift for you. Take it."*

"California Love,"
2pac, Dr. Dre, Roger

We've been driving for more than six hours, and I'm getting tired, so Abi texts Eric and tells him to stop at the next rest stop. I've been following a Penske truck in our Ford Explorer, which is stuffed to the gills with all our stuff, all three kids, Abi and I, and has a black metal porch bench awkwardly strapped to its roof. Eric is in the Penske truck, with Onyx in her cat carrier in the seat next to him and the rest of our stuff in the back. He also strapped our toilet plunger to the truck's back bumper to complete our "rednecks on the road" aesthetic.

Six months ago, Eric applied for another Navy educational program, this time to earn an advanced practice degree in pediatric nursing. Obviously, the main idea is for him to advance his career and pay grade, but this also means we get the chance to move somewhere further away. So, over the last few months, we've been purging and packing our stuff (again) so it will all fit in one box truck and my Explorer. We left several hours later than we intended to today, and we do have something strapped to the roof, but at least it's a yard bench and not a kid.

I knew to expect that a long trip with all our stuff and people and staying in truck stop hotels for about ten days straight would be hard, and even this first day has pushed me to tears twice. The cleaners we hired to perform our move-out cleaning for the home we'd rented in

Virginia Beach did a terrible job, skipping one room entirely, among other things. I ended up borrowing a vacuum and cleaning supplies from a neighbor to finish the job this morning, and we left behind a lawn mower we had tried to sell on Craigslist but got no takers. Then, Henry lost his "phone," which is really an iPod Touch. When we didn't find it, we had to tell him we were leaving without it, which resulted in Henry angry-crying for the first 20 minutes of the trip, and then I got a call from a neighbor who'd found it in her yard and had to drive back. By the time we make it to our first hotel reservation in Nashville, it's almost 2:00 a.m., and in the morning, we need to be back on the road by 8:00. We have to move the bike rack around to open the back hatch on the Explorer and get our suitcases, so by the time we get to bed it's closer to 3:00 a.m. It's going to be a long trip.

"Route 66," Chuck Berry

We've arrived at the stop I've been looking forward to most on our moving trip to San Diego. We're in Tucumcari, New Mexico; I know that doesn't sound too exciting, and I suppose it's not. But we'll be here for three whole days, and there's a rockabilly and vintage car show happening. They also have fun mid-century space race-style hotels, but of course, we're not staying in any of those because they're too expensive and we have to get two rooms. We're staying at the only hotel in town that has absolutely no visual appeal whatsoever.

When we arrived, we found out why it was the only hotel in town that still had vacancies on the weekend of a rockabilly festival: it's nasty. The rooms are tiny. There's barely enough room to walk between the bottom ends of the two double beds and the TV stand/dresser, the sheets feel greasy with other people's old sweat, and the water in the shower is lukewarm at best. I could go on. But there's nowhere else we can go.

There is a mini fridge, which allows me to store my healthy groceries so that I can make my meals in the room while we're here and pack up my food in Ziplock bags to eat when we're back on the road. (Not that the room is clean enough for that. I line the countertop with paper towels before I set anything on it.) The rockabilly festival wasn't much, but it was kind of cool. Abi and I both put on pinup-style dresses and did our hair, and a few of the men displaying their old cars let us take pictures with them like old car advertisements with pretty girls, and Eric took the kids (and himself) for ice cream after dinner. The hotel pool isn't fancy, but it's cold and relatively clean.

But between the bugs and the scuzzy bedsheets and the blowing desert sand in my eyes, I'm ready to go on to our next stop. Today, we're going to drive through Amarillo, Texas. Muz grew up here, although I don't think she was in the city, more like the suburbs or maybe even further out than that. I remember telling her when I was little that someday I wanted to go to Amarillo to see her old hometown. She's passed away, but today I will finally get there.

We still have three, maybe even four more days on the road before we get to the house we've rented in San Diego. What I thought would be a fun, epic adventure to see America has been a draining, hot, boring, and oftentimes frustrating slog through hundreds of miles of desert and a whole lot of nothing—but it had its high points, too. Let's hope California is worth the effort.

"Californication,"
Red Hot Chili Peppers

It's our last day of driving, and we'll get to our new home soon, but Abi really wants to see a place called Salvation Mountain. It's located much further south, still in San Diego, technically speaking, but it's basically Mexico. At this point, I'm a little frustrated at the detour when we're so close to being home, but Abi showed me a picture of Salvation Mountain, and it's definitely worth the effort. It's a large, mountainous outcropping that is painted in a variety of pastel colors, kind of mod/hippie, 1960s style, with Bible verses in several places and hippie "flower power" type slogans in others. The rock outcroppings are high enough to be impressive but low and flat enough to climb on, so Abi, the kids, and I climb up. Definitely one of the best stops we've made. I thank Abi for convincing us it would be worth the short trip extension.

By the time we arrive at the house, it's getting dark, so we let ourselves in and take a look around. All I want to do is sleep in my own bed now— even my own mattress if that's all we can get out of the truck tonight. Tomorrow, Eric is leaving again. I'll be driving him and Abi to the airport in the morning, where Abi will get on a flight to Philadelphia, and Eric will get on a flight back to Virginia. His job there isn't done yet, and his official transfer date isn't until the first week of August. The kids and I will be on our own for just over eight weeks again.

Then, when we get the door unlocked and walk in the house, I'm pretty dismayed. On the whole, everything looks exactly like the photos we've viewed. But when I walk around and look closer, I realize I will have work to do to get the place clean. There is a thick layer of dust on every flat surface, including the stovetop and kitchen countertops, where the dust is also sticky, having adhered to whatever greasy grime remained on the counters after the last tenants left about two months ago. The toilets are dusty, too, and I can feel more of the sandy desert-like dust on the carpets when I take off my shoes. I am disgusted and exhausted, which is not a good combination. Then, I find shampoo, makeup, and even a prescription bottle that still contains pills in the master bathroom, and dust in the shower as well.

I'm already feeling grimy and dirty from days of long drives through the desert, from staying in cheap hotels where the level of housekeeping reflects the nightly rate, and I'm hungry, but even though I have the food I need on ice in a cooler, the sticky countertops are hardly ready for food prep. When I burst into exhausted tears, Eric suggests we go to the famous "In-N-Out Burger" closest to our house. It will mean an even later night for Eric, who plans to unload the truck into the garage before he sleeps, but we all need food.

We set up a litter box for Onyx, the sweet black cat who became ours when Abigail lived with us for those brief months in the fall of 2007. Onyx was the only piece of Abi we had to hang onto when our custody experiment failed, and she stuck with us through our reunion with Abi a year and a half ago. I can't say Onyx is enjoying this trip, but she's here, and she remains steadfastly attached to the rest of the family.

Much to my chagrin, when we return from In-N-Out, Eric insists on emptying the moving truck now rather than in the morning. He also puts our bed frame together, which is no easy feat on his own. I always wonder how he can push himself for so long without losing his temper or giving up, but over the years, I've noticed that he does lose his temper; he just takes it out on stuff instead of people. He certainly made quite a racket loading and unloading stuff we needed at each stop on our way from east to west, but when I finish putting sheets on our bed, sit down on it, and feel the floor shake a little, my heart stops for a second. Did he try to back the truck up to put it closer to the garage and end up backing into the house that hard?

But as soon as I manage to complete the thought, Eric comes running into the bedroom and says sharply, "What did you do?!"

Before I can protest his accusation that I have somehow moved the house, I feel it again, but a little less this time, and I recognize the feeling.

"It was an earthquake," I tell him. I only know this from my memory of the strange anomalous quake that happened in Washington, D.C. a few years ago. Tomorrow afternoon, the next-door neighbor would ask me if I'd felt it and if it was my first one, and I would tell her about the one in D.C. But for now, I laugh because this is the sort of thing that could only happen to me: an earthquake on my first night as a California resident. The neighbor would also tell me that this is the first one they've had in this area in several years.

Surely, our time in California will be momentous if the earth is moved by our very presence.

"Cake By The Ocean," DNCE

I am relishing the time on weekday mornings lately because Henry is in morning kindergarten, and I have a few precious hours alone in the house, just me and Onyx. Of course, the school year is almost over, but it's been a nice time to spend with Henry before he starts first grade next year. Every day, I walk him up to the elementary school, only a quarter of a mile from our house, and just before noon, I walk back again on my own and wait for him on the front porch of the school. And now that the weather is nice again, we usually walk about a half mile to the 7-11 store together, where I get him a treat and myself a Coke Zero, and then we walk home.

I have about 15 minutes before I need to start walking up to the school when my phone rings. When I answer, the caller identifies herself as a collections agent, and I start to panic. She tells me that my past-due bills have been sent to her agency, and she is calling to help me arrange payment with her agency's help.

"I wasn't aware that I had any credit card debt," I assure her. "I only have one credit card I don't use, and it isn't the one you just mentioned."

"Is your social security number..............?"

"Yes, that's my social security number, but I did not make those charges," I tell her. She says that if I believe the charges were fraudulent, her agency can help me prosecute the offender and pay off the debt. "Is there anyone else who may have access to your social security number?"

Angie, I think. She did this. But why would she have my social security number? I can't think of any time I would have needed to give it to her. With what I know about her, I never would. Could Eric have given it to her? But if he knows she used his cards without his permission, why would he give her my social security number?

My mind is whirling, and I need to go get Henry. I tell the collections agent that I will do some research to find out if any of my family members could have made the charges, write down the name and number of the collections agency, and start walking toward the school.

I don't understand credit card debt. I mean, I understand what it is. I don't understand why someone would use a credit card to pay for something when they know they will never be able to pay it back. Is that thing you want, whatever it is, worth a minor crime? I can see their usefulness if there's an unexpected hardship that must be fixed immediately. You either take on debt in order to fix that problem, or you use the money you have to fix the problem but fall into debt with other things until you can somehow catch up again. Why even let yourself get to that point unless it's a matter of personal safety or something?

When I get close to the school, I try to calm myself down. I've been crying, and Henry will be able to tell I'm upset even if I didn't have tears on my face. And he worries when I'm upset. Once, when he was three, shortly after Dad died, I was crying, and he sat down next to me and asked, "Mommy, are you happy to me?" Of course, my heart melted, and now Eric and I both ask each other that question when we're concerned for each other.

I pray in my head while I walk with Henry to the 7/11. I consider telling him we can't go to 7/11 today, but I'm learning that it is better to work on solving problems when I am calm. In the past, if something like this came up, I would plow into the problem like a runaway freight train, unleashing all of my fear and anger as if I could force an unembodied problem to submit to my dominance. It's still my first reaction when bad things happen. But this time, I realize, my desire to keep Henry from worrying about what I'm upset about has actually stopped my own worrying. I have to remember that next time something like this happens.

After Henry gets his treat and we walk back to the house, I feel my heart rate increase, so I take a few deep breaths before I call the collections agency again. When I do, they tell me that the social security number, name, address, and phone number on the account match my information, but when I ask if they can give me information about the amounts of the individual charges and what they were used to purchase, I catch it. A good number of the charges are from the D.C. area where we lived or the parts of Maryland and Virginia that we were often in during the time we lived in the house in the city. The most recent ones are from the Virginia Beach area where we live now.

It's not Angie. It's Eric.

Social security numbers are not a carefully concealed personal matter for people connected to the military. We use them for our IDs, especially for the active duty member, and since the kids and I are all on Eric's health insurance, he has all of them, and has his own and mine memorized. He must have opened a credit card in my name and then ignored all the bills after using it. By my calculation, based on the charges the collections officer indicated, he's been using this card—my card—for more than five years.

When he gets home, I ask my neighbor to keep an eye on the kids while Eric and I work this out in private. We go to Denny's, which is definitely not private and definitely not a great place for a compulsive overeater to be when she's upset. But my frustration covers up my hunger pretty well.

After I tell Eric about the phone call and the clues I put together from it, I tell him that I initially thought it was Angie, but the local businesses paid match our locations, not hers in Pennsylvania, and so I knew it was him who had done this. Then I map out a plan to make sure we can communicate about money since right now we don't talk about money at all.

I propose that we meet together to consider our bills and budget every Sunday night for a while. He says that a weekly meeting is overkill, but I insist we at least start there and then maybe do monthly when we get more comfortable being honest with each other about some things; although by "we," I really mean him. I can tell he hates this whole situation. I have never successfully called him out on anything before. I've called him out on lies a few times, and every time he swore he wasn't lying. Then, when I got confirmation from someone else that he had been lying, at least in part, I confronted him with it and he just stonewalled me. No response or explanation, and no eye contact for a while either.

We sit and eat our food, mine taking longer than usual. He's quiet, and I remind him that I love him and I'd rather he tell me "no" than use credit cards for bills he can't pay. Then, when I take the next bite, a sudden connection comes to me.

"Eric," I say gently, "You did this to Angie, too. Am I right?"

"Yes," he says meekly, without looking at me.

"So, does that mean that all the stuff you told me, how Angie had used your credit cards and racked up all your credit debt, that those things were actually things that you wanted, or at least that you were in agreement about buying? Does it also mean that you lied to her in the same way, and she dumped you because of it?"

"Yes," he says softly, "But there are a lot of reasons we broke up; it wasn't just that. But yes, that's true."

I feel as if someone has picked me up by my feet and is dangling me upside down. This changes a lot and brings in a whole new side of Eric that he's hidden from me for 18 years. But it changes everything I thought I knew about Angie herself. I have been hating Angie for years because Eric led me to believe that she was the reason he was financially destitute. I've treated her poorly because of it and looked down on her. All based on a lie. Eric maintained my belief in that lie and used it to his advantage to get custody of Abi. He even showed me checks that Angie had endorsed in his name, telling me they'd been mailed to her by accident. In reality, they had been mailed to Angie because that was the address on the account since Abi lives several states away and the bills were for copays on dentist appointments, but it was still his job to pay them.

"Did you tell Angie to sign your name to endorse those dental service repayments?"

He says nothing, and I take that as my answer.

"Another Brick in the Wall," Pink Floyd

I suppose it may have briefly come to mind that we were moving to the opposite side of the country, and everything any of us know as home, while my two neurodivergent kids are in middle school—arguably the most awkward and uncomfortable part of childhood. We intentionally only looked at rental homes in areas with good school districts nearby, but you have to take those school rating websites that people submit their reviews to with a grain of salt. I know I've been in the position where something I experienced was less than I expected, allowed my frustration to turn into rage, and then went to a review site and posted a rant that wasn't really a review at all. The school websites, I would think, get a lot of ratings that are more or less anger dumps.

Well, we should have given more credit to the angry parents and students who posted their frustrations about this middle school because we've already experienced worse things than anything on the review site.

Because Daniel has ADHD (a diagnosis we'd expected for years that was finally confirmed by a doctor in Virginia), he has a very specific plan that maps out what sort of positive and negative behaviors he has and where and when he may need some extra accommodations in order to perform on the same level as his peers academically. Taking tests in a room where he is alone with only one adult rather than surrounded by other students, for example, helps him focus on the test and not the environment.

Ida, on the other hand, has autism, so she has an Individualized Education Plan (IEP) that any school she goes to must use with her, but a new school or teacher is free to interpret the less concrete goals and accommodations. With an IEP, the school is legally required to provide what's in it.

Neither of these is happening, but that's the least of my worries. Ida and Daniel are being outright bullied—and not entirely by the students, but even more so by the teachers. Daniel reported to us that because his science class has an odd number of students, the teacher made Daniel the only student without a lab partner. Ida, who has been reluctant to shower and wear deodorant as often as she needs to, has had teachers send her out of class because of body odor, telling her that she can't come to class again until she takes a shower. This was said in front of other students.

I am shocked by this, not because I didn't expect them to be bullied—because, in some ways, they have always been bullied—but that teachers are intentionally shaming my kids in front of their classmates. I had so many problems in middle school, with bullying in particular, but I don't think I was ever publicly bullied by a teacher. My goodness, have none of these teachers seen *Carrie?*

It's only been a month since school started, but I've been in at least five meetings at the middle school to try to make this all stop. Part of the problem is that Ida and Daniel are not nearly as upset about it as I am, and it seems that the bullies, student and adult, take that to mean that they either don't care about the bullying or are too dimwitted to understand it. Of course, no one notices the tears on their faces. Another part of it is that the teachers interpret the IEP and behavioral plan as suggestions at best, and sometimes ignore them altogether. More than one teacher claimed she had no idea they have special needs. Ironically, we picked this area to live in part because of this school's strong reputation for its work with special ed. kids. I can only conclude that that information was an outright lie.

After both the special ed. coordinators and I were completely shut down by teachers refusing to even care about Ida's IEP, we gave up. Eric and I have submitted paperwork to the school indicating that we are withdrawing them and enrolling them in online school, just as we once did for Abi.

Still, I can't help but worry about all of this for a whole bunch of reasons. I mean, middle school and being a middle schooler is hard and awkward for everyone, and my kids were in that environment five days a week for a month, so they have to be hurting from it, even if they don't show it. Also, because Eric's graduate nursing classes fall mostly on weekday evenings and Saturday mornings, we had been happily enjoying our school day hours alone in the house. Now that goes away, too.

Heavy sigh. Just when I think I'm done being a stay-at-home mom because my kids are in school all day, they're not. I spent all of August, from the time we arrived here until a day or so before Eric came back after finishing his required time at the Virginia hospital, soul-searching about what I want to do now that all the children would be in school. With my MA complete and my thesis published, I'd like to find a job working with music therapy and special needs kids or their families. I'd been planning to start an online course that would allow me to become a licensed advocate for parents negotiating IEPs with school districts. Turns out, I should have spent that time getting ready for my own battle with that.

"Christmas in the Sand,"
Colbie Caillat

I'm having a bit of a struggle right now on two fronts. First, I am sitting here at the Christmas lunch picnic that Ida and Daniel's online school classmates and families and teachers have put together for them for the last day of "school" before winter break. The idea that online school even has a winter break is kind of funny, but part of the benefit of online school is that following a curriculum and a school schedule helps my kids keep their school day vs. no-school day routines in place, even when both happen at home.

My first struggle right now has to do with my nose. There are stacks of Pizza Hut pizza boxes, many with a few remaining slices still inside, sitting right next to me, and I am desperately refraining from eating them.

My second struggle is that it is the middle of December, and we're all still wearing shorts as often as we wear pants. It's warm here, even in December. Not as warm as July and more humid than the summertime here, but winter isn't winter here; it's flash flood season. In San Diego, the seasons are hot, unbearably hot, and rainy.

Ida and Daniel's teacher, the one person who teaches all the California Virtual Academy middle school students in this area, asks me if I like winter in southern California, and I tell her "no" right away. How could anyone raised on "Winter Wonderland" enjoy "Mele Kalikimaka"? It just seems wrong to me.

We made the right decision when we enrolled Ida and Daniel here. I miss the four or so hours Eric and I were alone together, but this is what Ida and Daniel needed to get through middle school. A lot of their classmates are neurodivergent, too, which is an even greater indicator that this was the right choice.

"Run Like Hell," Pink Floyd

Picture it: Lake Cuyamaca, California, October 2017. A California resident for only one year, I am tasked with providing aid by means of refreshments to streams of sweaty, nauseous, and often ill runners attempting to run a 100-mile race within two days. When asked, I willingly hold a freeze pop up to one runner's mouth while she changes her socks. For the next, I pour ice cubes into a baseball cap and help him get it back on his head without losing too many.

This job is totally weird and oddly fun. In his early years of running, people would sometimes ask Eric if he ever considered doing an "ultra," the runners' term for any race longer than a marathon. Eric always gave the same answer to this question. "I've never gotten to the finish line of a marathon and thought, 'Let's do that again right now.'" He laughed off even the idea of ultra races. And now here we are.

This is Eric's first 100-mile race, but not his first ultra; he's done a few shorter ones as he worked his way up, training for this one. Since the race has been going for a few hours, he is somewhere out on the course, hopefully upright and breathing. But the kids and I are at one of the aid stations on the course, doing our best to help out. I've also helped out at some of his road races, but it's a much simpler job at those. Typically, during shorter, less tactical road races, the only concerns you have as a volunteer are passing out water and energy drinks and letting the posted medical crew know if someone is hurt. At an ultra, I'm learning that everyone working the aid station is a part of the medical crew, and the runners need you to fill multiple bottles with water or energy drinks—or, strangely, pickle juice. Already today, I have cut open multiple freeze pops for full-grown adults to happily suck on like three-year-olds. I don't just feel excited for Eric but for each of the runners I've given aid to, and that feels good. A picture of Thomas the Tank Engine, Daniel's first major obsession, comes to mind, along with his railway-based terminology. Today, I am a very useful engine.

By the time Eric arrives at our aid station, he is looking pretty rough. I ask him what I can do, but for the most part, I let the other volunteers cater to him while I sit on the ground next to him so he can use a chair. I have never seen him this beat up during a race, and he still has quite a ways to go. He asked me not to tell anyone, but a month ago, he was struck by a car during a training run, and he is recovering from a concussion. I didn't want him to do this race because of that, and I am worried now. I tell a couple of the aid station leaders the truth, not to betray him, but because I want them to help me track him on the race GPS system and make sure that if he ends up in a first aid tent with a DNF (that's "did not finish"), I can get someone to drive me to him.

All the same, when Eric insists on getting back out on the course, I'm glad to keep serving the other runners. Ultra trail runners and the people who support them, who are often the ultra trail runners themselves at other races, are tough, obviously, but there is also a sort of redneck tree-hugger mixture that I really relate to. I'm never going to run an ultra—I didn't even enjoy my two marathons—but over the last year, I've fallen in love again with the woods, the wilderness, camping, gardening, and getting dirty. Although California isn't, and may never, feel like home to me, it's awakened me to a part of me I'd forgotten: the farm girl who rode on the backs of flatbed trucks and swam in a pond while minnows nipped painlessly at her toes. I missed that girl, but she's back now.

"High Hopes,"
Panic! At The Disco

The worst part of moving is having to clean up the empty house after you move all your stuff out of it. First, you can't really move *all* of your stuff out until you're just about to leave, which means there will be random junk that you're still using in the house while you're trying to make it look like new. It's always random junk and basics, like one lamp, a random pen lying on the carpet, or that one fancy thing you have that's too weird to pack and will have to make the trip sitting in your lap in the car. I brought a tiny cactus with me from Virginia to San Diego, and it rode the whole way in a cup holder on the center console of my Explorer. Every time Abi or I, or whoever was in the passenger seat, would try to reach something from the floor behind the front seats, we got stabbed by the cactus. At one point, Abi got so tired of it that if one of the kids was causing a problem during the drive, they had to hold the cactus. It was the Punishment Cactus.

Right now, we are moving away from our rental house in Poway, California. The landlord increased our rent when our original two-year lease was up, and it was no longer worth what we'd be paying. We found a different rental house with more space in a town about 40 minutes away. At the same time, Eric convinced Ida to try out for the cross country team at the high school she'll be attending next year, and it turns out she didn't even have to try out; they took anyone willing to put forth their best effort.

Ida has the perfect runner's body. She's short and thin but has good muscle tone when she's active. But she also still has that unusual habit of walking on her toes, as if she were pretending to wear high-heeled shoes. Sometimes it even helps us judge how she's feeling because if she's toe-walking, she's generally feeling happy. Just as Eric once predicted, all the toe-walking has strengthened her legs and developed in her a habit of leaning forward and using a springing sort of step when she runs. Eric's been wanting to see her run for years now.

So Ida is enrolled in El Capitan High School in Lakeside, California, for this coming year. Daniel will continue with his last year of online middle school, and Henry will go to elementary school two miles away from our new house.

"Blessings," Laura Story

I can't really think to put sentences together—or even two words—but I'll try.

Okay. To start with, I feel like crap, and I've felt like crap for almost ten days now. At least, I think it's ten. I don't know what day it is right now.

I can't say I remember when this started, but I got a headache. That's simple enough. I've been getting headaches since I was a kid, but this headache is different—excruciating. I think it started around the day I went to the dentist, but at this point, I can't remember if that was a week ago or a month ago. I can't keep track of time. When I get up to go to the bathroom, it feels like I'm in a boat, rocking back and forth. My head is pounding sometimes, and other times it feels like there's a big, flat rock sinking into my brain and squashing it like a pancake.

Eric took me to the ER at the naval hospital, and they gave me an IV infusion of something that helped me enough to fall asleep and then go back to sleep for the night when we got home. But the release only lasted about 24 hours, maybe a little more, and then I was standing in the kitchen and had to grab onto the counter and bend over and lay my head on it. It was cool, so I stayed there for a few minutes.

It's most certainly a huge migraine, my first diagnosed one, but not actually my first. They were never this long or this bad before, though. I am lying here wondering what damage this pain might indicate. My brain hurts. What if this is the beginning of a lifelong, devastating disability for me? How will Eric work, take care of the kids, and take care of me, too? I don't want that for my family. I'd rather die.

Maybe this is my very dramatic way of getting Alzheimer's. That horrible disease has haunted me ever since I was six years old, and now that I know I have a 50% chance of getting it, it's pretty hard not to assume that this pain is an indicator of what's to come. But it's too soon, and I don't know that I have Dad's gene mutation. Did Dad get migraines when he was in his 30s? I think he did, actually. I remember a few times when I was surprised to come home from school and find him in bed asleep during the day. He wasn't the napping kind. Did Mom tell me then that Dad had a headache? I know something like that happened. I remember feeling surprised that my big, strong dad could even get a headache bad enough that he needed to lay down. But I don't remember him ever doing that for ten days.

I keep thinking about snow. I told Eric last night that I wanted a tiny snowstorm that only covered a single 20-foot circle in our backyard so I could get naked and lay in it. My body is a furnace, yet I don't have a fever. I hope this never happens again if it ever leaves, but I'm pretty sure it will.

"You Don't Know How It Feels,"
Tom Petty

Mom is texting me right now, telling me I should watch *60 Minutes* tonight. Apparently there is a long segment on Alzheimer's research with a focus on a family in Columbia (the country) who are carriers of a gene mutation similar to the one that Dad had, if not the same. I get forwarded emails with articles several times a week about Alzheimer's, all from my mom. She means well, but I really don't feel well enough to believe that my mental health would withstand taking in too much information on it. I don't cry every time I think about Dad and about my potential to have the disease, but when I do, it often puts me into a deep depression for a little while. It's not worth it.

But after I get off the phone with Mom, I feel unsettled. Maybe I should watch it, even if I only do it to make her happy. I can always turn it off if it upsets me too much.

But as I watch, I find myself riveted. First, I want to cry for this poor, huge family who share my "curse"—well, the curse that I might share with them. I wonder how they felt when the youngest children were born. Did they question the choice to have a baby, given the risk of this disease? I did, and that's why Henry's here. Back then, Eric and I said that no person's worth is determined by the length of their life or how it ends. But when Dad died, I still felt guilty for having had children.

Then, during the final portion of the segment, the reporter gives the contact information and website address for the scientists leading the study of genetic Alzheimer's and drug trials to see if they can find a cure. *If they find a cure, especially if they find one soon, my kids would be saved,* I think.

According to the Dominantly Inherited Alzheimer's Network website, there are three types of involvement—a registry, where a person at-risk or diagnosed with genetic Alzheimer's can provide their information to help inform any of their familial connections and the scientists about who is connected by blood to whom; an observational study group of people who are at risk for a gene mutation like the one I might have, where the participants come in periodically for interviews and cognitive-behavioral testing, and their results are tracked over time; and a third group of people enrolled in clinical trials, which means that those are the people who are the human guinea pigs, taking drugs that aren't approved yet but that scientists think might help do *something* for Alzheimer's. The clinical trials are what provide the most valuable data for finding a cure, I guess. Those people are laying their lives on the line, in a way. I mean, no one knows the side effects of an untested drug. I'm sure there is a process to confirm its safety before they give it to actual people, but still.

Against my better judgment, I write down the phone number for DIAN and leave a message asking for a call back.

"Float On," Modest Mouse

I like grocery shopping when I have plenty of time to do it, and the store isn't too full. When I go to a regular, commercial grocery store, this time of day (early afternoon on a weekday) is a good time because it's after the first-thing-in-the-morning rush and before the late-afternoon-crap-I-have-nothing-to-make-for-dinner rush. But I keep forgetting that the commissaries—the name for grocery stores on military bases—have a late morning rush, too. Except in this case, the store is full, but I'm the only one rushing. When all the retired ladies leave the base gym for lunch, they all go to the grocery store and continue chatting together, so the aisles are full of a lot of women stopping their carts to talk. I know I'm complaining, but it isn't that big of a deal. I sometimes chat with them, too.

I'm standing in aisle six (soup, broth, canned sauces, and "ethnic" foods) when my phone rings in my purse. I don't recognize the number, and my first reaction is to ignore it, but I notice that the phone says the call is coming from St. Louis.

I answer, and I am flabbergasted. Dr. Grossman, one of the two lead doctors for the U.S. division of DIAN, has called me. It's as if a minor celebrity just called me out of the blue. I'm talking to a world-renowned neuroscientist who is a front-line doctor in finding a cure for Alzheimer's. And when I answer, it really is him.

I walk to a quieter corner of the store and talk to him for about 20 minutes, mostly asking questions about the drug trials, their safety, and the logistics of getting involved as a participant. My main concerns are avoiding the possibility of contracting a debilitating illness or injury from a reaction to a study drug and the logistics of how to be involved in the study while Eric is still on active duty and we expect to be moving every few years. But Dr. Grossman answers those questions quickly and easily. Although the drugs used in trials are untested for their effects on Alzheimer's, they are still thoroughly tested for safety. And even if only one person has a bad adverse reaction to a drug during a trial, they will immediately put things on hold for participants and reevaluate their dosing methods and the effects of the drug itself to determine if it's too dangerous to continue.

The other good news is that the study is truly worldwide, with sites on three different continents. Although the main American study center is where he is in St. Louis, there are satellite sites throughout the country, and if I get involved, I would be assigned to the closest one to me—the one at UC San Diego. They are still recruiting for the third "arm" of the drug trial, searching for ways to combat amyloid plaque development in the brain.

He also tells me that he himself has family members who have suffered from brain diseases, so it is personal to him, too. We even chat about our kids for a few minutes—not what I'd expect from a neurologist leading drug research for one of the deadliest and most debilitating diseases in the world.

I tell him that, yes, I would like the St. Louis study coordinator to call me to get started, and while we're at it, have the UCSD coordinator call me as well. After the call ends, I take a few deep breaths to calm myself and get my mindset back to grocery shopping. I just made a decision that could change my life, and possibly millions of others, and now I have to figure out whether I want to get the fresh chicken breasts or the slightly cheaper ten-pound bag of frozen ones, and that takes some adjustment.

"Everybody Eats When They Come to My House," Cab Calloway

I love Pinterest; it's like a digital file cabinet with infinite space, so I can have dinner recipes in one box, cute clothes in another, and memes in a third. But right now, I'm looking at my board labeled "Cats." I have at least a hundred pictures of black cats saved, all since we lost Onyx. Last month, a door was left open, and she must have wandered outside. She never came back. I miss her. I didn't give her much attention when she was with us, and she didn't require much, but I feel sad without her around and a bit guilty that we couldn't keep her safe.

I do not like Next Door. It's got its good points—when I had a migraine last week, and a neighbor's dog was barking so much I couldn't get myself to relax and rest, I posted a kind but clear message on Next Door, a respectful request that the dog either be brought in or occupied in a way that kept him from barking. Minutes later, the barking stopped. Then, a few weeks ago, I was mindlessly scrolling through the new posts from my neighbors and found a cat. Zazz: a big tabby and calico male who weighs 15 pounds. One of my neighbors needed to rehome him because one of her kids had been diagnosed with asthma, and Zazz's fur had become an irritant. I've been telling Eric for the last couple of weeks that, while London and Paris are still pretty new to us, we haven't had a boy cat in ages since Cheese died in 2011. If I remember correctly, I told him we should get "a big, stocky boy cat and name him Houston." A cowboy name to contrast with London and Paris, which both sound pretty posh. Since he's just around the corner and free to a good home, I think I found our Houston.

It took me a few days to convince Eric, but the cat formerly known as Zazz is now with us and renamed Houston, and he's definitely big like Texas—over 15 pounds. I know a too-fat-to-be-healthy cat when I see one, so Houston's first job is to lose weight. But all is well, and London and Paris are starting to get used to him being here. Henry, in particular, is in love with Houston and tries to get him to willingly sit on his lap. So far, that hasn't lasted more than a couple of minutes, but I told Henry to be patient and he'll adjust.

We're moving to Lakeside in a few months, a different town about 40 minutes away and more inland than Poway. The rent is cheaper, and the house is bigger and better suited for the kids. It's a true four-bedroom, unlike this one, which was advertised as a four-bedroom, but the smallest bedroom is more like a closet. At the new house, all three of the kids' bedrooms are small, but still big enough for comfort, and roughly equal. Henry has already said that Houston is going to sleep in his room.

"Just Breathe," Pearl Jam

T his afternoon, everything about my future and my family's future might change. I've been working with the DIAN study coordinators, doctors, nurses, and other specialists for over a year now. I'm still a participant in the observational branch of the study, which only involves periodic visits for memory testing, vital signs, interviews about life changes or other health issues, and things like that. After the third "arm" of the last drug trial was dropped, I agreed to do the observational study and move over to the next drug trial group when one becomes available. But today, I am here because of me, and while the nurse and counselor I'll be seeing has worked with DIAN patients and the drug trial staff, she is not a doctor or nurse, and she is not a part of the study. She is a genetic counselor.

The first time I requested genetic counseling, which DIAN study members are eligible to receive freely and confidentially at the study site, the first automated referral sent to me to the genetic counseling clinic, and it was kind of a nightmare. It hadn't occurred to me before we walked into the waiting area, but one of the most common reasons a person seeks out genetic counseling is health concerns about her unborn baby. So, when I walked into a waiting room filled with young mothers with strollers and baby carriers, or pregnant mothers who just seemed nervous, my heart dropped. It got worse for a little while from there. I approached the intake desk and explained that I had an appointment and was from the DIAN study. The receptionist didn't know what that meant but said she could notify the counselor that I was here anyway. Then she handed me several intake forms to fill out, and I started to freak out again. First, because my membership in DIAN is kept confidential, and because DIAN would pay for the counseling and genetic testing expense, my name should remain anonymous. Second, because I was looking at a form that had questions like "What is your concern for your unborn baby?" and "Indicate your best known date of conception for this pregnancy." I tried to hand it back to her, telling her that I wasn't pregnant and I wasn't here about a pregnancy, but she insisted that every patient had to fill out the form. So I sat down and filled out the form while I cried on it.

When I did meet with the counselor, who was also pregnant, she sincerely apologized and said that they are working on finding a way for counselors to meet with DIAN patients outside of this particular clinic. But at that particular appointment, the counselor felt that my answers indicated some fear that I should work on before I seek my genetic status. So that's what I did.

Just over a month ago, I got an appointment with another genetic counselor—one who had already worked with several of the other DIAN study participants at UCSD. She asked me a few questions first, but by last month, I was more than ready to just get the whole thing over with.

Deciding whether or not I wanted to know if I have a genetic mutation that leads to Alzheimer's was one of the hardest decisions I've ever made, of course. But I have wondered, worried, and felt anxious about this possibility in some way since I was about eight years old. As I grew older and started to better understand what Alzheimer's is, what it does to the brain and the body, and that my family's estimated age of disease onset is around age 50, it started to worry me. And when my dad got diagnosed, and his doctor officially confirmed the dominantly inherited gene mutation present in his body, I panicked.

Certainly I haven't been panicking since 2005, but it haunts me and keeps me up at night and distracted during the day. I'm worried about our finances and the kids, all the practical extensions of a deadly genetic disease. But I'm also worried about myself. What if Eric doesn't want to take care of me? What if I've passed this to my kids? What if I become violent and hurt someone? What if I do something incredibly embarrassing or inappropriate because I don't understand where I am or how to act there? What if I take off my clothes in public or flirt with a young man because I don't know that I'm 50-something? I once saw a news story about a man whose wife had Alzheimer's and lived in an assisted living facility while he remained in their home nearby. One day he'd come in to see his wife, and she was kissing another man, calling him her boyfriend. She knew her husband's face but not his name or how he knew her. And the husband didn't try to correct her. He visits his wife while she talks about, hugs, and kisses another man, and he's weirdly okay with that.

I don't want to be that lady. But if I am, or could be, knowing that now will give me time to grieve that possibility and for my family to do the same. There are also financial reasons that knowing is better than not knowing at this point. Because of this possibility, we took out a life insurance policy on me, enough to at least give Eric and the kids some time to grieve without having to worry about paying the bills for a bit.

Last month, Eric and I met with the counselor in the same room we are sitting in today. The conversation then was brief because the decision had been made. I spit into a plastic test tube until it measured out to one tablespoon of saliva. The test tube was sealed in several layers and mailed to a DNA testing facility, and the results were returned here.

Eric and I pray together before we enter the building. We had to drive here in separate cars, him from work, which is closer to UCSD than our home, but he will come home driving his car again as soon as we're done. When the counselor comes in with a manila envelope, she asks us a few brief questions to make sure I'm still ready to know my status. When we give her the go-ahead, she opens the envelope.

"Unfortunately, it's not the result we hoped for. They did detect the genetic variant."

As a little kid, I cried a lot for a lot of different reasons, and I never felt the need to hide my tears. I remember each of my parents, separately and together, complaining that I cried over everything. That's not true for me as an adult, though. I hate crying in public or even in front of my family, really, although that's a little easier. When something upsets me in public or in front of others, I may let a few tears slip out, but when I know I need to really lean into a cry, I make sure I'm alone.

So as Eric and I walked out to our cars, I cried quietly and sniffed a bit, and I cried a little more while we talked, leaning on his car. But when we both drove our separate ways, and I was alone for a long rush-hour drive home, I wailed. I yelled and told God I was angry with him. I got out all the frustration and fear and dismay that I could in the first 30 minutes of that drive. And then I turned on the radio.

"Don't worry.... 'bout a thing....every little thing...gonna be alright,"

Seriously?!

It really is kind of a dumb song. Life is friggin' hard, not just for me. And every little thing is *not* going to be alright. Some things are, and always will be, completely and uncontrollably *wrong*. But when I hear this song, I picture Ida on that one sunny afternoon by the window, playing with the Little People school bus and singing; my little girl with autism, who I'd worried over and prayed over because I was so afraid that something within her was wrong, and that it was wrong because of me. As it turns out, nothing was wrong. She's at track practice at her high school right now. Knowing I have Alzheimer's hurts right now because I just got the news I have worried about getting since I was in grade school. Now that worry is over. Now my job is to grieve, trust God, and move forward in faith. God was faithful to me in the past, and I trust him. I'm sad, but I'm not worried.

"Runaway," Pink

I regret ever even thinking about getting a dog. But I can't think about that right now because the one I got is running in traffic.

I know for sure that I'm a cat person. Cats are generally quiet and demand little attention, and are really quite easy to take care of as long as you recognize that your cat believes you're *his* pet. But for the last few years, Eric has been gushing over photos of a couple of huskies that belong to a friend of his in Ouray who's the photographer for that deranged 102-mile mountain race he goes to. So he wanted to adopt a husky, and he charmed me into wanting one, too.

We just got back from Ouray, so any effort either of us had put into avoiding the addition of a dog to our three-cat household is gone, and Eric had already been calling a California rescue before we ever left for this trip. A few hours ago, that rescue, one in Los Angeles, returned his call and left a voicemail that they have a young female husky we may want to meet.

So naturally, after coming home from two days on the road and two weeks away from home, Eric and I dropped off the kids and the luggage and got right back in the truck to drive to Los Angeles and adopt a dog.

I heard at some point that huskies are very smart and independent, but that's all I knew about them before we adopted one. A smart dog sounds like a good thing. But huskies are smart, fast, and *very* independent. Right now, our husky, Imogene—named for one of the mountain passes in the Ouray 100-miler—is winding her way around several buildings that contain rentable storage space. I've been following her around here for hours, and while I am angry and worn out and incredibly dehydrated, Imogene shows no sign of being the least bit tired. Actually, being able to even follow her around these buildings is a relief, because two hours ago, she was running in the street dodging morning commute traffic, with only eight-year-old Henry to keep track of her.

There are no school buses here unless you purchase your ride to school with actual money. We're close enough to the high school that it's not a long trip, and because Ida goes to either track or cross country practice both before and after school, she can't take the bus because she needs to be there earlier and stay later. But now that Daniel's a freshman, I need to drive him the six or seven miles to school in the morning. Some days it's no big deal, but other days it is.

Today I made the mistake of letting Henry, who is very mature and responsible, stay at home with the pets while I took Daniel to school. I should have put Imogene in the dog crate, but the only one we have is too small for her height, and she screamed bloody murder in it last night. Yes, dogs can scream, especially huskies. Look it up on YouTube if you don't believe me.

So I told Henry to just make sure he didn't open any doors. But somehow, when Henry went to his room to get dressed for school, she found a way to get on the back porch and then climbed and jumped over the six-foot fence in the backyard to run in the street. Again. She already did this twice last night right after we brought her home.

When Henry realized what had happened, he ran outside to find her, still wearing his pajamas with only one sock on one foot. Thankfully, a good Samaritan neighbor came along and reminded him to never get in a stranger's car, "But do it just this one time so we can try to get your dog back." When Imogene made it to a busier road, a few other people pulled over to help, and another neighbor of ours walked down to help as well.

We're at the tail end of this particular escape attempt right now, I think. It's getting very hot now, and she's tired. She keeps plopping down in the shadier spots, but if I get too close, she gets up and starts trotting again.

When I do finally manage to wear her out enough to allow me to put the leash on and walk her home, I am bitter and angry, but how can I really be angry with a puppy that has never before been someone's pet and is only doing what she knows how to do? If you've spent your entire life in a small kennel, a house is just a much larger kennel. She wants freedom, which I can respect, but freedom needs rules and limits to work. For a dog, anyway.

"Country Roads," John Denver

Today, Eric and I bought a house that we've never actually seen in person. If someone else had told me that they were going to do something like this, I would have thought they were a moron.

It's time for Eric's next duty station rotation, and usually it's August when he has to officially report to his next command. The Navy gave us the option of staying in California, but I knew I didn't want to stay in California about two months after we arrived here, so we turned that down the moment it was offered. After that, there was a little discussion about whether we would be returning to the coastal Virginia area where we lived prior to California, or the D.C. metro area where we lived prior to that, but in the end, Eric's next—and last—duty station will be back at Portsmouth Naval Medical Center in Norfolk, the first hospital he was stationed at after becoming a nurse, and the area we were living in when my dad died. It's great news for us; we really enjoyed our time there and the military-friendly environment, even off base.

The only problem we're having now is the same one everyone on earth is having now. COVID has messed up everything for everyone, to be sure, but just to clarify, here is one way that it messed us up: neither Eric nor I will be able to actually go to Virginia to find a house. Normally, I would go look at houses so that Eric doesn't have to use up days of leave for house-hunting, but now, even that is out of the question. So, in these unprecedented times, we hired a buyer's agent to look for us, and every day or two she sends us photos and videos of available houses, and when we find one we want to consider, she goes to the house and video calls us for a walk-through. In between video call home tours, Eric and I look through the real estate listing websites and save the ones we're interested in seeing.

I found myself going back to look at this one weird house that I loved for some reason. It isn't even ideal for us, but something about it kept my interest more than the others. It's a ranch-style house built in the early 1970s and later remodeled to expand some of the rooms and add a second living room area to the back. There's a big fenced yard for the dogs, and it already has mature perennial plants in the flower beds, which I love. And part of me likes this house because I want to change it. I like the structure and size of it, but not the décor and colors inside. And, as I told Eric, I think we can get a really good deal on it. It's smaller and older than some of the comparable houses we looked at—and, more importantly, there are deer heads.

In one of the main rooms of the house—a sitting room with a gas fireplace right next to the open-space kitchen—there are mounted deer heads all over the place, hanging on the walls in rows. I'm pretty sure one of them is actually from an ibex. I can only imagine that any other person who toured this house looked at it and later remembered nothing about it but the mounted heads. When I was in high school, after Dad got out of jail, he won a trip to Montana to hunt elk, and when he got one, he was awarded a huge model elk head that hung on the wall in our living room until my mom moved out. The antlers were the only thing actually from the elk my dad shot, but that doesn't matter. He called it his trophy. Mom, Scott, and I named the elk Julio and hung garland and Christmas balls on its antlers in December, much to Dad's chagrin.

Anyway, the point of that story is that I can easily recognize what a wall full of deer heads would look like without the deer heads, but other people may be too shocked to try.

We got the house easily at a very good price. Next week, I'm going to get on an airplane for the first time in many years and fly to Virginia to spend five days inspecting the house, cleaning up what needs to be cleaned, and getting started on some of the improvements I want to make. I've been saving home improvement and design ideas on Pinterest for years, so this is my chance to apply some of the bigger projects I have in mind. My plan is to paint the kitchen cabinets and install new handles, paint the fireplace and grate, paint the master bedroom, and hang peel-and-stick wallpaper in the master bathroom. I'm super excited.

"Old Town Road,"
Lil Nas X, ft. Billy Ray Cyrus

I'm pretty sure that after we completed our two-week-long drive when we moved to California, I said I would never move across the country by driving myself and my stuff again. But here we are five years later, and not only are we doing it again, but we're upping the ante.

We are going to move across the country together, without a moving truck or any help at all for now. Last week, we had shipping boxes stationed in our driveway, which we gradually filled with most of our stuff, other than the things we needed to keep until we made the move. On Christmas, we did the things: relaxing, eating cookies (not me, though), and staying in our pajamas. But we were up bright and early on December 26, filling those shipping boxes, locking them up, and then packing up Eric's car and the pickup truck. And let me tell you, this is awful.

Mind you, we're doing this while COVID is still raging everywhere, and frankly, I think I have it myself, but I haven't gotten a test or anything. I'm exhausted. Before we got on the road, I had been lying on the carpet in the not-quite-empty-yet master bedroom, sleeping. That is not like me to be able to sleep on the floor with the light on and everything around me going crazy. But when it came time to start driving, what was I supposed to do? According to what they're saying, my kids and husband were already exposed before I started feeling sick, but Eric was one of the first people I knew of who got the vaccination, and my kids don't have any symptoms. So I packed the truck and the shipping boxes when I could, slept on the carpet when I couldn't, and now we're on the road, COVID or no COVID.

Last time, when we made this trip in reverse, we scheduled days of downtime and checked out some of the sites and tourist traps along the way. This trip isn't that. We get in the car, drive, we make stops for gas, the bathroom, and food, and then drive again. We're staying in cheap but pet-friendly hotel rooms and clearing out as early as possible— which is like 9:00 a.m. in this family. We like to sleep.

There is an additional complication for this trip: his name is Richmond. After some really hard and unpleasant training with Imogene, she is certainly better behaved now, but her energy level is still off the charts. I thought that, maybe, if we got another dog for her to play with, they could get their energy out together and not rip up the house or clothes or books. Because somehow, that made sense to me at the time. Struggling with your dog's behavior? Get another dog; that will fix it! Yeah.

In October, Imogene and I drove out to Arizona to meet a lady who owns a little ranch and animal sanctuary so we could meet a husky-malamute mix she'd named Terry. She had found him abandoned and in a shelter in Tijuana. Who adopts a husky in Mexico? Anyway, Imogene and I visited him, signed on the dotted line, and Terry became Richmond—who is now in the backseat of my truck, trapped between Imogene, the back of the driver's seat, and our TV, which Eric strapped to the back cushion of the back seat.

Fun times.

"100 Bad Days," AJR

Today's my birthday.
I hate my birthday.
Especially this one, and not just because I'm 40 now.

I have been in catastrophe mode since before we even arrived in our new house in Virginia, and we got here on January 3. I knew it was a bad idea—not the move, but the aftermath—because I would have no way to let my guard down after the stressful move. After Eric unloaded both vehicles and chased the dogs around the new neighborhood several times, he got in his car and left to drive back to California. As I said before, this whole trip was insane, and only partially because of COVID. Getting out of California as soon as possible was a motivator, too.

Every day of leave that Eric can save is precious time with us, and since he won't be with us for a while, he is saving leave he might have otherwise taken. I had to get the kids enrolled in school and their records transferred from California. I had to find and hire someone to reinforce the backyard fence since Imogene could so easily escape. I had to assemble new furniture. I had to drive Ida to track practice twice a day and the boys to Boy Scout meetings and events. I had to make sure the bills got paid, which Eric mostly did online for me, but I always double-checked.

I did my best, I suppose, but it was nowhere close to good enough. Ida and Daniel probably missed more school than they ever have, and

Henry definitely did. On the days he did make it to school, he was late, and I had to drive him in. And the lateness and missed school was almost always my fault, not theirs. It wasn't only that I overslept, staying up too late to watch movies and calm myself down from the daytime stress—sometimes they missed school just because they wanted to, and I wanted them to. I wanted them to stay with me because I was tired, stressed, lonely, and often sick, and the kids understand that because, frankly, we've grown up together.

I did some good things, too. Ida had a boyfriend, so I monitored that situation, and when they started having philosophical differences, I tried to help Ida make decisions about that. Lately, she and her boyfriend have been arguing a lot about Jesus. I think it started as general discussions about religion, philosophies, and science but transitioned into arguing when her boyfriend started hinting at sex. Mind you, Ida doesn't come right out and tell me things like that, but I paid attention when I drove Ida to his house or him to ours, listening to them talk. They both enjoyed talking about deep stuff, which is something Eric and I bonded over, but her boyfriend wanted to debate with her about her faith, and it was becoming too much for her. Sometimes, in the car, he would ask me questions or tell me his thoughts about whether or not there's a God, and over time, he got more aggressive about it—not in an angry way, but in a way that I could tell it was bothering him.

Then, just two days ago, he asked me if I would come pick him up at his house and drive him to ours so he could see Ida. It was something he hadn't done before; I'd driven him home plenty of times, and I'd picked him up with Ida in the car, but I didn't think much of it at first. I allowed the two of them to be alone in Ida's room, but only with the door open so I could listen in, and yesterday, I heard Ida crying. So when he walked up to me, with Ida still in her room and still crying, I knew what he was going to tell me, but I was surprised by his reasoning and, frankly, proud of both of them.

As you can imagine, the first 10 or 15 minutes of the drive was silent. I asked him if he was okay and if anyone was home at his house so he wouldn't be alone. I could tell he was upset, even though it was he who broke off the relationship. He told me he was okay, but then there was more.

"It's just that you can't really know if God even exists, so why would you make choices because it's what God wants? We don't even know where the world came from, so how can someone guess that there's a God, and then know that God made the world, and how he made it, and everything about every person, and that God said you can't have sex if you're not married? It's just not… realistic. I just… can't."

I didn't argue with him. He was crying now for sure, so the brokenness that God uses was there, and God was using it because he had him thinking. I said, "If you want, you can ask God to show you in some way if he's real or not. You can ask that question without actually believing in him. The chances that you'll hear a booming voice from the sky are pretty low, but he'll let you know if you tell him you're willing to find out."

"Yeah," was all he said, and then he opened the door to leave. "Take care of yourself," I told him. "Do something that either makes you happy or helps you relax." And then I drove away. By the time I got back home and checked on Ida, letting her know I was around if she wanted to talk about it, she said she'd already sent messages to her friends from her church small group who were supporting her. I was very impressed.

"You know, I just drove him home. He's much more upset than you are right now. And I'm proud that you withstood temptation and told him why you were doing it. He's thinking about it. You challenged him."

"Yeah," was all she said, but she smiled.

That big success was a few days ago, and today, I'm a mess. It started first thing in the morning. I had told Henry he could bring his friend from across the street over to our house today to celebrate Henry's birthday, which is his tenth. I even went to one of the military bases and rented a moon bounce for the day, so Henry and I went together to pick it up this morning. Like I said, though, I woke up a mess, with self-pity and anger that COVID makes so many things more complicated, that I have Alzheimer's, and that it's not fair, and all the usual tirades I go on in my head. I was already ugly-crying on the way to pick up the moon bounce, and on the way home, I confessed to

Henry that the darn thing was so heavy there was no way I would even be able to get it out of the car.

There was no party. Henry's friend did come over, but they just hung out playing video games while I cried on the phone with Eric and with a few other people, too. I also texted my therapist because I'm beginning to feel like I'm not me. Like I am another person watching myself from within, the way a first-person video game works. It's called disassociation, and it's a sign that I need to just give up for the day. So I do.

Not every day is this bad, but there are more bad days than good ones.

In a few weeks, Eric will be able to move in.

"You're on Your Own, Kid," Taylor Swift

I remember when I graduated from high school, my mom was more excited about it than I was. I was excited to graduate, but graduation, the event, wasn't very important to me. It wasn't unimportant either, but Mom wanted to have a graduation party for me, and I didn't really want one. We had one anyway.

I haven't been in my mom's position in the sense that I have not been the mom of a high school graduate. When Abi graduated from high school, she was still doing online school, and as far as I know, if there was an in-person graduation ceremony, she didn't go to it.

This year, I will be in that position. Ida is graduating from high school in June 2022. But right now, we're celebrating one of the earlier "lasts" of her school career. Eric, Henry, and I are at Ida's very last cross country meet. This meet really isn't any different than the others, though, and most of the seniors on the team will also compete in one more year of spring track races.

Eric got stuck later at the hospital than he'd intended, which happens more often than not, but Henry and I are here. We made it in the traffic, but we were barely on time to catch the beginning of the senior boys' race. Thankfully, Ida's race will be a little later.

Ida was never the fastest runner on her team, or even one of the fastest. That actually matters less than you'd think, depending on the race, and in a team scenario like this, the goal for each runner is to do well enough to earn points for their team. To be honest, I never asked too many questions about the points thing. I just know that even if Ida doesn't look like the type to be a cross country or track star, she does when she runs, and she runs because she is part of the team, and her efforts are included in the team results.

What I love about Ida—well, one of the things I love about her—is that she is a team player. She's not a very social person (most people with autism aren't), but when there's a group that needs to work together toward a common goal and when her role in the group is clearly defined, she is totally independent. She genuinely loves her teammates. As I write that, it kind of sounds insignificant, the equivalent of a participation award given to kids after a Little League game. But now that I think about it, it's not insignificant at all. It's small, but it's big. Ida supports the people she cares about, even if it means she's cheering on the runner that she will never catch up to.

Eric made some silly signs for the team to see during the races as they go by, but they aren't really being used. Henry, who is 11 now, is teasing Ida, calling her "Bad Ida." It's a joke between them. Henry likes to tease with nicknames, and Ida and Daniel will happily play along with this, calling Henry names back. He usually comes up with his goofy names spontaneously, but a while ago, he told me quietly that he just couldn't come up with one for Ida, and he was concerned that if he did, she might get angry if she didn't like it. Eventually, he settled on "Bad Ida." I'm sure there's more to it than that, but there it is.

Henry has always been a bit shy about yelling and cheering when we're at races, but since this one is special, he says he wants to do something to tease her. I grab a marker and one of Eric's signs. "Write 'Bad Ida' on it and hold it up when she goes by."

And he does. He isn't as socially awkward as Ida and Daniel are, but it seems to me that Henry's incredible all-around intelligence has made him an old soul. His abilities are far beyond what he's studying in school, and his maturity is catching up with his thinking. Sometimes when I talk to him, I forget that he isn't an adult or that he doesn't literally know everything. He's still my baby, but I see in him a wonderful combination of Eric's intelligence, my hard-earned emotional skills, and some things that are truly all his own.

Much to our chagrin, Daniel is the only one of the three kids who never came to enjoy running, but he has his own passions. He's not in Boy Scouts anymore, but he still loves camping, hiking, swimming, and outdoorsy stuff. Last summer, he worked at the local Cub Scout camp, which he plans to do again this year. He played guitar for a while, and though he isn't taking lessons anymore, he still picks it up sometimes and picks out a tune from thin air. His musical ear is ten times better than mine. He was the only junior in senior English class this year, and next year he may be able to start taking some classes for college credit. He's planning to study psychology after graduation.

I got news the other day that the next drug trial the DIAN organization is offering will be one that tackles tau tangles in the brain—proteins that accumulate in the brain of Alzheimer's patients and prevent the brain's communication synapses from working properly. It may be several months before they're ready for me to start, but they know I'm ready and want in on this study as soon as possible. I'm taking Aricept now, and it's helping, I think, but when your brain isn't working properly, it's difficult to trust your own observations of things like that.

I'm grieving my own life as I live it and while I forget it, but grief isn't so bad now. I've grieved about a lot of things, and I'm not saying any of that—the bad stuff I've been through or the grief that came from it—is something we should enjoy or make into a hobby. But to be honest, I have spent a lot of time grieving something or another for most of my life. I don't know the dictionary definition of grief or the psychological or neurological meaning of it, but I do know grief, and I know it like I know my husband and my kids. Grief, I think, gives a voice to the part of my soul that remembers Eden in all its perfection and knows that it can't return to it. Grief is the thing that reminds me that I, like all others, am a broken creation, full of potential for both great integrity and great evil. Grief, like love, is what makes me human.

Made in United States
Orlando, FL
11 August 2024